IN SEARCH OF NEW AGE
SPIRITUALITIES

The search for an adequate understanding of the New Age phenomenon is fraught with difficulties when examined within the perspectives of sociology of religion which have shed light on religion in modernity.

New Agers cannot be located easily in the secularisation narrative; they move through fluid networks rather than settled collectivities; they assemble personal syncretisms of belief, myth and practice rather than subscribe to codified doctrines and prescribed rituals. New Age is quickly found to be a label that is unacceptable to many of those designated as New Agers.

This book advances our understanding of the so-called New Age phenomenon by analysing accounts of insiders' religious experience and orientations. This approach is brought to bear not only on the study of written documents relating to New Age and its putative antecedents, but on the analysis of in-depth interviews with thirty-five spiritual actors.

ASHGATE NEW CRITICAL THINKING IN RELIGION, THEOLOGY AND BIBLICAL STUDIES

The *Ashgate New Critical Thinking in Religion, Theology and Biblical Studies* series brings high quality research monograph publishing back into focus for authors, international libraries, and student, academic and research readers. Headed by an international editorial advisory board of acclaimed scholars spanning the breadth of religious studies, theology and biblical studies, this open-ended monograph series presents cutting-edge research from both established and new authors in the field. With specialist focus yet clear contextual presentation of contemporary research, books in the series take research into important new directions and open the field to new critical debate within the discipline, in areas of related study, and in key areas for contemporary society

Other Titles in the Series:

Ancient Taboos and Gender Prejudice
Challenges for Orthodox Women and the Church
Leonie B. Liveris

Metaphysics as Christology
An Odyssey of the Self from Kant and Hegel to Steiner
Jonael Schickler

In Search of New Age Spiritualities

ADAM POSSAMAI
University of Western Sydney, Australia

ASHGATE

Published by
Ashgate Publishing Limited
Gower House
Croft Road
Aldershot
Hampshire GU11 3HR
England

Ashgate Publishing Company
Suite 420
101 Cherry Street
Burlington, VT 05401-4405
USA

Ashgate website: http://www.ashgate.com

British Library Cataloguing in Publication Data
Possamai, Adam
    In search of New Age spiritualities. – (Ashgate new critical thinking in religion, theology and biblical studies)
    1. New Age movement – Australia 2. Spirituality – Australia
    I. Title
    299.9'3

Library of Congress Cataloging-in-Publication Data
Possamai, Adam.
  In search of New Age spiritualities / Adam Possamai.
    p. cm. — (Ashgate new critical thinking in religion, theology, and biblical studies)
  Includes bibliographical references.
  ISBN 0-7546-5213-0 (hardcover : alk. paper)
  1. New Age movement—Case studies. I. Title. II. Series.

  BP605.N48P675 2005
  299'.93—dc22

2005007230

ISBN 0 7546 5213 0

Printed and bound in Great Britain by MPG Books Ltd, Bodmin, Cornwall

Contents

List of Tables   *vii*
List of Figures   *viii*
Acknowledgements   *ix*
Preface   *x*

INTRODUCTION   1
Methods   2
For a Weberian Approach   4
Three Working Assumptions   6
Contents   11
Presentation of Participants   13

1. A PROFILE OF THE RESPONDENTS: SOCIAL AND SPIRITUAL
    ASPECTS   17
    Who are these Spiritual Actors? : The Conflictual Actor   18
    How do People become involved in Alternative Spiritualities?:
        Alternation rather than Conversion   23

2. A PROFILE OF THE RESPONDENTS: NETWORKING ASPECTS   29
    How do they Organise Themselves?: The Networking Capital   29
    The Cultic Milieu and the Network Paradigm   31
    Well-Being in the Cultic Milieu: An Application of the
        'Cultic Milieu' Grid   36
    The Portrait of the Urban Australian Alternative Spiritual Actor   37

3. KEEPING NEW AGE AT BAY   39
    Etic and Emic Approaches: Categorising 'New Age'   39
    Philosophia Perennis   48

4. PERENNISM   53
    Evidence from the Field   53
    Monism   54
    The Human Potential Ethic   57

Spiritual Knowledge   62
The Triad   66
For a Sociological Appropriation   71

5. THE SPIRITUAL KNOWLEDGES   73
    Marilyn and Spiritual Knowledges   73
    Esotericism Unveiled   76
    Esotericism Simplified   82

6. A SOCIOLOGICAL CHART OF THE AGE OF AQUARIUS   85
    The Age of Aquarius as the New Age   85
    New Age as the Age of Aquarius: Its Genesis   87
    The Critical Mass   91
    The Second Coming   95

7. NEO-PAGANISM AND PRESENTIST PERENNISM   99
    Neo-Paganism   99
    Neo-Pagan Rituals and Covens   102
    Presentist Perennism   108

8. THREE PERENNIST SPIRITUALITIES   113
    The Three Perennist Sub-Types Back Together   113
    Modernity/Postmodernity   115
    Individual Level   118
    The Perennist Trinity   125

9. PERENNIST RE-ENCHANTMENT: THE CULTURAL LOGIC OF
    LATE CAPITALISM AND COMMUNICATIVE ACTION   127
    The Space of Perennist Symbolism: Consumerism and Re-enchantment 128
    Resistance   134

CONCLUSION   139

Bibliography   *143*
Index   *155*

List of Tables

I.1	Informants' spiritual praxis	3
I.2	Mystico-pneumatic experiences reported	8
3.1	Perception of NAS	44
3.2	Attitude towards NAS	46
4.1	Informants' belief in perennism	70
4.2	Informants' belief in the perennist triad	70
6.1	Informants' teleologies	94
7.1	Solar celebrations – Sabbats	103
7.2	Aquarian perennism versus neo-paganism	106
8.1	Informants' affiliations	113
8.2	Characteristics of the three perennist sub-types	114
9.1	Neo-pagan sub-categories as listed in the 1996 and 2001 censuses	131
C.1	Summary of the differences among perennist sub-types	140

List of Figures

2.1   The cultic milieu and its affectual networks   35

3.1   The Moebius strip   50

8.1   Perennist genealogies   114

Acknowledgements

Some of the chapters of this book have their origins in some articles and book chapters published previously. These are:

Possamai, A. (1999) 'Diversity in Alternative Spiritualities: Keeping New Age at Bay', *Australian Religion Studies Review* 12 (2), 111-124; reprinted as Possamai, A. (1999) 'Diversity in Alternative Spiritualities: Keeping New Age at Bay' in Gary Bouma (ed.), *Managing Religious Diversity: From Threat to Promise*, AASR editions, Melbourne, 111-124; reprinted as Possamai, A. (2004) 'Diversity in Alternative Spiritualities: Keeping New Age at Bay' in J. Lewis (ed.) *The Encyclopedic Sourcebook of the New Age*, Prometheus Books, New York, 425-438.

Possamai A. (1999) 'The Aquarian Utopia of New Age', Beyond the Divide (3), 68-79.

Possamai, A. (2000) 'Nature Religions' in P. Hughes (ed.) *Australia's Religious Communities. A Multimedia Exploration: CD-Rom Standard Edition*, Christian Research Association, Melbourne.

Possamai, A. (2000) 'A Profile of New Agers: Social and Spiritual Aspects', *Journal of Sociology* 36 (3), 345-358.

Possamai, A (2000) 'A New Look at the Cultic Milieu' in Oakley et al. (ed.), *Sociological Sites/Sights TASA 2000 Conference Proceedings*, Adelaide, CD-Rom.

Possamai, A. (2001) 'Not the New Age: Perennism and Spiritual Knowledges', *Australian Religion Studies Review* 14 (1), 82-96.

Possamai, A. (2001) 'A Revisionist Perspective on Secularisation: Alternative Spiritualities, Globalised Consumer Culture, and Public Spheres' in C. Cusack and P. Oldmeadow (eds), *The End of Religions? Religion in an Age of Globalization*, Sydney Studies in Religion (4), 200-215.

Possamai, A. (forthcoming) 'Les Spiritualités Alternatives De La Phase Du Capitalisme Tardif: Logique Culturelle, Colonisation Du Monde Vécu Et Agir Communicationnel' in M. Geoffroy, M. Gardaz and A. Bouchard (eds.) *La Mondialisation du phénomène religieux*, Presses de l'Université de Laval, Québec.

Preface

For Judith and Angelo, these wonderful parents and people who have always supported me in everything I wanted to do. Without their support, my migration from Belgium to Australia to do a PhD would not have been possible.

For Rowan Ireland, a top PhD supervisor who proved to be a dedicated mentor and a wonderful sociologist.

For my wife and my children in Australia, Alphia, Natasha and Cameron, who are never short of support and understanding.

For the rest of my family in Belgium, Philippe, Ingrid, Faustine, Geena, and a soon to be born nephew.

Thanks also to the colleagues and friends from the then School of Sociology, Politics and Anthropology from La Trobe University who were a great support in the writing of my PhD: Johan Arnason, Peter Beilharz, Ken Dempsey, Doug Ezzy, Francesco Formosa, Arnaud Gallois, Trevor Hogan, Joel Kahn, Beryl Langer, Wendy Mee, Graham St John, and Evan Willis, and thank you to the colleagues and friends from the then School of Sociology and Social Justice who provided great advice in the process of turning my PhD into referee publications, and, in turn, these publications into this book: Michael Bounds, Mary Hawkins, Rob O'Neill and Murray Lee. Thanks to other sociologists of religion who have provided me with great advice and help: Alan Black, Gary Bouma, Grace Davie, Philip Hugues, Michael Mason, Ivan Varga and Liliane Voyé.

Introduction

The term 'New Age' is highly problematic. In 1996 in Melbourne, on the first day of 'prospecting' for voluntary participants, a shop owner (of what I would have called a New Age shop) told me explicitly that he had nothing to do with 'New Age' Spiritualities. On top of this, during the course of my pilot interviews, I realised that participants were negatively disposed to the term New Age. The term not only lacks a clear denotation in the academic literature and among the likes of the spokespersons (e.g. Edgar Cayce, Shirley McLaine) of these spiritualities listed by York (1995, 48-88), but creates problems when used in the field (see Chapter 3). Indeed, as Lewis realised already in the early nineties:

> For anyone researching the new age movement, the reflections found in "Is 'New Age' Dead?" raise several important issues. In the first place, because individuals, institutions, and periodicals who formerly referred to themselves as 'New Age' no longer identify themselves as such, studies built around a distinction between New Age and non-New-Age become more complex (Lewis, 1992: 2).

Questions quickly arose after this first experience in the field. What is New Age? Why do people not refer to themselves as New Agers? If they do not refer to themselves as New Agers, how do they refer to themselves?

These questions led to the writing of my PhD (Possamai, 1998) which gave a sociological account of these spiritualities in Australia. Since working in this field much additional material has been published. During the writing of my PhD, seminal accounts such as that of Heelas (1996), York (1995) and Hanegraaff (1996) appeared and marked the field of study on New Age, and became part of what Sutcliffe (2003b) calls the first wave of 'New Age' studies; that is, they share a consensus that beneath the diversity of what is 'New Age' there is nevertheless an enduring substantive core. Sutcliffe then reinforces the idea that a second wave of studies has started; this one offers additional localised ethnographies to detail the heterogeneity and diversity of these contemporary practices. This book, which is greatly inspired by my thesis and by the articles listed in the acknowledgement section, situates itself within these two waves of studies. It details a localised ethnography in Melbourne and then revises the 'enduring' substantive core for an Australian perspective; to be able to offer a localised ethnography of the diversity of alternative spiritualities in the city of Melbourne, I had first to find the common core to those spiritualities to be able to pinpoint afterwards each sub-type's specificities. The key argument of this book is that New Age is being used in the literature and in everyday life as a meronymy; that is New Age is being used as the single descriptor for a range of distinguishable religious phenomena which comprise a family of which New Age is a member. By combining both empirical and theoretical approaches to provide a rigorous account of a contemporary phenomenon, this book discovers a new type of postmodern spirituality (what I will call presentist perennism) and demonstrates the validity of the groundbreaking theory of 'perennism' to explain today's alternative spiritualities, e.g. Aquarians and Neo-Paganism; specifically in the Australian context.

Methods

To reach these discoveries, I conducted a type fieldwork in the New Age which is lacking according to Sutcliffe (2003a, 2003b) and Corrywright (2003). I simply engaged in open research that allowed New Age actors to express themselves through discussion and not through percentage distribution of responses to closed questions (e.g. Donahue 1993; Houtman and Mascini 2002; Rose 1998; York 1995, 179-223). My approach is a micro-sociological, V*erstehen* and action approach: action because I wish to consider the reflectional work of New Age actors on themselves, and on their social relations, and V*erstehen* because I want to grasp what made sense for them, their construction of meaning. In sum, I do not want to paint a static (quantitative) picture of New Agers but a vibrant (qualitative) portrait of how New Agers interact and negotiate meanings. The description of two methods used in this research – anthropological immersion and interviews follows:

Immersion

It is impossible to grasp this phenomenon immediately and adequately as a coherent, distinctive spirituality. Initial impressions and fluidity in belief and practice suggest complexity close to chaos. In the search for whatever coherence there might be, I have found it necessary firstly to take in all the complexity, searching all the while for any clues to an underlying thematic coherence in the complex elements themselves. My assumption has been that there is no code for deciphering these spiritualities outside of the complex of diverse practices and discourses constituting it.

I have had to proceed like an anthropologist investigating a newly discovered culture. So I have immersed myself in an ocean of 'New Age' books, researched these spiritualities on the Internet, visited many psychic fairs and 'New Age' festivals, attended lectures and conducted informal interviews. I have attended workshops, to learn, for instance the basis of Tarot cards and astrology, always attempting to think on, or close to, the wavelength of these spiritual actors. Furthermore, I have found it necessary to study the work of predecessors – e.g. occultism, spiritualism, Guénonism (see Chapter 5) – so as to grasp the diverse cultural transactions between those religious practices which have led to the genesis of these contemporary spiritualities.

Of necessity, then, the first characteristic of my research has been respectful personal immersion in all aspects of this phenomenon. This, I believe must be a characteristic of any research on exotic phenomena such as these spiritualities.

Interviews

The second method is long semi-structured interviews. I interviewed 35 people (to preserve their anonymity, I have changed their names) and taped them, with their full knowledge. They were interviewed between July 1996 and August 1997. These interviews lasted between 40 minutes to 3.5 hours. Those who were more keen on talking, generally, had longer experience in the so-called 'New Age' scene and were interviewed in quiet surroundings conducive to reflective conversation. The conversations were later transcribed verbatim and this enabled me to look at each case as a whole.

I decided to conclude my field work at 35 interviews, because I realised when I had reached 30, that I was not gaining any more relevant information or insights. The five supplementary discussions were conducted partly to gain a margin of security.

My method of selecting people for interviews was inspired by my immersion in this culture: I simply networked. Indeed, 'both the New Age and Neo-pagan movements operate through word of mouth and extensive networking links' (York 1995, 224). Instead of studying in depth a couple of more or less homogenous groups, I purposely wanted to discover the different and heterogenous layers of this phenomenon. The volunteer sample was collected in the city of Melbourne through a 'snowball' technique. I have followed the assumption that New Age networking is mainly an urban phenomenon. There is indeed a lack of research in the sociology of these spiritualities focusing on its individual actors. To redress this, it has been necessary to sample individuals located outside any organisational context.

I have tried to grasp the most different perspectives and practices of my interviewees. This was to prevent the study of these alternative spiritualities from a single vantage point. I have found these actors involved in many religious practices, however each individual tends to specialise in one specific type of activity, as presented in Table I.1. This list, actually understates the diversity of practice: all my interviewees opted for more than one spiritual activity.

Table I.1 Informants' spiritual praxis

Spiritual Praxis	Number of informants (n=35)
Astrology	4
Automatic writing	1
Buddhism	2
Channelling	1
Crystals manipulation	1
Discussion group	1
Etheric surgery[1]	1
Feminist spirituality	1
Festival organisation	2
Meditation	4
Naturopathy	1
Neo-paganism	2

Spiritual Praxis (n=35)	Number of informants
Numerology	1
Palmistry	1
Parapsychology	1
Perennial philosophy[2]	1
Psychic readings	2
Reiki[3]	2
Spiritualism	2
Tantrism	1
Tarot	2
Urban shamanism	1

[1]   A medicine used on the etheric body, i.e. the physical body's template.
[2]   See Chapter 3.
[3]   A hands-on spiritual or psychic healing whose practitioner lets operate a form of spiritual energy through him or her.

My main aim in conducting these interviews was to elicit New Agers' own accounts of their spirituality, their own ways of locating their spiritual experience in their lives. In a study on neo-paganism (see Chapter 7), T.M. Luhrmann (1994, 22) mentions the case of a researcher who had passed out questionnaires to prospective subjects; and everyone was offended. I did not want to face the same problem. So it was necessary to avoid the trappings of the scientific survey or the social scientific experiment – at least in this sample. One interviewee, James, explained his views on rigorous scientific method:

> If you come to a science experiment with a determined idea, it is not difficult to prove that you can prove it, and that's why they have initiated procedures that they loosely call the double blind system. That is, you design, say a questionnaire, or you design an experiment, you give it to somebody else to set up and get another person again to actually conduct the experiment. So there's no connection back. So that the findings are as divorced from the initial as possible. Because if you started doing the experiment yourself you'd only prove your expectations.

Here was a further reason why the interviews had to be informal and conducted outside a scientific environment so as not to betray the hallmarks of scientific study.

For a Weberian Approach

This approach is in accord with a Weberian perspective; an approach that has not been used in previous studies on these spiritualities and which will shed more light on this phenomenon. Indeed, Wood (2003) points out that the knowledge of the field is not going to move if its analysis is not conducted in a different light. For Weber, the construction of a definitive and exhaustive system of concepts is impossible and therefore an illusion. Reality is a dynamic stream of events that is in a state of perpetual flux. Sociocultural disciplines are therefore endowed with eternal youth because culture in its endless progressions invariably leads these disciplines to novel problematics. From this, it can be inferred that these spiritual actors as cultural innovators require exactly that sociologists of religion trying to understand them have to formulate new problematics. Following a *Verstehen* approach limits a tendency to ascribe characteristics on these actors and therefore reduces what Weber calls a 'dogmatic' conceptual construct. Indeed, all analytical concepts are specific to a particular historical and cultural environment. It is therefore necessary to search for less ascribed concepts, that is those which are found in 'local realities and meanings' and minimise the cultural gap between insider and outsider's accounts. I therefore understand this research to be a study conducted by an outsider but included in the 'local reality and meaning' of these actors.

However, while following a *Verstehen* approach, I tend also to distance myself from the participants to gain an overall view. For this reason, I adopt a 'synoptic approach'. A discussion of this follows.

In the current academic world, it is impossible for a sociologist or an anthropologist to be a scientist following the positivist illusion of the social world completely amenable to objective study. On the other hand, the method of subjectivism of the researcher which is proposed as a remedy faces problems as well. J.P. Olivier de Sardan (1992, 8) compares this method as ethno-ego-centrism in which the 'I' of the researchers dominates the literature through their feelings or 'by cloaking their involvement in intrigue'. According to the author (1992, 161), 'subjectivism does not avoid ethnocentricity any more than positivism does' and 'the positivist approach which regards the involvement of the researcher as unproblematic, and the subjectivist approach which regards the first-person narrative as some of miracle solution often achieve similar results'.

The solution does not lie in either of these extremes. What this research follows is a 'synoptic approach' (Hanford 1975) in which objectivist and subjectivist orientations are not seen as opposites, but as complements. As Geertz wrote, the symbolic universe of the actors is to be the point of departure, not the final destination (quoted by Karcher et al. 1981, 22). Emic data (subjectivist) have to be strongly taken into consideration, not as an end, but rather as part of the process of obtaining valid etic categories (objectivist). As Karcher et al. (1981, 100) state:

> an objective viewpoint demands continual motion, back and forth between immersion in emic data and construction and reconstruction of etic categories.

This synoptic orientation does not exclude the approach to 'differences' in favour of unity; it includes both. This principle means that, in this case, these alternative spiritualities can be studied both from the inside view of participants and from the outside because that approach 'includes the rigour of empiricism without its reductionism and includes the challenge of the phenomenologists without their insufficient means for validity' (Hanford 1974, 219).

Three Working Assumptions

Networking in the field, conducting a qualitative analysis and following a Weberian approach were not enough to reach the results of this research. I also followed three working assumptions. They were used as a guide to my analysis of these spiritualities. They are inspired by my field work and are that:

1   The religious experience of my interviewees is in the first instance irreducible and must be placed in dialogue with concepts and models of spiritualities in use;
2   The assumption of the (hard line) secularisation thesis should be held at bay in the analysis;
3   Rich religious (or cultural) exchanges may be found in shifting everyday life networks rather then in religious organisations.

Before studying in detail these three assumptions, here is an account by Martina, a Tarot cards reader met in a 'New Age' festival, that exemplifies the need for them:

> Listening the whole time [to some voices in my mind] but trying to live a normal life at the same time. [They were] actually telling me things about what was going on with people and it was just really weird. I went to the doctor and said I think I've got a massive problem here. I've been a junkie, da de da de da, I've got these voices in my head and she said 'I don't think you're schizophrenic, I'll put you on this medication'. Didn't help it. All it did was make me really tired. Which was not good when you're working a 19 hour day. So I actually met someone coincidentally, because I used to come down to Melbourne twice a week to go to the wholesale fruit and fish market, and I met this woman. It was strange. I was standing there listening. I was buying some stuff and then all of a sudden I'm listening to what's going on in my head and it was about meeting someone who I needed to meet to fill the gaps. And I had quite a good rapport with this fruiterer by this stage after all those years. And he said to me Martina you're not here and I said no no, I'm not. I'm tired and da de da de da. And I said what I really need is a decent body relax because I don't relax. The meditations weren't working because they were just out of books. And he said look I've got this card of this woman who my wife sees, she's a masseuse. I said great, give it to me, I need one really badly. I rang her there and then and went to see her. And for the first time in my life I think I actually relaxed. And she said to me you're psychic aren't you? And I went no. And she said oh okay. And she said when your gut instinct is to do something do you do it? I said of course you do. Otherwise you know it ends up being detrimental to myself. And she said have you got noises in your head? Maybe, why? And she said because I think you need to find out who you really are. And she said do you? And I'm thinking I've got no idea. [...] I have no idea who I am. I have no idea what I'm doing. But I've never ever felt that I needed a purpose. [...] And she said I want you to go and see a friend of mine. And I said oh look I don't have much time and she said don't make excuses. And I thought ooh she knows me.

First working assumption: The phenomenological noumenalist approach

Martina had been listening to voices in her mind for a long time. Less extremely, many of my interviewees claim flashes of intuitions. What are we to make of these sorts of claims?; claims that from some interviewees have radically changed their life as in the case of Elizabeth. She went to a meditation group and believed at that time that this practice was trivial, and during the third meditation session, she received a conversion experience, 'an experience of light':

> The [meditation] teacher didn't know that anything had happened. In a way even I didn't know what had happened because something had changed. [...] I went from being an atheist to believing that there was something greater than the individual. [...] It was nothing that I knew anything about. I suppose that's what set me on the [spiritual] path really, was not so much even the group of people, it was more having an experience of light coming through me and around me and how on earth I could be so wrong for so long about something so important.

After this, she decided to travel and to discover many religious groups. She was looking for an understanding of what had happened. My conclusion about these claims is spelled out in the first working assumption: the emphatic acceptance of the extraordinary, a belief which has to be taken into consideration because it enters into the acors' negotiation of their religious quests and generally influences their social life. This assumption means that I employ what Garret (1974) has called Phenomenological Noumenalist approach. The approach followed within this research admits subjective reality as an independent variable in social analysis and focuses its research on the consequences of belief and behaviour generated by religious experiences. This school has its roots in the work by Rudolf Otto (1936), a German theologian, philosopher and historian of comparative religions, who has focused his research on the non-rational aspect of the religious dimension. Being both theologian and scientist, his purpose was to embrace the scientific paradigm and the religious interpretation of the world. He sought to determine the kind of rationality that is relevant to religious study and found in Kant the pertinent pair of noumenon and phenomenon. The noumenon is in the philosophy of Immanuel Kant, the thing-in-itself (*das ding an sich*) as opposed to what Kant has called the phenomenon, the thing as it appears to an observer. Though the noumenal holds the contents of the intelligible world, Kant has claimed that human's speculative reason can only know phenomena and can never penetrate to the noumenon. Eliade (1957, chapter VII) writes that Otto describes under the concept of *noumenal* the manifestation of the sacred, of an immense power that generates a sense of awe for the human race limited in its profane experience. Otto has called the 'numinous' – or noumenal – or 'Wholly Other', that which utterly transcends the mundane world. It is roughly equivalent to 'supernatural' and 'transcendent' in traditional usage. The phenomenological noumenalist school accepts the noumenal as irreducible experience and as producing effects at the individual and social levels. It fits with the *Verstehen* methodology mentioned in the previous section, because it focuses on the meaning contents of the religious phenomenon, meanings that are to be understood from 'within'. This approach can also be found in Bendle (2003), Howell (1997), Hume (1998, 2002) and Nelson (1987) but is not used with Garret's appellation.

For the purposes of this research, I use the adjective 'mystico-pneumatic' to describe these supernatural experiences, and will not dedicate more space on the explanation of the different mystical experiences ('mystico') or the different visions of spirits ('pneumatic').

Table I.2 Mystico-pneumatic experiences reported

N=35	Mystico-pneumatic experiences reported
21 people (60%)	Claimed to have had mystico-pneumatic experiences
6 people (17%)	Claimed to be intuitive or having a strong feeling of being connected to something higher than oneself.
1 person (3%)	Claimed that they never experienced anything but that they would like to.
7 people (20%)	gave no information.

Table I.2 presents the proportion of my sample having these kinds of experiences. A majority of them (21 people, 60 per cent) declare such experiences. Furthermore, if we add those who claim flashes of intuition and the like, we reach 27 (77 per cent) of my sample. Often, respondents who declared themselves to be 'more imaginative' do not know if they really experience something beyond the normal or not. For example, for many years, the interviewee Marilyn thought that she had a lot of imagination, and one day she came to the belief that she was a clairvoyant. As she said:

> Well I've always had a good imagination. I've always been what I now know to be clairvoyant. Didn't know it then but just thought it was my imagination. So I found myself in my imagination.

Hay (1982; 1990) researched religious experiences in England and found in 1976 that over a third of all adults in Britain would claim to have had experiences of this kind. In 1986, the overall total has risen to almost half of the national population (1990, 56-57).

In the next chapter, I present those kinds of mystico-pneumatic experiences that have influenced the lives of many of these actors, and that for some, provide a grounding for the beliefs and practices found in alternative spiritualities.

Second Working Assumption: Keeping Secularisation at Bay

While Martina, the informant who introduced this section, was denying her religious experience, she met people in a market who gave her the address of a masseuse. The masseuse finally convinced her that her perceived psychological problems were psychic abilities and put her in touch with someone who would help Martina. Later in the interview, Martina mentioned her interest in Kabala and after I asked her reason for this interest, she referred to an affinity she had with someone she had just met in a street:

Interviewer: How did you decide to study Kabala?

Martina: I actually met someone. I met a girl who had been in New York studying and we actually met in a bar just by coincidence. She came running into the bar, she wanted some money for a meter and they wouldn't give her any change at the bar. And I said to her look I've got a couple of dollar coins, here you go. And she said oh look I haven't got change for you, can I buy you a drink. And I said sure. So we just started chatting and she was saying she'd just come back from New York, where she'd been, at the Kabala Centre. And so I went searching. She gave me a couple of names of some books. Then all of a sudden all these people kept coming into me. I met Linda who's the Rabbi at the Temple of Bethlehem. Female Rabbi. And she just all of a sudden appeared in my life.

These interactions in a grocery market and in a street, which convinced Martina to follow a religious life, gave her the interest to study Kabala: it did not happen in the private sphere but in public places. Obviously, not too much can be made of this, but I use it here as a justification of my second working assumption because it suggests the need to leave open another interpretation: that new forms of religion flourish and are communicated in public spaces, albeit, as in this case, not in the spaces of institutional religion. Secularisation theory, at least of the hard kind that posits a public sphere devoid of religious communication and discourse devoid of religious content, must be kept at bay if informants like Martina are to have a say and their experience taken seriously.

Contrary to the recent argument by Bruce (2002), I follow the working assumption that, even if traditional Christianity is in decline and less people attend churches, the West is slowly moving to a post-secular phase. Richardson (1985, 104) compares secularisation theory as something of a 'sacred canopy' for a majority of researches in the social sciences of religion. However, this seems less the case in very recent years. Secularisation theory, not religion, now seems to be in crisis (ibid., 114).

For Gauchet (1985, 233-236), the Age of Religions as a structure is over, but it will be naive to believe that religion is over in terms of culture. This inclines sociologists of religions to understand secularisation as the 'privatisation of religion' (see Luckmann 1990, 132). T. Luckmann (1967) discusses 'invisible religion', a form of religiosity that has emerged in a period when the ecclesial religion was decaying, religion thus becoming a 'private affair'. As Beyer (1991, 373) notes this idea has been put forward by many sociologists since at least the 1960s, a time in which, for José Casanova (1994, 19), sociologists developed more systematic and empirically grounded theories of secularisation and distanced themselves from the past thesis that religion would eventually disappear from modern societies.

Gilles Kepel (1994) claims that if religion did become limited to the private sphere in a certain phase of modernisation in many societies, around 1975, there was a reversal of this process around the world. Revived religious traditions no longer tried to adapt themselves to secular values but proposed alternative ways of organising society around sacred values. Kepel analyses some of these movements inside Judaism, Christianity and Islam and describes these religions as containing a high proportion of people who have a secular education but want to submit reason to God's law. Following this line, José Casanova (1994, 65-66) uses the term 'deprivatization' which is:

the process whereby religion abandons its assigned place in the private sphere and enters the undifferentiated public sphere of civil society to take part in the ongoing process of contestation, discursive legitimation, and redrawing of the boundaries.

Rather than referring to the too concise terms of death and return of religion (Eslin 1997, 7), because as Brown (1992, 39) points out, religion, is not static, but adapts to different social and economic contexts, I follow the re-interpretation of secularisation in terms of religious change (Stark and Iannaccone 1994, 231). One of the key points in the contemporary study of religion is to study people who believe without necessarily belonging (Davie 1994).

The minimal conclusion to be drawn from all of this is that the sociological investigation of new religions and spiritualities in contemporary societies must be protected from assumptions about confinement to the public sphere and triviality implied in hard line secularisation theories.

One consequence of this working assumption is that we can expect that with the downfall of traditional Christianity, we might expect the growth of alternative spiritualities and other new religious movements. However, as Houtman and Mascini (2002) comment, we should not neglect the fact that besides these new religiosities, nonreligiosity is an important option as well for the church leavers. Indeed, as Bruce (2000, 233) points out in the case in the UK, 'even the most generous estimates of the New Age are unlikely to have the new spiritual seekers filling the space left by the decline of just one denomination'.

Third Working Assumption: Maffesoli's Sociality

Martina did not go to a cult, a sect or a church. Her religious views developed through her interactions in everyday life. Albert, another interviewee, is a born clairvoyant and as a child, his mother was hoping that his ability would go away with age. However:

> We were living in Ringwood at the time. And then we moved from Ringwood to Bayswater, Mum sort of thought oh well maybe this sort of ghost stuff will change. Well out of the frying pan into the fire. [...] Mum, thinking that this is taking me away, that maybe I'll lose interest. Well we'd move right in next door to a practising working clairvoyant. Spiritual medium. And so that was that. While the other kids were out playing footy I was in learning tarot and doing all that.

Hence the third working assumption that these actors live their religion not in institutions or other formal organizations but that they exchange their religious products (cultural and material) in everyday life. This working assumption concerns location of these spiritualities. As indicated, I quickly learned that they were not to be found in organisations but in everyday life networks. I was looking for something akin to what R. Towler calls 'folk theology' and came to assume that these spiritualities would mainly be located exactly as Hay (1990, 98-99) found folk religion to be:

> Folk theology does not appear in textbooks; it is passed on informally within particular groups in society. In my view it is an error to chart the decline of Western religious institution as the one true indicator of secularization. An alternative account [...] is to say that religious interpretations of human experiences are by no means disappearing. The fact that these 'theologies' are unsophisticated, naïve and superstitious means that they tend to be ignored by investigators. But they are there, mostly kept secret, in what is perceived to be a hostile environment.

This folk theology is generally characterised by decentralisation, oral liturgies, dynamic and syncretic belief systems, and consensus-based leadership (Houk 1996, 447). In Folk religion, the attention of the researcher needs to be focused on legends (stories which are presented as true) and memorates (personal stories of the believer) rather than on theology, philosophy and the study of group rituals as used when researching 'official' religion (Sutcliffe and Bowman 2000). Other terms refer to this kind of theology and they are reviewed by Dobbelaere (1987, 122-124) as 'popular religion', 'lived religion', 'common religion', 'implicit religion or 'diffused religion'.

However, the description and location does not entirely fit with these spiritualities. 'Folk' refers to uneducated people in subordinated classes. This does not correlate with my own and others' observation of literate spiritual actors in urban areas.

My working assumption about social location and the mode of communication to be investigated in the case of alternative spiritualities has been shaped by ideas about forms of 'sociation' in contemporary societies. In particular, Maffesoli's notion of sociality has guided me, a paradigm that has also been used in the field of religious studies (Rémy 1996):

> The social realm includes mechanical solidarity, instrumentalism, the project, rationality and finality. Sociality, on the other hand, deals with the development of organic solidarity of the symbolic dimension (communication) of the 'non-logical', the concern for the present (Maffesoli 1990, 91).

This spirituality, I have come to assume, is not to be found primarily in the social realm as Maffesoli conceives it: there are no religious, economic or political institutions which propound a 'New Age' vision of reality. There are no ecclesiastical elites, no manifestos which can move crowds, no structured organisations to spread New Age ideas, but these spiritual actors are here. Sociality, a kind of underworld which gives to 'affinity' a place of honour, is the space where I have found these actors evolve and is a matrix in which individuals find their various ways of being (ibid., 8). In this space there is much social effervescence, but it is elusive (Amirou 1989, 115).

Contents

While other researchers on this subject tend to treat 'New Age' as a whole coherent spirituality with a single underlying logic of belief practice (e.g. Heelas 1996; Hanegraaff 1996), I allow the possibility that the term 'New Age' is a meronymy, i.e. a label bunching together unlike entities (e.g. neo-paganism and what I will call later presentist perennism). I therefore seek to identify and discuss some ideal-type characteristics which at once allow us to see links between the diverse actors of the so-called 'New Age' movement, to discuss differences between them, and to distinguish between 'New Age' and other spiritualities included and hidden by this meronymy (e.g. neo-paganism). Here is the path I have chosen to pursue this aim:

Chapter 1 (A Profile of the Respondents: Social and Spiritual Aspects) addresses the literature from which New Agers are profiled as urban, educated, middle-class, with a majority of women – a portrait mainly based on quantitative analyses. This chapter aims at providing a richer sociological description through a qualitative analysis of 35 interviews. This qualitative approach describes these actors as religious individualists, as technical mystics, and as people who locate authority in their inner self. They tend to move in or toward New Age through crises and through a consumption of New Age symbols that predispose, provoke and reinforce alternation to New Age. However, as we will see in *Chapter 2 (A Profile of the Respondents: Networking Aspects)* even if they perceive themselves as unique in this spirituality, they also mix with other people in 'affinitive' networks. For the purpose of this chapter, I will merge together the cult typology with the network paradigm.

Chapter 3 (Keeping New Age at Bay) elaborates an heuristic tool, or ideal-type, which I call perennism and which is the element that links my respondents. It is constructed on the basis of my outsiders' thematic interpretation of a variety of texts.

Chapter 4 (Perennism) supports a *Verstehen* approach, which is returned to when the constructed type is made to confront insiders' accounts. The word perennism, inspired by Aldous Huxley's (1994) *Perennial Philosophy*, is used as a sociological tool, and should not be confused with this philosophy. Perennism is defined in this book as a syncretic belief in:

- Monism (a paradigm which recognises a single ultimate principle, being, or force underlying all reality);
- The Human Potential Ethic (the teleology of a better or superhuman being; also referred to as self-development);
- Spiritual Knowledge (a quest for the knowledge of the universe or of the self, the two being sometimes interrelated).

Chapter 5 (The Two Spiritual Knowledges) explores one differentiation among my interviewees found in the former chapter by analysing the putative ancestors (esotericism; including the Theosophical Society, Spiritualism, Occultism, Guénonism) of these contemporary alternative spiritualities. In this chapter (and in the following), a difference between esotericism and perennism is discovered.

Chapter 6 (A Sociological Chart of the Age of Aquarius) and *Chapter 7 (Neo-Paganism and Presentist Perennism)* compare what is commonly known as 'New Age' to other contemporary spiritualities with a 'family resemblance'. This is done through an analysis of its history and further analysis of the interviews. At this point, I attempt to show what differentiates the supposed 'New Age' actors and their different spiritualities. From this, I am able to refine the definition of perennism and indicate diverse sub-types of perennist groups; these are Aquarian perennists (Chapter 6), neo-pagans and presentist perennists (Chapter 7).

Chapter 8 (Three Perennist Spiritualities) summarises the findings from the previous three chapters, attempts to find more elements of dissociation among the three perennist sub-types, and finds theories of modernity/postmodernity helpful. Chapter 8 thus analyses perennism and postmodernity through their elective affinities and builds on a synchronic perspective of perennism. I argue that the sub-types of Aquarian perennism (a modern movement valorising the future and progress) and neo-paganism (an anti-modern movement valorising traditions, mainly pagan) were innovated in the 1930s among esoteric groups. Presentist perennism, on the other hand, has its genesis in postmodernity. It is a postmodern movement focusing on the present. These sub-types cannot be usefully conflated under the term 'New Age'. More specifically, these sub-types have a different genesis. The Theosophical Society (an esoteric group from the 19th century) has engendered Aquarian perennism, while Occultism (another esoteric group from the 19th century) has inspired neo-paganism. These two groups were formed in the 1930s and 1940s. Presentist perennism is not connected to a specific esoteric movement but, I argue, has grown out of a cultural shift in industrial societies. Post-industrial societies (including their counter-culture movements) are defined partly in terms of deep cultural changes occurring within them; these include declining belief in the idea of progress, radical individualism, and fluidity of movement between sub-cultures. Presentist perennism, even though it borrows eclectically from earlier esotericism, is to be understood as an expression, in the field of spirituality, of emergent post-industrial or postmodern culture.

Chapter 9 (Perennist Re-enchantment: The Cultural Logic of Late Capitalism and Communicative Action) attempts to evaluate the impact of these alternative spiritualities in mainstream culture, and argues that a re-enactment of a part of the world is occurring through their re-invasion in public spheres (mainly in consumer culture). It will be argued that even if these spiritualities are part of the cultural logic of late capitalism, some of their actors resist the full commodification of their spirituality through communicative action.

Presentation of Participants

The sample is not representative of the population of all social actors involved in alternative spiritualities from the Western world, and not even from Melbourne. It does not respect the unknown statistical distribution of these believers in the population as a whole or a function of gender, of age, of level of education, of professional situation. It is a voluntary sample and it over-represents actors using the full resources of the networking process, and correspondingly under-represents those exclusively faithful to one group. This sampling allowed me to explore these spiritualities in their diversity, but the extent of this diversity is unfortunately unknown.

Details of distributions on standard variables will be reported in later chapters, but I can now introduce my participants.

Alan: Early thirties, a sales assistant in a 'New Age' bookshop, is against many 'New Age' practices and believes only in meditation.

Albert: Late thirties, claims to be a born clairvoyant. He ceased to be interested in religion when he was 16 and came back to it 10 years ago to become a spiritualist. He works now as a full time clairvoyant.

Alice: Early thirties, organises a 'New Age' festival every month and hopes that this will make people aware of the relevance of alternative spiritualities.

Anne: Late twenties, university student, became interested in this spirituality after reading a book by Ruth Montgomery offered by her mother. From an atheist background, she became hooked into this way of thinking and she tried many different religious practices. She found her path in the form of automatic writing as a form of meditation.

Betty: Late twenties, studies history and is neo-pagan. She has gone through a neo-pagan initiation but she is not affiliated with any groups.

Christine: Early forties, is a minister of an independent spiritualist church. She has been clairvoyant since she was young and has a background in nursing. She now wants to cure people not only physically, but also emotionally and affectively.

Daniel: Late forties, practised yoga for many years and experienced a mystical conversion in his twenties. He wanted to understand more and followed a guru in India (whom he still respects). However, he has realised that it is important to find one's own path. He is an astrologer and teaches Tantrism.

Elizabeth: Late twenties, found herself isolated in a new place when she moved to a new job. She met a new group of people who were into alternative spiritualities. She only started to believe when she experienced what she called a mystical conversion. She left Australia to visit India and Findhorn (Scotland), to learn more. She is now an astrologer and an undergraduate student.

Fred: Early fifties, came to Australia from Malaysia twenty years ago. He thinks that Western countries are good places for spiritual development because there is easy access to 'New Age' resources.

Harry: Early forties, calls himself a perennial philosopher. His approach to this spirituality is strongly philosophical and he teaches philosophy and religions.

James: Middle forties, lived through the 1960s counter-culture. He tried drugs and claimed a few mystical experiences. He was interested in many spiritual practices until the death of his son. After many years of depression, he tried Reiki and became fully involved in it.

Jane: Middle thirties, postgraduate student, left Iran where she was a Baha'i. At university she became atheist. However, she came back to religion three years later as a Zen Buddhist. She is receptive to other kinds of spiritualities.

Jennifer: Middle thirties, is a Feminist Spiritualist (see Chapter 7) and first became really interested in this spirituality when she was pregnant. She dreams of living in a community of women but realises the problems that come with it.

Judith: Early forties, initiated Betty in neo-paganism. She searched for many years for a mentor and realised later that she had become one herself.

Julia: Middle forties, postgraduate student, tried Transcendental Meditation when she was 25 years old, but was not convinced. She explored other aspects of this spirituality and became Buddhist. However, this has not stopped her being interested in other forms of spirituality.

Julian: Early thirties, was involved in groups specialising in ritual magic. He left when the group started to be interested in black magic. He studies astrology with Sue.

Marc: 34, is a parapsychologist. He collects stories from people who experience the other world and is planning to write a book on this subject. He studied demonology and angelology.

Marilyn: Early seventies, was the daughter of a spiritualist. She has been involved in alternative spiritualities since she was 11 and her life is rich in experiences in this field.

Martina: Late thirties, has always heard voices in her head. She thought she was completely crazy and one day found that those voices were attuned to her spirituality. She practices tarot card readings as part of her living.

Ned: Early forties, defines himself as schizophrenic and as being part of the new Christ consciousness (a new interpretation of Parousia, see Chapter 6). At 21, he already thought he was Christ. After searching for, and reading, 'New Age' books, he has managed to rationalise his belief.

Paul and his wife Michele: Late thirties and early thirties, immigrated from Russia to Australia. They were totally agnostic until Michele was cured by a psychic healer. Since then, both have been searching for answers.

Peter: Middle thirties, was first interested in alternative spiritualities through the practice of martial arts. He often meets in a discussion group sharing points of view and reflections on spiritualities.

Phillip: 55, is a spiritualist and a numerologist. He owns a little business which produces 'New Age' artefacts.

Robert: Late forties, had a stressful job and felt relaxed for the first time in a Yoga session. Over the years, he developed a psychic ability and he is now a psychic counsellor, which is part of his living.

Robyn: In her sixties, organises many 'New Age' festivals in Melbourne. She is also the channeller of a Master, an important entity. She started 15 years ago with contacts with spirit guides and then realised that she was channelling this Master; he communicates through poetry.

Roger: Early forties, had some psychological problems 15 years ago. His psychologist advised him to study palmistry and ever since Roger has continued research in this field. He is now a psychic consultant.

Sandra: Early forties, is involved in crystal manipulation. She started to study 'New Age' practices after her divorce. She is always keen to discover new facets of her spirituality.

Sarah: Early thirties, comes from a hippie family. Her mother offered psychic counselling for payment. Sarah was completely disgusted by her mother's attitude of ripping off people. She stopped believing in this and other aspects of alternative spiritualities until she realised that there was more to it than what her mother presented to her. She reads Tarot cards as a form of meditation.

Steve: 34, started his religious quest when he was 7. He went to numerous occult and neo-pagan groups and does not want to be formally part of an organisation any longer. He calls himself an urban shaman.

Sue: Late thirties, was born into a Christian religion which was too lax for her. She wanted to understand more about spirituality and became a reborn Christian. She decided that this was too dogmatic and opted to study something she had wanted to for a long time: astrology. She is now a practitioner and a teacher.

Susie: Late twenties, went to confest (a gathering of alternative lifestyle and spiritualities held in Australian bushland) and discovered the value of many aspects of alternative spiritualities that she had considered trivial. One day, she was sick and cured by a Reiki practitioner. She now wants to learn more within this field.

Tom: 60, born in Canada went through a tough initiation in a group that he did not want to name. He was an ambulance man for many years; and he is now an etheric surgeon. He owns a clinic in Melbourne where he operates on the etheric body (the aura) of his patients.

Veronica: Middle thirties, first studied astrology. Her current interest is naturopathy. She has a degree in hard sciences and wants now to be involved in the more human side of life.

William: Late twenties, was an orthodox Christian and homosexual. He left his religion because his sexuality was not acceptable. He now studies astrology while retaining much of his original spirituality.

Chapter 1

A Profile of the Respondents:
Social and Spiritual Aspects

The social profile of what is commonly known as western New Agers is urban educated middle-class and middle-aged, with a majority of women (Champion 1993; Rose 1998). However, this portrait is based on quantitative analyses, and as Rose (1998: 20) claims: 'we will become better informed [about the spiritual actors] once more qualitative evidence is gathered'. The aim of this chapter is thus to provide a qualitative and richer analysis of the 35 respondents interviewed.

At the beginning of each interview, I asked the participant how they followed their particular spiritual path (or spiritual journey). Other questions were:

- What are the resources you have employed or employ to follow this path? What groups are you going to? What are you studying? What books are you reading? What techniques or meditations are you using? (If there have been some changes of methods in the life trajectory: Why?)
- Why did you choose these resources and not others? Why do you think that these could help you better than other techniques?
- Where do you think this path will lead you?
- If you were to advise someone who wants to set out on a spiritual path, what would you say?

While analysing the interviews, I wanted to answer the following questions:

- Who are these spiritual actors (from a sociological point of view)? What are their defining features?
- How do people become spiritual actors of the alternative type? How do people strategise in or towards this religious field?
- How do they organise themselves? What are the details of their organisation – if they have any – and how does it operate?

These questions are inspired by Lofland's (1995, 37) list of generic propositions used in ethnographic researches. The interviews were thematically analysed to give an answer to these questions. Other analyses of these interviews on anti-modern, modern, and post-modern values can be found in Chapter 8.

This chapter will address the first two questions. The next chapter will focus on the third one and will deal exclusively on the way these actors organise themselves.

Who are these Spiritual Actors?: The Conflictual Actor

Four cases of alternative spiritual actors follow. The immense social psychological differences are obvious and challenge any simple composite portrait. Anne, William, Sue and Sarah have been chosen as case studies because of their pertinent explanations of the conflict they experienced with any sort of religious organisation. They also come from different backgrounds (Anne was atheist, William Catholic, Sue got involved in a born-again Christian movement and Sarah was born in a family already involved in alternative spiritualities) and offer a good contrast for this research.

Anne was a confirmed atheist until her mother gave her a 'New Age' book written by Ruth Montgomery. This book made sense to her and she began to experience the different aspects of the religious and spiritual field. '*I started to be very interested in spirituality and I went to some churches and things.*' One day, she met a reborn Christian and followed him to his church, '*he was a very devout fundamental Christian*'. Conflicts appeared quickly. She did not fit in with the dogmatism of the church:

> I had a chat with the man who was taking the Bible study group, who was a priest, I explained to him my interest in psychic phenomena and I said: 'Does Christianity have a belief that this is evil to be interested in it?' He said: 'well', he didn't want to say yes, but it was more or less yes. [...] I just thought, you know, I had this big debate with him and I said to him: 'Okay, if it is evil, do I have to be evil to want to study it?' There's nothing wrong with wanting to study evil. It's like how lawyers need to study crime or else how are you going to have justice, you know. And they were sort of, oh, not very comfortable with that you know. So I went on my merry way.

She finally separated from her Christian friend who had become her partner, and decided to follow different 'New Age' workshops. She tried many different practices, including regression, to discover who she was in her previous life:

> I've tried to be regressed. Which didn't work on me. But then they say it can take, you know, many sessions before you sort of, and you need to feel comfortable with the person and whatever, which I never did. And at something like [AU] $120 a session you don't want to go to too many sessions before you know that something's happening.

She also went to a Buddhist monastery and was ready to become a Buddhist monk. She left this place because she perceived that the monks were not completely ascetic, or authentic at times; they were known to watch the *Star Trek* series on television. She admits that she was attracted by the 'glamorous part' (i.e. the part which offers 'mystical knowledge') of 'New Age'; she hoped to become enlightened. Although she never had any mystical experience, she still hopes that one day the light might come to her. However, if this was strong in her narration when she first started her quest, she does not consider this aspect as important as before. After having experienced many different practices, she now believes she has found what she thinks suits her better (for the moment); that is automatic writing as a form of meditation.

William was an orthodox Christian:

> I was quite a strict Catholic [...] for some years in round about 18 to 23. But abandoned that and I no longer go to church any more.

Even if he refuses the teaching of the church, there is a part of himself that still wants to stay with it:

> It's still in a way part of yourself that you haven't quite, I haven't quite, shaken off. I don't think I ever will quite shake off.

He decided one day to leave the church because he could not solve his inner conflict. His homosexuality could not fit with the Catholic moral dogma:

> I went through a very emotionally difficult time around 21, 22, until finally I thought one of these has got to have to go. And I couldn't picture it ever changing, my sexuality. And much of the response I was getting from the church I was involved in was either you'll grow out of it or you can be healed of it or it's just wrong and you have to not do it. Eventually I thought well I don't think I'm ever going to grow out of it. [...] That was the beginning of the end. And as I began to question that I began to question a lot of other things too about that. I still believe in God but I don't know what God is any more.

During this time he decided to explore his life outside the church. After a few years he decided to come back to a spiritual life; he found it hard not to live a religious quest. He started something for which he had been longing for a long time, astrology:

> But lately I'm feeling a sort of need for something in some sort of way. That's probably in part why I've started studying astrology, to try and find a meaning, of something, or to the world, because I mean, as I say I still believe in God, whatever it is and believe in there's a meaning to life and there's an afterlife and so forth. But it's not terribly structured. The beliefs are very hazy and eclectic. So it's trying to ground that a little.

He still considers himself a Christian and believes in reincarnation.

Sue was born into a background that was religious but not strictly so:

> I was about 19 when I really felt serious about finding some kind of other meaning to life. I'd had a fairly traditional but not a strict religious upbringing, but church was a fairly meaningless process and I thought there's got to be more to it than this.

When she arrived at Melbourne University, she explored Indian religions and yogic philosophy, but she also got involved in a born-again Christian movement:

> I'd go to their meetings and argue quite furiously with them about things and eventually it was kind of can't beat them join them. So I had a go at that for a while, which I found fairly repressive actually. It was a period where I felt like a lot of my own thoughts and feelings had to be suppressed because they didn't align with the dogma that was being preached. And whilst they were all very friendly and they had, I think what attracted me was the sense of security in the group and that they seemed to be really certain of what they believed, and I was certainly far from feeling certain about anything.

She stayed in this group for around 7 years. She was heavily involved with it for the first 4 years, but later started to distance herself from this movement. Conflicts started to appear between her and other members of the movement, even if she wanted to stay during her three years of doubt:

> I suppose what ended up being a crisis was meeting somebody who I fell in love with and who was totally anti-religion. So that ended up being a 3 year sort of struggle within me and the outcome of that was to do a lot of soul searching, abandoning it altogether and just thinking well if I'm wrong I'm wrong, but at least I'm being honest. And you know all these threats of hell they throw at you. Which it really is like that to some extent. You know if you abandon the path then there are all these consequences supposedly. But as I've said, I mean I found my personal integrity was more important. So no regrets.

Out of the movement, she decided to study astrology ('*I've had a lifelong interest in astrology. You know since I was about 14 I've always read books about it and been vaguely interested*') and tarot cards and she now teaches in these areas.

Sarah's mother was a fortune teller and her auntie was a professional witch. As a child she could see 'ghosts and fairies', yet also, she saw the tricks her mother performed behind the back of her customers:

> I had every kind of crackpot come through the house for fortune telling because she's [her mother] very much an airy person with no common sense or business sense. So anybody was allowed in the door at any time. [...] So it was a kind of household if you said I saw a ghost, oh yes yes. Oh yes we've seen that one or you know I've just been talking to the fairies down the back yard, oh what were their names. And I guess I saw a lot of things when I was little.

She eventually decided to leave alternative spiritualities:

> I kind of grew up because of that being a total sceptic. I'd seen every trick in the book. I'd seen what my aunty does and what my mother does while they may think they're genuine, you know it's a lot of body language, reading's a lot of feeding questions and I can read people fairly quickly, so my thing is the line between psychic ability and just being able to psychologically analyse someone.

She even became anti-religious but she continued to keep an eye on alternative spiritualities:

> I was kind of fighting against it but at the same time I loved reading things about paranormal and I always found myself, you know I would ask Mum to do readings for me and she always knew stuff that she shouldn't know. Secrets.

Despite her mother's tricks, she found that her readings were 70 per cent accurate and started to dissociate '*spirituality with kitchen magic*'. Four years ago, she met a friend who re-introduced her to magic:

> she was very down to earth and very natural. I guess that appealed to me and I got to like the idea of, I don't know, it's hard to express. Opening myself up, back up to spirituality again in a comfortable way. Where it wasn't about tricking people or it wasn't about power.

And ever since, she has decided to study alternative spiritualities in an intellectual manner, rather than the 'kitchen magic' of her mother and aunty.

As typified by these case studies, New Agers from my sample might have been born in a religious environment or been atheistic, but none of them follow the steps of their primary agents of socialisation. They can be an atheist, and suddenly meet someone, read a book or have a mystical conversion to become interested in alternative spiritualities. They may have also been socialised into a strong religious background, but they always conflict with the ecclesiastical authority. They may even have been educated in an alternative spiritual environment, but they still rebel against their (religious) upbringing. In my sample, I have not found a common religious background that could be said to have influenced their decision to follow 'New Age' ideas, apart from a common factor of conflict towards their socialisation – be it religious or otherwise.

On their spiritual paths, after having rejected their spiritual establishment, my informants have visited diverse 'New Age' and non-'New Age' groups and often continue to experience tension and conflict within those groups (e.g. born again Christians, Transcendental Meditation, Scientology), because they want to find their own subjective religion. Their discourse on religious establishment is often cynical and derides the perceived dogmatism. Cynicism in this context is possibly a 'detachment mechanism', a way of achieving a 'role distance'. It is often used by those who have become disillusioned with their work or religion (Ballis 1995, 140). However, I find the word 'cynicism' not precise enough to describe my interviewees. Many of my informants used humour to describe their rebellious act against their background - be it religious or otherwise. The cases presented above show, to a certain extent, a kind of satire used to describe their conflict: a kind of satire that I felt while conducting the interviews and which is not, unfortunately, as strongly reflected in their transcription.

In their satire, my informants can be regarded as cutting themselves off from their past upbringing and justifying their religious mobility. However, one may wonder what happens after this detachment. Do spiritual actors of the alternative type go to another group or do they refuse to be involved in any group ever again? Julian's interview extract below emphasises a strong independent quality in my informants:

This is a thing I wrote just after I met my girlfriend. [...] We met at a party in February and then at another party in May. At the party in May we talked about a lot of things. Philosophy, magic, spiritual path. Because I was looking for a magical teacher at the time and she was saying no you don't need a teacher, you have everything you need. So I wrote this afterwards. This is basically written a few days after, in early May. It's titled 'the search for spiritual truth' by me. [...]

Be a student but not to any self proclaimed guru.

Have teachers but not one teacher.

Partake of group activities but be not bound to only one group for this may limit your growth.

At the same time do not wantonly hasten down every spiritual path that is presented to you.

Rather use discernment.

Have the confidence to trust your intuition for your intuition is your higher genius.

It is the guidance of your guardian angel.

The conflicts these respondents have experienced and their satirical approach make them perfect individualists of religion. By this, I refer to the notion of individuation of decisions presented by Dobbelaere and Voyé (1990, S4-S6) in which people no longer accept a religious 'set menu' offered by 'traditional religions' (and even by New Religious Movements for my informants) but are more interested in a *'religion à la carte'*. Describing these independent religious individualists, Dobbelaere and Voyé argue that 'the adage, "I think and I choose my beliefs and practices to express my religious feelings" – [has] a tremendous appeal for them, and especially for intellectuals'. This idea of individuation conforms with what Roof (1993, 167) calls 'new voluntarism' and what Hanegraaf (1999) refers to an eclectic private symbolism. In this symbolism, new religious and spiritual syntheses are continually created via an individual manipulation of existing symbolic systems. It also describes individual autonomy in religious matters, and implies a greater voluntarism within a religious life. These new voluntarists free themselves from ascriptive bonds and thus, presumably, weaken social ties to any particular religious group.

To know better, in a sociological sense, who these actors are and their religious individualism, I have found the notion of Troeltsch's mysticism helpful. For Troeltsch (1950), mysticism occurs in established religious traditions but its experience occurs outside the regular forms of worship and devotion to these religions. The experience of the mystics, from this ideal-type, is the means by which they realise and appropriate the tradition of the religious organisation in which they belong. They do not detract from the existing sociological forms of religion even if mysticism embodies the form of the highest religious individualism (Bastide 1996, 197-206). They even legitimise and support established ecclesiastical structures.

Technical mysticism, on the other hand, makes a break with traditional religion. Technical mystics contest the religion within which they have been socialised. They understand themselves to be independent from every religious institution and principle. Technical mysticism sets up its own theory which takes the place of doctrine and dogma by undercutting the form and structure of the established religions. It discovers everywhere, 'beneath all the concrete forms of religion, the same religious germ [...]' (Troeltsch 1950, 231).

As individualists, my informants are critical of the first religion they encountered (even those who were brought up in alternative spirituality) and tend to be cynical towards it. They leave their first religious socialisation and search for other religious groups and beliefs, and consequently become technical mystics.

There is a further characteristic to reveal. Nearly all my informants locate authority in the religious quest in the inner self (see Heelas 1993, 109; and Kohn 1991). Extracts from the interviews indicate the aversion among my informants to any dogmatic message from an authority beyond the self.

Michele stated that:

I think you have to find what you can relate to. You can look at whatever appeals to you. Because to each person at each level would be something that would appeal to him especially. Something which will appeal to me might be different than would appeal to you. Because we're all different, we're all at different stages and we're looking for different things. In the same book you might find something which I will just glance over. I would say that yeah you have to look for what makes sense to you. You know whatever makes sense to the person and take it from there.

Daniel on teachers:

But in some ways now I would say that I'm a little bit wary of getting too involved under another teacher. I'm quite willing to take their experiences as help for myself, but I have learned that finding one's own path is really very important.

In total, 29 (83 per cent) of my informants locate the inner self as the arbiter of the spiritual quest. None of the remaining 6 (17 per cent) advocated doctrine or a school of thought or a leader as authoritative. Kohn (1991) refers to this allocation of authority as 'the self as authority' or 'radical subjectivism'. This subjectivism dictates that one should find one's own path (another characteristic of their spiritual individualism) and includes experimenting and exploring spiritual practices, reading a great number of books, etc., until one feels confident enough to decide which spiritual path to follow. This exploration can take many years and it is stressed that time is sometimes necessary before finding the most suitable path. This aspect is for Heelas (2000, 247) part of humanistic expressivism:

One should be true to oneself, trust one's sui generic authenticity, have faith in one's own 'intuition' or in what 'feels right', rather than simply relying on reason or tradition; one should trust what is integral to oneself, one's own experience, rather than depending on what the establishment might happen to dictate.

How do People become involved in Alternative Spiritualities?: Alternation rather than Conversion

How does one become such a spiritual actor? Is it through the process of conversion? I have demonstrated above that my participants are technical mystics and locate authority in their inner self. These two characteristics immediately suggest that, whatever the process, it is not one often posited by those who join 'cults' – Lien Bich Luu to be understood in this context as a negative religious group – in which the conjunction of dependency needs and intense social pressure result in conversion (see Richardson 1993). Because of their individualism and their mobility, my informants constantly explore new ideas and groups for their spiritual growth. They could be described as seekers, i.e. explorers of different metaphysical movements and philosophies for whom 'seekership constitutes a social identity that is positively valued by the individual and his significant others' (Balch and Taylor 1978, 54-55).

This notion of the seeker with his or her path (rather than his or her cult or group) could describe each case from my field work.

York (1995, 16) underscores the work by Richard Travisano who distinguishes the terms conversion (defined as 'a radical re-organisation of identity, meaning, life') to alternation which involves a less radical and complete transformation. Travisano (1970, 601) defines 'alternations' as 'relatively easily accomplished changes of life which do not involve a radical change in the universe of discourse and informing aspect, but are a part of or grow-out of existing programs of behaviour'. Alternation is the outcome of what York (1995, 17) calls 'religious market consumption'. My participants move to one group and leave it after a while. Afterwards, they might visit one or many other groups or simply stop 'seeking' for a while. 'Alternation' involves constant mobility: there is never a radical change but a constant 'flip flopping' among, or back and forth 'visits' in and out' of, many groups.

How do my informants get into alternative spirituality apart from 'seeking'? They have experienced mystico-pneumatic experiences; everyday life crises; have encountered 'New Age' ideas in their family, in leisure time, through a significant other or in the counter-culture movements, and these have led them to their alternation. I have included in the 'everyday life crisis' category: divorce, conflict with traditional beliefs, loss of a job, and pregnancy; and in the 'leisure time' category: the reading of 'New Age' and Science-fiction books, the participation in 'New Age' workshops for fun, and martial arts.

Below are two extracts which exemplify two different ways of being influenced by alternative ideas:

Susie was sick and cured by crystal manipulation:

> At the time I didn't take a lot of ['New Age'] stuff seriously, so you know I thought oh well crystals, yeah well someone can hold a crystal over me and I don't really know if it's going to have any effect on me or not and so I'm not really going to take much notice. And I kind of didn't really get into much of it since then, but late last year I was really sick and really confused and a friend of mine started using crystal stuff with me. And I found, I think because I was really ill I was actually more sensitive to universal energies and environmental energies and things like that, and I felt lots of sensations from people using crystals and not all of it was positive. [From this, her interest in alternative spiritualities started to grow.]

Julian expressed his interest in alternative ideas more from a cultural perspective:

> When I was about 8 I used to read science fiction books and I read about this thing called telepathy, and that [...] got me going. I've got the science books giving me ideas about philosophy [...]. I guess when I was about 16 I got very interested in trying to read minds and you know my friends and I used to try and send each other thoughts, and we had a certain amount of success with that.

The two extracts above represent two broad ideal-types of entrance to these spiritualities: 1) one can experience a crisis (as Susie) and become interested in alternative ideas, and 2) one can start as a consumer of 'New Age' products and practices. These two entrance points to alternation are explored below.

Crisis and Mystico-Pneumatic Experiences

Sarah elaborated on crises in her spiritual path:

> And spiritual development for me is the same way. You go through these continual crises. Spiritual vertigo I used to call it. You know, oh my God, who am I, I'm nothing. [...] Which part is me and go through these horrible times. And then you come through it and then you're better for it, but then if I go through the next one, whatever that is.

Eleven (31 per cent) of my informants reported the cause of alternation is an everyday life crisis.

For ten (28 per cent) of my sample, this alternation is mainly due to a mystico-pneumatic experience: a specific type of crisis as argued below. There is 'extraordinary' experience, and from this, a spiritual quest follows. The 'seeker' tries to understand (and/or rationalise) his or her experience. However, a mystico-pneumatic experience does not necessarily mean that someone will begin to 'seek' in a straightforward manner. For example, Phillip and Albert believe they were born clairvoyant and for years had mystico-pneumatic experiences but did not try to explore them. They tried to push them aside and to not speak of them to any great extent. It is only after years of dealing with these experiences, of meeting people also involved in alternative spiritualities, that they began to practise their spirituality.

Are the factors of crisis and mystico-pneumatic experiences linked? Lynch (1978, 102-104) does not categorically dissociate them. Kellehear (1996) argues that the academy should acknowledge the link between Near Death Experiences (one of the mystico-pneumatic experiences) and everyday life crises. Hay (1990, 75) offers a useful insight into how crisis can affect the perception of everyday life and its taboos towards mystico-pneumatic experience:

> On examination of the secular culture in which we live, what one encounters is a narrowing of vision caused by social taboo. Much more interesting than triggering, is to remind oneself again of the occasions when this taboo is broken. One of the points that turned up very early in the examination of the accounts of [mystico-pneumatic] experience that were sent in to Alister Hardy Research Centre is the number of them that seem to be associated with times of great personal distress. [...] It became clear that around 50 per cent of all the accounts we received were associated with a time of disturbance, such as the loss of a loved one, the loss of a job, the fear of death, or severe bodily injury.

Ten (28 per cent) of my participants declared their mystico-pneumatic experiences as processes of alternation, whilst 27 (77 per cent) of my informants admitted to having had those experiences. For 17 (27 – 10) or 49 per cent (77–28 per cent) of my interviewees, these experiences could be considered as a predisposition or a reinforcement of their alternation, and not as the main cause. Only ten of the interviewees experienced this as a crisis.

The 11 (31 per cent) of my participants describing their alternation in terms of everyday life crises and the ten (28 per cent) in those of mystico-pneumatic experiences (i.e. those who experienced this as a crisis) could be united in the larger category of 'crisis' (21).

The Consumption of 'New Age' Symbols

As seen before, some people alternate to alternative spiritualities because they were brought up in a family that valorises these ideas (though they still rebel against them), because they were influenced by some significant others and/or by the counter-culture movement. It could be argued that these people were socialised into alternation in their family and/or by significant others. The problem is that my informants (being technical mystics) tend to rebel against any form of teaching. They may have been socialised to become individualist, but not an alternative spiritual actor *per se* and in fact appear to be resistant to religious socialisation as commonly understood. One of my informants, Sarah, was born in an alternative family, and completely rejected what she was taught and came back to alternative spirituality years later, but with a profound change. Rather than speak of socialisation, we would better refer to an *influence* of 'New Age' ideas communicated by an alternative family or significant others in a case like this. However, going further on this point would take us too far afield in the realm of social psychology.

It is hard in some cases to pinpoint the precise influence that has operated on my informants. However, in terms of triggers and/or longer processes of alternation, I would argue that 14 (41 per cent) of my informants were influenced by 'New Age' symbols transmitted in a family, in interaction with peers, in diverse movements, in leisure. Using this deficient term for the time being, by 'New Age' symbols, I refer to any material objects, beliefs, ideas, words that carry a 'New Age' connotation that is recognised as such by its 'consumer'.

These 'New Age' symbols can cause some of my participants to alternate but may also predispose people to alternate at a later date. Jennifer is a case in point. She alternated after a crisis (in her case: giving birth) but was predisposed by long familiarity with New Age symbols and practices:

> So around the time my daughter was still young and I felt, I guess discovering tarot, astrology, witchy poo sort of stuff, it felt very much at home to me. So it didn't feel like anything too new. So that's why it's so hard to pinpoint everything. It felt like a carry-on of my whole life.

The four case studies presented at the start of this chapter are instances of similar conjunctions of crisis and influence by consumption of 'New Age' symbols. Another example can be found with another informant, Sue, who went through a crisis when she left her born-again Christian movement and decided to 'seek' a new spiritual path by studying astrology, a discipline that she wanted to study for many years because she encountered it when she was a teenager. In these cases, as in the rest of my interviewees, it is very hard to 'pinpoint' everything.

Thus, two ideal-types of alternation to alternative spiritualities were found: one centred on crisis and the other on a consumption of 'New Age' symbols. However, the types are deeply interrelated.

How does the 'New Age' culture that has influenced my interviewees operate? Taking a small step beyond information provided directly by my interviewees, we can trace the path to alternation in terms of a production of 'New Age' symbols. As Mike Featherstone (1991, 117) puts it:

Rather than deal with the question in terms of a void in belief which needs to be filled to produce some meaningful moral order and adequate social bonding [...], we need to inquire into the specific ways in which beliefs, especially those produced by specialists in symbolic productions such as priest, intellectuals and artists, played a central role in holding together everyday life.

Chapter 9 will analyse this production of 'New Age' symbols, its specialists in symbolic production (with some insights from my interviewees who promote New Age symbols) and will even argue for a kind of re-enchantment of a part of everyday life (mainly in consumer culture).

Chapter 2

A Profile of the Respondents:
Networking Aspects

As seen in the previous chapter, authority is located in the inner self and no one has to follow a road already taken by someone else. However, this does not mean there is no mixing with peers in the spiritual quest.

How do they Organise Themselves?: The Networking Capital

As Judith explains:

> [...] I'm a solitaire [...] I don't belong to any group, no. I don't belong to any rigorously defined group any more than most people would say, somebody may be a computer programmer and they belong to the group of computer programmers but they don't necessarily know them. But they'll have a lot of friends who are. They'll all pull together. And if somebody's particularly good at some particular part of that job then they'll probably teach the others. If they're particularly strong in some other area the information is passed on. And it is more about information being passed on. It's a network I suppose more than anything else. A bit of a Web.

There would thus be a network, a web, in which people in alternative spiritualities exchange ideas. Technical mystics, even if they are religious individualists, are not isolated. My participants attend seminars, workshops, conferences, reading groups, and exchange ideas. They visit many kinds of religious associations and very few stay all their lives in only one. They also visit psychic fairs and New Age festivals for a 'bit of shopping' and select the new books and/or new practices on the market: always out to discover something new and to enrich their spiritual experience. However, as indicated above, they also experience many religious groups or ideas until finding 'what feels right to them'. The mobility of these technical mystics among various spiritual groups can be expressed as networking as mentioned by Judith and as described by others in the following extracts:

Elizabeth on networking:

> I suppose what characterises the New Age movement to me is a networking thing. Where you can just turn up to a place like Confest[1] on your own and meet lots of people and immediately identify with them.

Molly, a feminist spiritual actor, uses the expression 'widespread community' to describe her experience of network:

> And a very specific group of women who are still, like they're out there and you know you go to certain things and you know those women will turn up to it. It's a movement. It's a particular movement and it doesn't have a name or an address or anything. It's just that you know that if you go to one of those thing you know that such and such will be there and such and such. And there's ones that have been there for 15, 20 years, and then there's other ones who I knew. But there's a sort of a constant population of that community. It's a community. But it's a widespread community that connects via maybe women's spiritual magazines sometimes or these gatherings or whatever.

My informants were disinclined to stay in one organisation indefinitely. They wander. They network. Unfortunately, there is insufficient evidence from my interviews to allow more precise analysis of the structure and longevity of the networks. Furthermore, only seven of my participants use explicitly the term 'network' in their interview (whereas all of them indicate in their narration that they do indeed network). This underlines the fact that there is no consensus on a specific term to describe their mode of 'organisation'. Moving to the academic literature, we are faced with the problem that the classic Church-Sect-Cult typology is not adequate when dealing with these social actors (York 1995). One way to face these problems is to shift to a paradigm within sociology, which accommodates the fluidity of the New Agers, i.e. the network paradigm. This paradigm includes concepts such as the Bund (Hetherington 1994), neo-tribes (Maffesoli 1988), situationalistic networks (Lipovetsky 1987), and the Segmented Polycentric Integrated Network (York 1995) and the Web (Corrywright 2003; 2004). Explaining these terms is beyond the scope of this book, and I will thus work more specifically with that of the Bund; the reason being that this concept seems to be more appropriate to describe the affective and intuitive forms of associations of New Agers.

This term was created by the German, Schmalenbach in the 1920s. Hetherington (1994) summarises it as:

> An elective form of sociation, in which the main characteristics are that it is small scale, spatially proximate and maintained through the affectual solidarity its members have for one another in pursuit of a particular set of shared beliefs. (1994: 2)[2]

The Bund has its solidarity more focused on affective-emotional links. It is elective and for its members 'Schmalenbach shows that it is an intentional act of joining together with strangers that is the basis of their common feeling and mutual solidarity' (Hetherington 1994: 13).

This term better characterises the form of organisation chosen by my participants than 'network'. Indeed, the term Bund has, as its central theme, the affect and the emotional elements which appear to correlate with the intuitive form of authority located in the inner self favoured by my interviewees. Indeed, when my participants describe how to follow a spiritual path, they often underline the importance of listening to intuition, to know what feels right for them, i.e. if they experience an affinity with a group or a person, it is worth listening to their 'gut feeling' about whether to stay with this group or person. The mode of locating authority in the inner self facilitates 'spiritual mobility', i.e. the eclecticism (often affectual) in spiritualities. In some interviews, the affectual factor was not made explicit but emotional (and spontaneous) reasons were still recurrent in accounts of joining or leaving groups. This is exemplified in the former accounts by Elizabeth on the immediate identity (i.e. an emotional sense of connection) she finds with strangers from Confest, and by Molly who refers to the idea of widespread community (a term used by her to express a rather romantic vision of communities nurturing the emotional).

However, I would argue that the notion of cult – taking aside its pejorative connotation in everyday life (Richardson 1993) – is still valuable because it describes various cells within the network paradigm, and thus should not be forgotten. As York (1995) claims in the conclusion of his book, the challenge to have a 'viable sociological tool that is applicable to contemporary late twentieth-century developments and study' is to combine the church-sect-cult typology with the network paradigm.[3]. Such is the task of the next section.

The Cultic Milieu and the Network Paradigm

The cultic milieu is a concept which takes into account the fluid form of aggregation of New Agers. This term was coined by C. Campbell (1972) who refers to it as the cultural underground of society. It includes all deviant belief-systems and their associated practices, e.g. unorthodox science, deviant medicine, the world of the occult and the magical, mysticism, and alien intelligences.

A major flaw of this concept is that it focuses on the belief that there is a lack of organisation in this cultic milieu; accordingly it does not take into consideration more organised cults (York 1995). The task for this section is thus to take the more organised cults into account, and to combine these cults and the cultic milieu with the recent network paradigm.

As a first step towards this, Stark and Bainbridge (1981a; 1981b; 1985) provide a typology which includes three levels of cult activities supposedly covering the whole cult environment; in this typology (see below), cults vary in terms of their level of organisation. However, Stark and Bainbridge's perspective tends to focus more on the production of spiritualities and takes less into consideration the different modes of consumption of these spiritualities, i.e. the plurality of reasons why spiritual actors visit these cults.

These actors do not consume spirituality passively, and, they do not necessarily take it for granted. Inspired by de Certeau (1988), the production of spirituality is indeed not received passively, but is contested and again reappropriated. And if we compare spirituality to a message, there is a resistance from the original message and as de Certeau writes about texts in general, '[t]he reader takes neither the position of the author, nor an author's position. He invents in texts something different from what they "intended" (ibid., 169). Indeed, as described in the previous chapter, New Agers no longer accept a religious 'set menu' offered by 'traditional religions' – and even by new religious movements – but are more interested in a 'religion *à la carte*'. They free themselves from ascriptive bonds and thus, presumably, weaken social ties to any particular religious group. This type of subjectivism dictates that one should find one's own path and includes experimenting and exploring spiritual practices, reading a great number of books, etc., until one feels confident enough to decide which spiritual path to follow. This exploration can take many years and it is stressed that time is sometimes necessary before finding the most suitable path.

These spiritual actors are seekers (Balch, Taylor 1978: 54-55; Sutcliffe 2003a) and they network. They shop around in these cults – and in the cultic milieu – and they consume spirituality on offer. Their inner self appears to be the arbiter of their spiritual quest. These actors focus on constructing their own identity, their own personality, and on generating their own knowledge. These consumers are mobile and their tastes fluctuate. They are part of what Bauman (1998) calls post-modern religions; they consume products to gather and to enhance sensation.

Explaining the cultic milieu only in regards to the production of spirituality does not aid in the understanding of the movements of spiritual seekers among ideal-types of cults. A way to explain this networking would be thus to focus more specifically on the movements of these social actors between what is produced and what is consumed.

Thus, to provide a more comprehensive look at cults – some more organised than others – within the cultic milieu, I wish to build a two-dimensional model – production and consumption of spirituality. I will apply three works (Stark and Bainbridge 1985, B. Campbell 1978, Gillen 1987) which are highly significant for the understanding of cults (see below).

First Axis: Production of Spirituality

Stark and Bainbridge's (1985) conception of cults is especially relevant for the description of the cults' structure, i.e. their type of organisation which produces spirituality. The authors propose a typology of three ideal-types of cult: the audience cult, the client cult and the cult movement.

Audience cults are the most diffuse and least organised kind of cult. They often do not gather physically but produce cult doctrines entirely through magazines, books, newspapers, radio, and television. There are virtually no aspects of formal organisation to these activities. They 'deal in myth, weak magic, and esoteric entertainment. Audience cults operate primarily through the mass media but sometimes attract crowds of consumers to lectures, fairs, and the like' (Stark and Bainbridge 1981a, 430). These audience cults will be involved mainly in what the Jorgensens (1982, 375) call *psychic fairs*; a synonym with 'New Age' festivals.

> The obvious function of psychic fairs is to make money and disseminate information, yet they also provide a crucial basis for social network and solidarity. In the course of psychic fairs, members of the community make new friends, exchange ideas and services, reaffirm established relationships, develop business arrangements, present positive images to the public, make converts, and recruit members.

However in this kind of fair, I find not only audience cults but also sometimes client cults that are more organised, but which also need to sell their 'spiritual' products.

Client cults are considered by Stark and Bainbrige (1985, 26) as audience cults organised among those offering the cult service. No successful effort is made to weld the clients into a social movement or to have their all-embracing mobilization. The leaders dispense magical services – e.g., those of astrologers, tarot card readers, psychics, healers, water dowsers. The authors compare the relationship between those promulgating cult doctrine and those partaking of it as the relationship between therapist and patient or between consultant and client. 'Indeed, client involvement is so partial that clients often retain an active commitment to another religious movement or institution' (ibid., 26).

Cult movements (ibid., 29-30) are full-fledged religious organisations. Many of them are very weak organisations, others can function much like conventional sects and attempt to cause social change. The degree to which these movements attempt to mobilise their members differs considerably within this ideal-type. However, unlike the other cult types, these movements tend to provide a meaning of the universe for their members.

Stark and Bainbridge (1981b, 322) summarise their typology as follows:

> In general, cult movements are higher in tension with the sociocultural environment, because they present more total challenges to conventional beliefs and practices than do client cults (which focus on narrow areas of human concern) and audience cults (which tend merely to offer vague vicarious satisfactions and entertainment).

Second Axis: Consumption of Spirituality

Bruce Campbell (1978) defines his ideal-types of cults through the way they handle the tension between the sacred within and the profane. He posits two ideal-types: the illumination cult and the instrumental cult.[4] Campbell developed this typology to describe different forms of aggregation, whereas I will 'paraphrase' his typology to analyse the different modes of consumption in the cultic milieu.

The author describes what I call the teleology of the being, i.e. that these spiritual actors will try to reach what they believe is the ultimate way of being; and this will influence their mode of consumption. If one person believes his or her salvation is in the extramundane, by developing his or her divine spark he or she will consume certain means in relation to this soteriology, e.g. use of yoga for meditation. If another person fixes a goal in the intramundane to reach a state of well-being, of realisation, he or she will consume other mediums, or he or she will consume the same means but with a different conception, e.g. use of yoga to diminish stress. I have also found, in the work of Paul Gillen (1987), another kind of teleology offered by some cults that is mainly entertainment, e.g. use of Tarot cards to socialise and have fun.

Because of this teleology of the being, the spiritual actor will shop around cults to find what can help him or her. There is not one teleology or mode of consumption shared by them, but many; those are what this axis explores.

The Illumination Cult

Referred to by others as the mystical form of cults, the illumination cult corresponds to Troeltsch's technical mysticism: a timeless, universal religion concerned with the development of the eternal self. This type emphasises detachment from the personality and the search for direct inner personal experience of the divine within. (B. Campbell 1978, 233).

Campbell suggests that this kind of cult gives to its members a belief in a sacred within that influences their teleology for illumination, i.e. a mystic, a wise man, a wise woman, a sage, a saint, etc. Spirituality is here an end in itself, and will be consumed to fulfil this goal.

Thus, by 'illumination', I refer to a quest for a direct inner personal experience of the divine within, or for a greater individual potential.

The Instrumental Cult

Referred to by others as the self-adjustment type, the Instrumental cult offers the individual techniques by which to better himself [sic] and his [sic] place in the world. Inner experience is sought for its effects, its ability to transform the everyday empirical personality so that it can better meet the demands made upon it (ibid., 233).

The teleology of their members is to become a more 'powerful' person in the intra-mundane and focus their attention, not on an inner experience, but on concrete effects, e.g. to develop their intelligence, their charisma, and to feel better in their body. The spirituality consumed, in this sense, is a means to external ends.

Thus, by 'instrumental', I refer to some techniques an individual uses to better himself or herself, and to become more effective and efficient in worldly pursuits.

The Entertainment Cult

It is a concept borrowed from Paul Gillen (1987) which originally dealt with the pleasure of Spiritualism. Some people will involve themselves in a cult to develop their higher self (illumination cult) or to gain more power (instrumental cult), but others will go to some meetings just for a good time. The author describes the context of the spiritualist cult and in his observations, he realises that 'spirit messages entertain in many ways, but most distinctively by the evocation of a suggestive indeterminacy. Like the patterns of the Rorschach test, they provoke interpretation but refuse to support a definite meaning' (ibid., 226). He also describes the activity of the medium as an attempt to hold the interest of his or her audience, like a television channel will do to raise its ratings. In another research, Luhrmann (1993, 222) argues that people turn to modern magic, 'because they seek for powerful emotional and imaginative religious experience, but not for a religion per se'. Heelas (1993, 111) also refers to yuppie (like) people who consume a more Disney-esque – i.e. entertaining – spirituality.

The Grid

The first axis shows the level of organisation of the cults (Audience, Client and Movement) and describes the production of spiritualities in the cultic milieu. The second axis describes the reason behind the consumption of these spiritualities (illuminational, instrumental and entertainment). The crossing of the axes gives nine ideal-types of cult which are at the meeting place between the production and consumption of spirituality, and which cover the whole cultic milieu. Spiritual actors of the alternative type mainly network among these ideal-types and it will be impossible to associate any of them with strictly one ideal-type.

Figure 2.1: The cultic milieu and its affectual networks

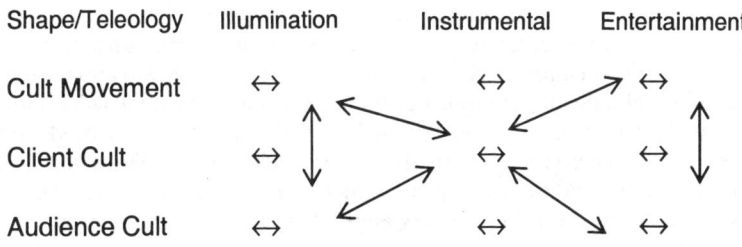

This figure describes what the cultic milieu is.[5] It is an imaginary place of many cults with different organisations and teleologies which offers a space of networking for spiritual actors. Some of them attract members, others, clients or patients, and others, spectators. In this milieu, many needs (e.g. seekership of spirituality, healing tools, having fun) of seekers are fulfilled: however, these needs vary. One person might visit a cult movement, e.g. the Theosophical Society, to develop his/her 'higher' self and another one might just enjoy the talks and workshops that this society offers. On the other hand, someone on a 'deep' spiritual path might go to an audience cult to discover new techniques of enlightenment. Accordingly these nine types of cults portrayed within the grid demonstrate not only the different reasons why spiritual actors use them, but also the plurality of actors who evolve in the cultic milieu.

However, even if these actors could be described as being involved in a cultic milieu, they are not restricted to it. The cultic milieu, being underground, is not the only place these seekers visit to enrich their spirituality. As already seen in the previous chapter, my respondents might have been born in a particular religion or been atheistic, but none of them follow the steps of their primary agents of socialisation. On their spiritual paths, after having rejected their spiritual establishment, my informants have visited many 'New Age' and non-'New Age' groups and often continue to experience tension and conflict within those groups, because they want to find their own subjective religion. For example, Anne, the first case study of the previous chapter, went to a born-again Christian movement (not an element of a cultic milieu). Some spiritual actors sometimes go to church or are interested in Buddhism and visit its temples. They can sometimes join a sect and stay in it for a few months. When one of my informants, Tom, said in his interview that the best way to learn spirituality was to 'get out into life and live it', he was referring to a life beyond a cultic milieu. Alternative spiritualities are thus not restricted to this cultic milieu and are spread in mainstream society as well. Indeed, according to a recent Australian survey, one in five [Australian adults] practice Eastern meditation, but less than half of them practice it frequently. One in ten turn to crystals and other new age practices, but again, for many their use is only occasional (Hugues 2002).

Well-Being in the Cultic Milieu: An Application of the 'Cultic Milieu' Grid

Current research on religion in general and subjective well-being (Daaleman et al. 2001; Eungi Kim 2003; Peach 2003; and Witter et al. 1985) tend to show a significant and positive correlation, and claim that the relation between religion and subjective well-being is stronger for religious activity than for religiosity measures. Specifically to this field of study on alternative spiritualities, spiritual actors are more interested in the experiential side of religion, i.e. they focus their spiritual work more on experience and relationship, than on gaining knowledge about religion or identifying themselves with a specific sub-alternative group. Indeed Champion (1995) shows that among these spiritualities there is more focus on experiential techniques, that is techniques that focus on a direct knowledge of the self, rather than on a taught knowledge. Moving quickly in my argumentation on this religious activity, it can be argued as a working assumption that alternative spiritualities is a factor that can positively influence well-being (Garret 2001). These spiritualities can regulate health-relevant behaviour in ways that decrease the risk of disease (e.g. promotion of ethos of moderation with substance use/abuse). They can provide in this cultic milieu a source of social contacts through these affinity networks which could be argued to give them a sense of meaning external to themselves and thus lead to a better well-being. They can offer psychological resources through aspects of their spiritual involvement with feelings of self-esteem and personal efficacy. Further they can offer resources for coping with certain types of stressors and health problems.

If we come back to the previous grid (Figure 2.1), we can observe that there are three ways to consume spiritualities, these three types can also be adapted to three types of ways of attaining well-being. Within these types, spiritual actors aim to develop themselves beyond their typical human condition and this leads to strong processes of self-enhancement. They follow rituals such as meditation and contemplation of symbols that act through and change the body and increase their subjective well-being.

These three ideal-types of consumption of spirituality which lead to different types of well-being are closely interrelated. One can decide to cure himself or herself through a Reiki practice and decide at a later stage that he or she is interested in a more spiritual path. On the other hand, someone who wants to follow this more spiritual path, has to develop his or her being to be able to reach other stages of perceived spiritual development. He or she might have to heal himself or herself first through a more instrumental practice. Consuming a spirituality, just for the fun of it, might also lead people to come back to certain of these practices for illuminational and/or instrumental purposes.

Further to these discussions on well-being, and moving my argumentation quickly to the work of Giddens (1991) and Beck (1992) on risks and well-being, these practices might be able to contain the growing sense of ontological insecurity that has developed in our Risk Society. It appears that since humans have secularly taken control of nature (industrialisation) and themselves (emancipation), risk, which at one time was the responsibility of an omnipotent God (e.g. war, famine, plague), would now be the sole responsibility of human kind. In the early days of industrialisation, risks were evident to the senses – they could be smelt, touched, tasted or observed with the naked eye (e.g. explosion in a factory). These risks were evaluated, predicted and calculable. In contrast many of the major risks today largely escape perception and calculation, for they are localised in the sphere of physical and chemical formulas (e.g. toxins in foodstuffs or the nuclear threat). They are no longer constrained within the constructed boundaries of nation states; indeed, the explosion of Chernobyl has affected diverse countries in the world and we are still suffering from the unknown consequences of this accident. Living in such a society affects people's sense of their self, and can increase their existential anxiety, or as it is also called, their ontological insecurity; that is, an obsessive exaggeration of risks to personal existence, extreme introspection and moral vacuity. The opposite of that state of being is ontological security; that is, a sense of reliability of persons and things aided an abetted by the predictability of the (apparent) minor routines of day-to-day life. It incorporates trust in the reliability of persons and things. Trust, therefore, may be regarded as a means of dealing psychologically with risks that would otherwise paralyse action or lead to feelings of engulfment, dread and anxiety.

Catherine Garrett (2001), a sociologist who immersed herself in three alternative practices – Transcendental Meditation, Yoga and Reiki- argue that these techniques provide a sense of ontological security by taking the practitioners beyond their current subjectivity by progressively reconnecting them to a sacred unknown which has been secularised by the advent of Modernity and the Risk Society. Indeed, in recent research in Australia, it was discovered that new forms of religion may provide a source of ontological security and thus be conducive to well-being (Possamai-Inesedy 2002).

If it can be claimed that alternative spiritualities provide three ideal-types of consumption of spirituality which are conducive to the subjective well-being of their practitioners, it is of course hard to evaluate the same process of the occasional users of alternative spiritualities. A comparative analysis between 'hard core' spiritual practitioners and 'occasional' practitioners would be tempting to conduct for future research, but it is unfortunately beyond the scope of this book.

The Portrait of the Urban Australian Alternative Spiritual Actor

After having detailed the sociological characteristics of my respondents in Chapter 1 and 2, here is a 'sketchy' portrait to summarise the findings.

York (1995, 57-58) notes that one of the criticisms of 'New Agers' is the charge of narcissism, i.e. that they indulge in the deification of the isolated self. This view has just been argued against. These actors are indeed religious individualists, but they exchange their cultural and material products in both a cultic milieu and in everyday life. They perform this exchange by 'affinity' networking.

Who are these actors? They are satirical cynics, religious individualists, technical mystics who locate authority in their inner self. However, even if they perceive themselves as unique in this spirituality, they also mix with other people in Bünde. They network across all different types of 'cults', but this networking is far from being limited to cults and the cultic milieu alone.

How do people move in or toward alternative spiritualities? Through crises and through a consumption of 'New Age' symbols that predispose, provoke and reinforce alternation to these spiritualities. Crises (with mystico-pneumatic experiences) and consumption of 'New Age' symbols are factors of alternation that are deeply interrelated.

Notes

1 Confest is a bi-annual gathering of alternative lifestyle and spiritualities, and radical political movements, held in Australian bushland and often comprising 8000-10,000 people (St John 1997).
2 A longer definition is presented in Hetherington (1994: 16) but it complicates the phenomenon unnecessarily.
3 His claim is more elaborated than this; but this is beyond the scope of this chapter.
4 He also posits the service-oriented cult which is on aiding others for their spiritual growing. But because this cult tends to be found to a greater or lesser degree in all cults, and because the author does not have a high regard for this ideal-type, I will posit the service-oriented cult as a non-independent type, and therefore, will omit it from my work.
5 C. Campbell (1972) who coined the expression 'cultic milieu' refers to an 'instrumental-expressive orientation axis' which is included in my 'illumination-instrumental-entertainment orientation axis'. Campbell also bounds the cultic milieu with a 'religion-science axis.

Chapter 3

Keeping New Age at Bay

To study these spiritualities is to face a major problem. As will be detailed, they are a customised religion, constructed by individuals. These spiritual actors visit one or many groups, read books, watch related television programme(s), listen to lectures, assist at workshops,... and then, as will be shown, seem to interpret, select and construct by and for themselves their own idiosyncratic spiritual culture. Furthermore, these actors might be ignorant of certain cosmological ideas and their theoretical underpinnings that are taken to be key elements of 'New Age' culture. The implication of this is that it appears that there will be as many different beliefs as there are spiritual actors, because every one of them may create his or her own syncretism out of a range of doctrines, theologies and experiences.

Some authors refer to esotericism, occultism, gnosticism, neo-gnosticism,... as the heart of these spiritualities. But, though various mixes of all these spiritualities are consumed by these actors, none of them appears close to being a unifying principle for 'New Agers'.

In this chapter, I continue the task that was set in Chapter 1 and 2, that of finding the common characteristics of my interviewees. Thus, I now search for a conceptualisation (or a tool of understanding) that is the closest possible to the representations of those involved in this spirituality and which can encompass their spiritual ideas. This chapter argues that neither etic (i.e. objectivist, or from the point of view of the researcher) nor emic (i.e. subjectivist, or from the point of view of the participant) conceptualisations alone are of much use in developing this sociological investigation. It therefore proposes to combine those two approaches to produce a conceptualisation which at once, faithfully reflects self-representations, and opens the specific spirituality of these spiritual actors to further comparative investigation in the following chapters.

Etic and Emic Approaches: Categorising 'New Age'

Many etic definitions of 'New Age' exist in the literature. They have already been analysed and commented in two recent studies (Kemp 2004; Sutcliffe 2003a). For example, Sutcliffe (2003a, 21-25) embarks on an analysis of the various etic understanding of the 'New Age', addressing for example the works of Hanegraaf (1996), Heelas (1996), Bloch (1998). He concludes about the sum of these works that it is 'a complex overview that – as one might expect – is strong on texts, beliefs and ideas, but less sure, even contradictory, on ethnography, genealogy and empirical structure'. There is no point here to re-invent the wheel and I thus invite the reader to consult these works for a detailed analysis of the current critiques on definitions on the 'New Age' from various disciplines (e.g. anthropology, studies in religion, psychology) and other religions (e.g. Christianity[1]). In sociology, there are different ways to describe 'New Age'. In France, Champion (1995) gives a descriptive classification for this New Age spirituality. She defines 'mystico-esoteric nebulae' as consisting of:

> the heterogenous ensemble of new groups, waves, networks, of a mystical and esotericist type, which have been affirmed since the 1970s. Those networks can be attached to some religions: eastern religions (Hinduism, Buddhism), or more exotic religions (notably shamanism). They can reactivate diverse esotericist practices, or correspond to new psychoreligious syncretism as 'transpersonal psychology'.

Michael York (1995) focusing on structural form, has developed the conceptualisation of 'SPIN (Segmented Polycentric Integrated Network)' to describe the segmentation and the boundary-indetermination associated with this spirituality. His research led to that of Corrywright (2003, 2004) who makes reference to a Web instead.

These characterisations focus on the structural aspect of New Age and do not fit with the intention of this research which is to develop a conceptualisation which is inscribed in the local 'reality' of those involved in this spirituality. Indeed, as described earlier, this book uses a Weberian approach and adopts the perspective that the key to explaining human conduct lay in adopting the actor's point of view.

It is important to note at this stage that Heelas (1996) and Hill (2004) have also researched a conceptualisation of New Age, which does not focus on a structural characterisation, but this will only be addressed at the end of the next chapter.

The attempt to construct an emic characterisation of these spiritualities faces challenges. There is the danger of trivialisation which arises when informants represent themselves in terms of exotic aspects like crystals and channelling. Similarly, there is the problem that the apparent kleptomanic behaviour of these actors may obscure whatever there is of an inner logic or telos involved in this spirituality. Sutcliffe (2003, 122-125) attempted the same line of work with the 'New Age' literature and faced the same problems as myself with my informants. He suggests that since the 1970s the past conception of 'New Age' which tended to be unified is now widely diversified; as it will be demonstrated in this chapter.

There are also problems in what would be called 'New Age' literature. As will be seen in Chapter 6, for some actors, the 'New Age' is at the top of a long and spiritual evolution process that leads to the Age of Aquarius. However, believing in spiritual evolution does not mean being a 'New Ager'. Wilber (1981, 327), a transpersonal psychologist (see Chapter 8) who believes in spiritual evolution, even perceives 'New Age' as Dark Age. Other writers who would be called New Agers also show some ambivalence towards the word (as seen by York (1995)). For other so-called 'New Agers', including those I have interviewed, 'New Age' is a pejorative term.

New Agers' detachment from systematised belief and practice poses one among the many problems confronting emic representations already raised in the literature (e.g. Feleppa (1986) and Karcher (1981)). Another overlapping problem is these actors' extreme individuation, including the rejection by many that they belong in the category 'New Age'. Practitioners offer indeterminacy rather than determinism, diversity rather than unity, difference rather than synthesis, complexity rather than simplification.[2] Their experiences are so specific and various that using their vocabulary will be like writing a phone book so that the aim of useful conceptualisation recedes as the self-representations multiply.

Sutcliffe (2003) in his analysis of the 'New Age' in the UK points out two different time periods. Before the 1970s, the 'New Age' currents tended to be ascetic, puritanical and other-wordly, whereas after, they became emotionally expressive, hedonistic and firmly this-wordly. Those before the 1970s tended to be subcultural pioneers and were serial seekers; those after are countercultural baby boomers and multiple seekers.

> A 'serial' seeker has changed religious or spiritual allegiance, typically more than once. Adhesion to each 'spiritual path' may last months, years or decades, and any number of sequential affiliations may be pursued over the course of a lifetime. [...] In contrast, multiple seeking proceeds multi-directionally and synchronically: an array of spiritual resources are exploited more or less simultaneously. Ideas, methods and techniques are decontextualised and reconstituted in new settings and adventurous juxtapositions (Sutcliffe 2003, 204).

These multiple seekers are far more extreme in their individuation approach to religion and this makes them harder to study from a more classical sociological approach than the serial seeker. These difficulties were evident in the field. As already discovered by Steyn (1994) in South Africa, in Australia, not many people identify with the term 'New Age'. At the end of the interview, I would always ask (if the topic had not been covered before): 'What do you understand the New Age to be?'. The answers were almost invariably negative. 'New Age' was:

A Misnomer

'New Age' is not 'new' at all. It includes beliefs and practices that are traditional. Here are a few accounts:

> *Christine*: 'But really it's old age and it's called new because they're breaking away from the religious dogma and Christianity itself'.

> *Julia*: 'I suppose that's the way I feel about the term New Age. Because it's not new'.

> *William*: 'Well first the New Age probably isn't all that new. I mean a lot of the concepts and things within it are quite ancient'.

> *Judith*: 'New Age now tends to be applied in two ways. Those people who are within it saying oh isn't it wonderful and new and therefore it will work this time, and those from the outside saying oh yes New Age, that stuff! Which is very dismissive and very oh yes well it's useless and it will go away again. A passing phase. New Age to me is really almost an oxymoron'.

A Business (often shady)

This spirituality allows some spiritual con-people to exploit the credibility of others. 'New Age', in this context, is also put down in terms like: 'they don't do this with the heart' or 'their price is too high'. New Age itself is viewed as a spiritual supermarket:

Albert: 'The financial side of things. Like with the New Age type of people'.

Sue: 'A typical New Age, I suppose the worst type will be the supermarket variety'.

Martina: 'I went to this New Age shop. Without it being from their heart. It's all from their head and their money. And look, I'm the first to admit I make money out of crystals [...] Because I believe in them. Not because I necessarily need to make the money as well'.

Sandra: 'It's like a train labeled New Age and everybody's jumping on it. And it started off very good, a very good term. But now there's a lot of people out trying to make big money on it for all the wrong reasons. Oh it's not wrong to make money, but they're just, their heart and souls are not in it'.

A Grouping of the Weak

This spirituality involves naive, shallow, gullible people, but also persons lost in the airy fairy who believe in everything without a critical mind. 'They are self deluded':

Alan: 'She [a friend] is hiding the unhappiness or the suffering or the emotionally confusion side underneath all these barriers of New Age rubbish. Although I do think it has its place. But gee it can be abused by some people'.

Albert: 'Yeah a lot of the New Age people basically spend too much time with their head in the clouds'.

Elizabeth: 'And the other thing I find most irritating about the New Age movement is how gullible people are'.

Superficial

There is a predisposition from people to touch everything superficially and not studying thoroughly one or two spiritual practices. 'There is no effort'. 'It's a lazy path'. 'New Age' is also dismissed as a certain fashion which trivialises spirituality in general:

Marc (speaking on some eclectic practices): 'And so that's what I feel is probably the dilution or a pollution of the true faith. And so that's why new Age is frowned upon'.

Julia: 'I suppose to me New Age tends to trivialise what's going on I suppose'.

Sue: 'I guess I'm a bit of a, you know I'm not your typical New Age, totally immersed in it sort of person [...]. I mean my personal feeling is that I like to keep my feet on the ground a bit [...]'.

Sarah: But honestly my definition of New Age is probably my definition of people who go to church every Sunday just because they do. It's just a nice watered down and easy way without much effort of getting involved in'.

Judith: 'They [New Agers]'re looking for an answer and they want a quick easy one. There are no quick easy answers so they'll fake it [...] well, they're weird but they're mostly harmless'.

Some of the characterizations were less obviously or less strongly negative. 'New Age' is described by my interviewees variously as:

The Age of Aquarius

It is synonymous with 'New Age' (see Chapter 6). In this sense, 'New Age' is characterised as a belief in a better world:

Alice: 'The New Age actually refers to the Age of Aquarius'.

Phillip: 'It's like a new way of living where New Age is where you've got people who are looking for something that religion, our man-made religion is not teaching. And that's why people go into what they call as New Age. You hear the Age of Aquarius and all this'.

Paul: 'Every age is a new age. The only reason they're calling it that is because we are coming out of the old age which is the Age of Pisces and we're coming out into the next [the Age of Aquarius], it's really the new age, it's the next age'.

An Awareness

There is today a tendency for persons to be interested in spiritualities and it has a positive aspect for the respondents, even if it involves the critics as mentioned above. The knowledge kept secret in pre-modern societies (see Chapter 5) is now open and allows everyone to have a grasp on alternative spiritualities:

Christine: 'To me New Age is the door, it is unlocking the old religions of the past'.

Sue: 'I think it's wonderful that the resurge of interest in all these things [New Age], which are often very old things that are coming more to the fore'.

Judith: 'To me New Age at the moment basically means people who are seeking something other than what they perceive to exist already'.

A More Loving Attitude

People involved in this spirituality are more loving and caring than people in dominant culture. They are happier and less stressed. However, in some interviews, 'New Agers' are 'charming but a bit silly':

Alan: 'It's [New Age] telling people about, well to open themselves up to all kinds of emotional and intellectual possibilities. Now I think that's a fantastic thing. Although enough, it can do damage to some people'.

Alice: 'I don't think our education system really teaches people that they are worthy. And to me that's what the New Age is. It's saying okay you know, we're going to give you all these things, you are a wonderful thing, run with it'.

Robyn: '[New Age] opens, broads mindedness you know. Non-judgemental. Just totally open'.

Roger: 'Well I think that the connecting principle to all this New Age movement is love. Is unconditional love. Spiritual love. Acceptance and appreciation'.

There were other descriptions not included here because they were so idiosyncratic or contradictory as to be incompatible with representations of 'New Age' by the other interviewees.

Table 3.1 lists the informants who mentioned these perceptions. Many respondents cross-over the different understandings. The two most used descriptions are that of a shady business, and superficial; both very negative.

Table 3.1 Perception of NAS

Perception of NAS as (n=35)	n respondents
A shady business	14 (40%)
Superficial	11 (31%)
Being for weak people	10 (28%)
Raising awareness	10 (28%)
Synonymous with the Age of Aquarius	8 (23%)
A misnomer	5 (14%)
A more loving attitude	4 (11%)

This result is quite different from that obtained by Rose (1996), as underlined by Kemp (2004, 172-173). Rose conducted a large survey of U.K. readers of a New Age magazine, and to the question, 'In a few words please describe what you think the New Age is', he found five types of answers: 1 – Greater awareness, 2 – Growth in spirituality, 3-Recurrence and renewal of aspects of life which have become distorted, 4- Reaction against materialism, and 5 – More holistic outlook on life. This is quite different from my results above. We could perhaps argue that the sample in Australia is different than in the UK, however the literature seems to point out the problem is with the word 'New Age' itself (e.g. Lewis and Melton eds. 1992, Introvigne 2001). My qualitative methodological approach, unlike that undertaken by Rose (1996), allowed me to gain the confidence of my participants to the extent that they opened themselves to this contentious issue.

Some interviewees proffered positive and negative characterizations. For example, Daniel links the 'shady business' and 'awareness' aspects of 'New Age', and he also offers us a good joke:

[...], certainly the New Age has got its hands dirty. I mean it saddens me. Like for instance when I went to Byron Bay, originally it was a very spiritual place, and now when I went there last it seemed to be very promotional. It's all you know become very money orientated. Not that there's anything wrong with money but as long, I don't mind money as long as I say there's an equal amount of give and take, and I just don't feel that that's always the case. And certainly things like that exist in the ordinary world too. And at least the New Age is maybe striving to make an effort to make people more conscious. So you know I have mixed feelings about it. But as far as truth is concerned, New Age, the only thing that I can think of is a story that I heard once. There was a guy who went to a guru and he said I'm ready for the highest truth, now you can give it to me. He says thou art that, you are the self, etc. And he said oh, great. And he said but is that all, that's it? And he said yeah, sorry, that's the truth. You asked, I told you. I don't feel satisfied with that and he said well there's a guru down the road a couple of kilometres and you might go check him out, maybe he can tell you something that I can't. So he went to that guru and he said you know I'm ready for the highest truth, will you give it to me and he says well first you have to do 12 years of service. I just don't give it out that easy. So he says oh okay. So he shovels cow dung or whatever for 12 years and at the end of the time he went back to the guru and said okay I've done my service, what's the highest truth, and he said well you are the self, you are consciousness, you are a perfect being. He said the guy down the road told me that 12 years ago. And he said well truth hasn't changed in 12 years. So yeah that's how I sort of feel about the New Age. You can redress it up and put it in different clothes and whatever, but it's still the same and it always will be.

However, most of my informants, contacted because of this supposed interest and involvement in 'New Age', describe 'New Age' in terms of the negative aspects they find in alternative spiritualities and the groups promoting them. The term 'New Age' seems to be like a mirror which reflects only worries, frustrations and pejorative sentiments regarding the unethical practices and beliefs associated with alternative spiritualities.

The following extract summarises in a way the concerns of a large majority of my respondents about 'New Age'. I put my question to Steve who is so totally disillusioned not only with 'New Age' but with all alternative groups and systematised teachings that he now rejects them all and relies completely on his own judgements:

Interviewer: 'I would like to have your opinion on the word New Age'.

Steve: 'Oh, it can be anything you want it to'.

Interviewer: 'But your conception'.

Steve: 'Oh, I don't worry. As far as I'm concerned, with every one of these fields of knowledge, most of it's crap. In the middle of it is something really great. I try and find the venerable in all things, yeah. I don't have any problems with the New Age. A lot of occult people think they're more advanced than New Age people. But I mean how can you tell?'

Following this discussion on the different ways that insiders interpret the 'New Age', Table 3.2 presents the distribution of their attitudes towards it. Twenty-five (71 per cent) of them had pure negative feelings on 'New Age'.

Table 3.2 Attitude towards NAS

Attitude towards NAS (n=35)	n respondents
Negative	25 (71%)
Positive	4 (11%)
Positive with negative aspects	2 (6%)
Positive but respondent does not identify as a New Ager	3 (9%)
Not clear	1 (3%)

My informants, by and large, were so anxious to distance themselves from what they took to be 'New Age' that it is impossible to use their responses to my questions about the meaning of the term as the basis for reconstructing an insider's understanding of 'New Age'. That, of course, does not mean that my informants do not share some sort of spirituality which can be characterised with reference to their own representations of their beliefs, practices, orientations and social relations. But it does mean that, to be faithful to their representations, the label 'New Age' must henceforth be dropped. Since, as Kemp (2004) and Sutcliffe (2003a) find, none of the academic 'etic' categorisations of 'New Age' is entirely satisfactory, it seems necessary to undertake the task of conceptualisation anew; at least for as long as we remain convinced that there is indeed a spirituality out there, shared by sympathising minorities in many countries that is worth trying to adequately define and conceptualise. Succeeding in this task will allow us to draw some findings when analysing sub-groups from within the sample of this research. This will be examined in later chapters.

The task will not be easy. Reference to adepts' own representations of their spirituality is especially difficult because of the profuse unsystematical terminology they use and the various emotional loadings that some of the more frequently used terms have.

For example, an informant, James, used the term 'higher self' to express what I initially understood to be a higher state of the self. Later, I interviewed Julia who shared a house with him for a while. During the interview I tried to use the language of my informants as much as possible, so I referred to the term 'higher self'. She rejected the term because of its suggestion of hierarchy, and was reluctant to employ it. Three months later, I taped their friend's (Peter) conversation, and while the two earlier interviewees did not call themselves 'New Agers', Peter proclaimed himself to be one. Three people who have lived together still did not share the same vocabulary or place the same connotations on common terms. As James ended his interview:

> I mean it's just my thoughts. Someone else will describe it in a completely different way. [...] I mean it makes little difference. It's the process and the communication that's important. The labelling's not.

And as Veronica also mentioned:

> Labels get in the way I think. Because everyone starts arguing about what the labels mean. So I'm not a label person.

Some changes in terminology appear to be market led. When I asked my informant Albert why he was involved in psychic fairs when he had declared himself to be a spiritual medium clairvoyant, he answered:

> We call them psychic fairs. Now we have advertised a couple as medium days. People don't come. No. They come to psychic fairs but they won't go to medium days. Even though they're exactly the same thing. People like the word psychic for some reason.

In the face of all those difficulties, I think it is clear that any conceptualisation of the spirituality under investigation cannot be purely emic. It is tempting, indeed, to bring the quest for conceptualisation to a close with the conclusion that this spirituality is essentially and exclusively individualistic; that there is nothing shared except the exaltation of individual eclecticism in what Lipovetsky (1987) would describe as a frivolous economy, i.e. consumers of cultural fashion who set their own goals and design their own lives guided only by hedonistic values. They eschew available macro-identities. They are mobile and their tastes fluctuate.

Adopting the notion of 'New Age' as a frivolous economy of religion would lead us to describe these spiritual actors only in their micro-identities, perhaps to the extent of dedicating one chapter per actor. This is not the path I propose to follow, despite the difficulties of defining 'New Age'.

As suggested above, it is impossible to define 'New Age' exclusively in emic terms. Indeed, the different discourses of my interviewees read like a post-modern intertextuality inviting the reader to wander in imagination and interpretation. How then to arrive at a conceptualisation which, while being informed by practitioners' representations of their spirituality, locates unity and allows characterisation so that this spirituality may be compared with others? As a first step, I propose to eliminate the phrase 'New Age' and to construct, with the help of a body of literature on perennial philosophy, an ideal-type of spirituality which, I believe, helps discern thematic unity in the plethora of emic representations. Aldous Huxley's (1994) work on world religions and spiritualities is the only work that is recognised as an insider's text by these spiritual actors and that can help this task. Other works by 'New Agers' are not openly aimed at an analytical (in the academic sense) approach of what the 'New Age' is, or if they do, they tend to focus on one sub-type of New Age spirituality (see forthcoming chapters). Further steps, of course, involve shuttling backward and forth between the ideal type construct, those emic representations, and indeed other etic representations. This will be discussed in more detail in Chapter 4.

The body of literature from which the ideal-type will be constructed includes the work of Nicholas Coleman (1994), Aldous Huxley (1994), Alan Laibelam (1992), Linda Olds (1992), Ted Peters (1991), Janice Rushing (1985), Huston Smith (1989), Eugene Thomas et al. (1993) and Ken Wilber (1981, 1996).

Philosophia Perennis

Aldous Huxley (1994) believes that rudiments of perennial philosophy may be found

> among the traditionary lore of primitive [sic] peoples in every region of the world, and in its
> fully developed forms it has a place in every one of the higher religions. A version of this
> Highest Common Factor in all preceding and subsequent theologies was first committed to
> writing more than twenty-five centuries ago, and since that time the inexhaustible theme
> has been treated again and again, from the standpoint of every religious tradition and in all
> the principal languages of Asia and Europe.

Every page of his book attempts to demonstrate, through a qualitative analysis of
relevant texts, the proposition of a transcendent unity of religions. Laibelman (1992)
searches for evidence from the mathematical and physical sciences to prove the
existence of this supra-religiophilosophy, as do Wilber (1981, 1996) and Thomas et
al. (1993) with their reflections on their field of knowledge: transpersonal psychology.

I am not concerned here with asking if such a tradition has existed – or still does –
in reality. Rather, I am attempting to take advantage of a construction of a perennial
philosophy which these authors believe to have existed for the purposes previously
outlined.

The phrase, *Philosophia Perennis* is believed by Huxley to have been coined by
Leibniz. But in Faivre (1992, 43), the reader will find that Huxley was mistaken.
Around 1450 in Florence, Cosimo de Medici (1389-1464) asked Marcilio Ficino
(1433-1499) to create a Platonic Academia. Cosimo organised a methodical search
for ancient manuscripts both within Christendom and, with Sultan Mehmed II's
permission, in the East. The goal was to search for a *Philosophia Perennis* through
history and/or myths from stoicism, gnosticism, hermetism, neo-pythagorism, etc.
Riffard (1990, 310) also mentions the book by Stenco de Gubbio, *Philosophia Perennis*
published in 1540 and compares it to that of Huxley.

Perennial philosophy includes in its paradigm all-embracing knowledge from all
cultures. Those who write about it recognise perennial philosophy in every religion
because, according to them, there is the same 'truth', the same 'mystical faith' which
underlies each grouping, be it Christianity, Buddhism, Gnosticism, Orphism,
Scientism. This syncretic perspective is not limited to churches, sects or cults, but
also takes in secular philosophies:

> Many philosophies have no place for parapsychology, Jungian archetypes, or even
> phenomenology; many theologies have no place for mysticism, other religions, or what
> falls under the rubric of folk religion. In the perennial philosophy these are accorded a
> respectful place; science too, of course. It is as if the perennial philosophy were to say to
> the others: You are right in what you affirm. Only what you deny needs rethinking (Peters
> 1991, 63)

Perennial Philosophy expresses perfectly *panthénosie* (from French: reconciliation
of differends) and thus, at least in Peter's version, rationalises eclecticism in the
'supermarket of religious commodities'.

Huxley (1994) describes the essential character of perennial philosophy as:

- The metaphysics that recognises a divine Reality substantial to the world of things and lives and minds;
- The psychology that finds in the soul something similar to, or even identical with, divine Reality; and
- The ethic that places Man's [sic] final end in the knowledge of the immanent and transcendent Ground of all being.

It is not the task of sociology to elaborate on these three characteristics or to test them as truth claims. But they do have the makings of an ideal type which will be of use in the quest for adequate conceptualisation of the spirituality here under investigation. So I have condensed each of the three characteristics in three short expressions which correspond intuitively to themes in my informants' testimonies and in what is known as the 'New Age' literature. The inscription, of course, remains to be validated at a later stage.

Departing from Huxley, I now propose as defining characteristics of the spirituality I am investigating:

- Monism
- The Human Potential Ethic
- Spiritual Knowledge (or Gnosis)

Monism

There are several subthemes constituting the metaphysics of perennial philosophy such as holism, wholism (Melton 1990), holarchy (Smith 1989), panentheism, acosmic pantheism and cosmic unity (Peters 1991). This metaphysics is variously termed:

> *Intelligible Reality* (Plato), or the *divine Mind* (Plotinus), or the *Buddha Mind* (Zen), or *Cosmic Consciousness* (R.M. Bucke), or the *Logos* (St. John), or the *Omega-point* (Teilhard), or *Mind-at-large* (Huxley), or the *Collective Unconscious* (Jung) (Coleman 1994).

One fundamental notion seems common to all these variations of Huxley's metaphysics and the various modes of expressing it: this is 'monism'. The word comes from the Greek *monos* meaning *single* and signifies a theory or system of thought which recognises a single ultimate principle, being, force, etc, underlying all reality.

Monism is in contrast with dualistic classical theism that conceives God as separated from the world, and mind as segregated from body. Peters (1991, 62) defines monism, as 'the doctrine of an underlying cosmic oneness that incorporates and unifies the apparent plurality of things existing on the surface of reality'. Monism is a generic term to describe this specific perception of the world and there exists also many sub-types. Here are two examples. Spinoza refers to 'logical monism' in which the world as a whole is a single substance, none of whose parts are logically capable of existing alone (Russell 1957, 600). William James refers to 'neutral monism', i.e. the belief that 'the material of which the world is constructed is neither mind nor matter, but something anterior to both' (Russell ibid., 841). On the other hand, Wilber (1996) would argue that monism is only a sub-type of an 'Ultimate State of Consciousness', but we will not go further into this. Suffice is to say that describing monism (or other similar concepts) is not a simple task and leads to many theological complexities.

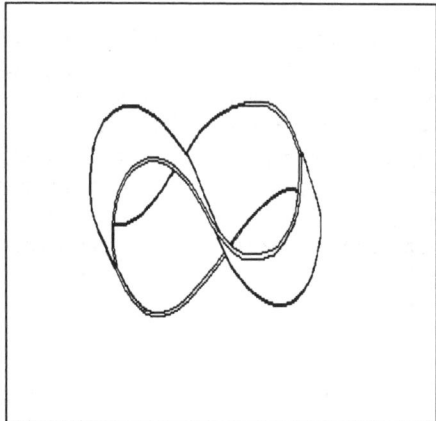

Figure 3.1 The Moebius strip

The metaphysics of perennial philosophy are found across space and time borders. Monism is variously expressed as God, One, Unity or even without theistic reference. These variations of expression are taken by Huxley and others to be variations of a common metaphysics conditioned by particular historical-cultural situations.

One expression of the monistic theme is expressed in the figure of the Moebius strip (Figure 3.1). In this image, there is no beginning and no end, no difference between the interior and the exterior. These opposites are combined in one image and there is no sense of domination of one opposite over another. A variation on the Moebius strip is found on the cover of *The Aquarian Conspiracy* (Ferguson 1981).

The Human Potential Ethic

The psychology underlined by Huxley finds in the soul something similar to, or even identical with, divine Reality, and this is performed by an inner adventure. People can find a divine spark within themselves and to find and ignite it, the spiritual worker only needs to be spiritually trained; this leads to the realisation of human potential.

There are various terms expressing this inner adventure. There is the description of a Jivanmukta in Smith (1989, 253-256), or Eliade's '*coincidentia oppositorum*' or the portrait of an androgyne (Eliade 1962), or Jung's 'process of individuation'. René Guénon (1958) (see Chapter 5) refers to the adventure of realising the 'universal man [sic]' which is the affirmation of pure being. Hermann Hesse's (1965), *Steppenwolf*, is a classic account of the inner adventure.

This inner adventure is not necessarily that of searching to become a god, or more than human, but it can be understood as the realisation of a higher self. By understanding one's body/mind/soul, by operating on the self through meditation, preventive healing, or other praxes, it is possible to feel better, happier, equilibrated or higher. In Jung's terms, this is to go through the process of individuation. Huxley (1994) claims that:

> Based upon the direct experience of those who have fulfilled the necessary conditions of such knowledge, this teaching is expressed most succinctly in the Sanskrit formula, *tat tvam asi* ('*That art thou*'); the Atman, or immanent eternal Self, is one with Brahman, the Absolute Principle of all existence; and the last end of every human being is to discover the fact for himself, to find out Who he [sic] really is.

Spiritual Knowledge (or Gnosis)

Spiritual Knowledge (or Gnosis; however this term is so overloaded (Faivre and Hanegraaff 1998) that it will be avoided) connotes knowing the ultimate reality or the secret of everything. And when the secret of everything is discovered, the inner adventurer will fulfil its Human Potential Ethic. Peters (1991, 81) quotes Jonas to emphasise this transformational effect of the discovery of the secret:

> Gnosis [i.e. Spiritual Knowledge] 'is not just theoretical information', writes Hans Jonas, 'but is itself, as a modification of the human condition, charged with performing a function in the bringing about salvation'. [...] The ultimate 'object' of gnosis is God: its event in the soul transforms the knower himself by making him a partaker in the divine experience.

Because of the monistic paradigm, Spiritual Knowledge can be found in the self and:

> To know oneself is to know the true Self of everything; for all things and lives and minds, including our own, participate in one and the same divine nature, the Logos or Nous. That divine nature is the origin, essence and perfection of the universe part and whole. So, to gain spiritual wisdom or self-knowledge is to achieve a proper comprehension of the eternal reality of oneself, and the world, and the divine (Coleman 1994, 38).

There are many ways to reach Spiritual Knowledge and according to the teachers of perennial philosophy, seekers of knowledge have to choose the path they think is the most suitable for them. In this paradigm, there is no purpose in being guided by a mentor throughout one's life. It is often said by perennist philosophers that in the case that one meets Buddha on one's road, one has to kill him (or her).

Each chosen mystical road is supposed to develop the seeker. By their questing, according to the literature, seekers are transforming themselves into a being following the human potential ethic. They amplify their skills by studying and searching and, at some stage, they will become sages, saints, or simply 'higher' beings and they will 'know'. This transformation 'which is the functional equivalent of salvation, is gained through knowledge, through gnosis' (Peters 1991, 80).

Notes

1   See for example the recent document "Jesus Christ the Bearer of the Water of Life: A Christian Reflection on the 'New Age'" issued in 2004 by the Vatican Pontifical Councils for Culture, Interreligious Dialogue and for Promoting Christian Unity. See comments by Dinges (2004) or Saliba's (2004) broader analysis of the various responses from Christianity.
2   Paraphrased from Rosenau (1992).

Chapter 4

Perennism

Evidence from the Field

In the interviews, I did not directly ask questions about the beliefs and orientations in this triad. Monism, the human potential ethic and the spiritual knowledge of the self can be described and interpreted in so many ways that using the terms is to invite misunderstanding on all sides. For example, after 7 interviews, I thought of using the term 'higher self' to describe what I now refer to as 'the human potential ethic'. I asked if people believed in the higher self, but it was soon evident that there is no consensus on the meaning of this term. Alice explained in her interview that 'quite often what you call your imagination is your higher self'; 'people call them angels', or 'little voices saying things to you. It's never pushy. It's only guiding', 'everyone has a higher self'. Phillip often referred to the notion of spirit in his interview, and after a few minutes I asked him what was the difference between 'spirit' and the higher self. He answered:

> Your spirit is your higher self. Because you are spirit. Get away from, which is very difficult for us to understand; get away from the human body. That's just a shell. You are spirit. Well it's very difficult to accept that fact. It's not at all that easy. But no spirit is spirit of your higher self, whatever you want to call it. There's many many names for spirit. But it's about a part of us.

I have realised that the notion of higher self does not correspond to that of the human potential ethic. The former term refers to the result of work on one's body and/or mind, to a human potential development, while the latter (for some informants) is already part of our very being. Once again, conceptual diversity appears to reign to the point of confusion. As interviewee Judith put it:

> The labels that we use tend to be unfortunately widespread and because they're being used by so many people they have many different resonances in people's minds.

The search for the perfect vocabulary with meanings shared between interviewees as well as between interviewer and interviewees was fruitless. This may please many post-modern thinkers who might well abandon the task of definition and characterisation at this point. However, I have continued the investigation with qualitative analysis of the interview texts, attempting to spot the triadic themes developed in Chapter 3 in a great variety of expressions. This investigation is now detailed under the sections of monism, the human potential ethic, spiritual knowledge and the triad (i.e. the three elements together).

Monism

Expressions that, in context, indicate a monistic view of self and the world were used as such by my informants.

Jane went to a meditation retreat and discusses her sensation of what I have labelled monism with the term 'connectedness':

> It's just almost like a sense of connectedness. Especially with other people. I mean it's very hard to describe. Like people I'm sitting next to or when we are walking meditation, it is a sense of flow. Not like me walking and this person is walking. It's almost like if he wasn't walking, I can't really describe it. That sense of connect. It's just a feeling, a very vague feeling. But that has been emerging very slowly. And like again after that same [Zen Buddhist] retreat, I came back and I wasn't a vegetarian and that's something I think could be connected to my meditation, but I'm not sure. But it almost felt like no I can't eat any more meat. I couldn't dissociate this food in my plate from the animals that were killed.

Harry explained monism in terms of energy:

> The presence and activity of some accountable creative presence, energy, dynamism, whatever, individuality, god, soul, something. And that presence will be found to permeate all areas of human interest and activity, and to unite everything.

Elizabeth on the contingence of everything:

> Everything is contingent upon everything else. And there are no such things as objects that have their own intrinsic existence. So this room for example is only a room based upon the relation of the walls to each other. And when you start to meditate on those kinds of conceptions you get a very strong sense of expansiveness.

Jennifer on embededness:

> Yeah I thought that book was good. The title seemed to be like it might be a Lyn Andrews book or something, but a bit NewAgey. It was actually, it's kind of just a view of cosmology that includes. What's the word she used for it? The embededness. Which is, she's talking about feeling a total connection between everything and in experiencing phenomenologically having a link with everything. So experiencing that flower there has really connected me to it and it to me.

A non-exhaustive list of the indicators of monism that were found in each interview follows. Only when one or other or several of these phrases fitted into context, as in the extract above, did I classify the informant who used them as displaying monism. When the voice of my informants was not clear enough out of its context, I have had some comments to clarify their view:

Alan: see the analysis of his case study below.

Albert: 'We're not something that's separate from spirit, from guidance and knowledge and wisdom that we're being offered. We're actually intertwined with it.

That's why it's actually interlinked instead of one being laid over the other or something, like they're interlinked, they're one. Spirit and the physical being one'.

Alice: 'I'm a seichim channel which is a form of energy healing and that's basically tapping into the universal life energy [...]', [energy which as Harry has mentioned above unites everything].

Anne: 'We are all fingers of the same hand'.

Betty: 'We've all got life energy. You know the force. May the force be with you, all sorts of stuff like that'. [She also uses the notion of goddess (another expression of monism) which will be presented only in Chapter 7].

Christine: 'God is energy, it's the universal energy of consciousness'. And also: 'I just wanted to be out under the stars again and feel like I was one with them. You know climbing into trees and pretending I was part of the branch'.

Daniel: 'From that time forward [after a mystico-pneumatic experience] there was another part of me that saw everything as just different levels of energy'.

Elizabeth: see above.

Fred: 'I mean everything God created is part of the earth. Because you are the final identity of all of it. You are, the sun is in you, the moon is in you. Every planet is in your body'.

Harry: see the analysis of his case study below.

James: 'The son of God is humanity. It's all people together, a son of God. We've all been, you know like a drop of mercury, scattered. Each thinks they're separate. That's the big trick. That's what's fooling everybody. We all think we're separate. I'm separate from you. And at a higher level, that's not true at all'.

Jane: see above.

Jennifer: see above.

Judith: 'I believe that there is a certain amount of life force in everything, everything natural'.

Julia: 'So I think you know if I become a better person and therefore the world will be a better person, then we're connected. Everything's connected. And I think it's important that those connections are recognised'.

Julian: no indication was found.

Marc: no indication was found.

Marilyn: 'The mind is no place at all. It's everywhere' [See also below].

Martina: 'And I believe that God, yes there is a God, but there's also God within us as well. Meaning that God's given us the opportunity to be responsible for ourself. He's given us the faith. And I have an enormous amount of faith. And it's not just in the universe, [...] but in the totality of existence'.

Michele: 'The whole world is energetic, it's all energy'.

Ned: 'Everybody, the universe is part of the I Am race'.

Paul: 'It's an energetic universe and the energy is passed down by those [who] stimulate their life. And energy steps down to those lower life forms'.

Peter: no indication was found.

Phillip: 'You got spiritualism in a blade of grass, in a brick, in a human being, in the air. It's everywhere you know'.

Robert: 'Everything we touch, everything around us has an imprint of our energy'.

Robyn: 'God's infinity, so I guess that we probably, as souls, we are, what's the word? Holograms. Yeah we're holograms [...] it's like him there, call it personalised, him, and all these little, break a bit of glass. Getting his reflection on a mirror. Say a man. Let's say God's a man. Getting his reflection. smash that mirror and all those little pieces are miniatures of him', 'And nature is God. It's in every tree'.

Roger: 'There's a connection there. It's not a typical, it's just that we're not aware of the cause, but on a subtle level there is a subtle connection principle, that we're drawn together. You know it's the metaphysical cause of effect. Still cause and effect. We're not conscious of it. You know what I mean? Collective unconscious. In the archetypal, collective unconscious'. [This collective unconscious refers to Jung which as seen in Chapter 3 is an indicator of monism].

Sandra: 'And also one of the other belief systems I've learnt along the way is about God as people call it. I believe there is an ultimate energy as such, but we've all got parts of that in us'.

Sarah: 'I guess I cheated again when I was 15 by taking LSD occasionally and getting sneak previews of the divine in everything without any hard work'.

Steve: 'Ultimately I believe in the oneness of all things, but I would never ever claim to be able to prove and manifest that'.

Sue: 'I think there is an energy'.

Susie: 'And my understanding of Reiki is that it believes in a thing called universal energy which means that for us to use and the way that we tap into it is to align ourselves to it, and the healing force, but it's also about being open to the universe means that you confront things in yourself as well'.

Tom: 'You exist on more than one plane at a time. You are on several planes at the same time'.

Veronica: 'I think all of life is one conscious thing and we're like a little splinter that's here to learn something and help this conscious mass [...]'

William: 'Often too sort of think whether the God I believe in is maybe not, in fact probably not a person as such, but rather some sort of unifying force or power which combines us altogether in our respective collective and yet also individual journeys'. 'I guess I've not read a lot of Jung but I know a lot of his principles. Similar to what he meant by the collective unconscious. [...] maybe that's what I meant also by God'.

Thirty-two (91 per cent) of my informants share the idea of what I call monism, an idea which is expressed differently in their expression.

The monistic themes presented by my participants can be summarised under these headings:

- Ultimate energy.
- God is a sort of unifying force which combines us altogether.
- The world is like a 'hologram' or corresponds to the 'collective unconscious'.
- Energy (divine) in everything.
- A sense of connectness.
- We are all fingers of the same hand.
- Nothing is separated, everything is connected to everything else, feeling a total connection between everything.
- Oneness of all things.

The Human Potential Ethic

As an indication of belief in and focus on the attainment of the human potential ethic, the respondents used expressions like 'intuition', 'balance', 'development' and 'healing'.

William stated in connection to his practice, astrology, that he valued it because through it he had become more intuitive: 'I know as I've studied astrology, so much of it is very psychological and looking at yourself and others, has helped me develop a lot of insight into myself, other people. Actually probably I've noticed I've probably become more intuitive'.

Betty on the development of the self: 'And yeah I do see [myself in] a process and I see myself in a permanent state of learning and developing, but I guess I don't see it as a single way'.

Robert on meditation and development: 'I think meditation is the key for all psychic development and spiritual development'.

Alice on healing the self: 'I'm a seichim channel which is a form of energy healing and that's basically tapping into the universal life energy all around and giving the body a boost of energy for it to heal itself'.

Martina on a balanced self: 'But now I study the Kabala for me. Because it teaches me to be balanced'.

We can already notice that there appear to be different levels of understanding about how to achieve the integral self. On the one hand, there is a search for a development (or increase of) human potential such as indicated by William (intuition) and Betty. And on the other hand, there is a search for healing (Alice), or a balance of (Martina), the human body and spirit. This difference has already been analysed with the consumption axis from the cultic milieu grid (see Figure 2.1) in Chapter 2. But through the different terminology and across different notions of appropriate practice, there appears to be substantial consensus about the central importance of the development of the human potential ethic.

A non-exhaustive list of some expressions used by my participants and interpreted by me as indicators of this belief and preoccupation follows:

Alan: see the analysis of his case study below.

Albert: '[...] for spiritual development I believe it can be fairly important to find out about your past life', [through this claim, Albert explained that he studied his past lives (what is called regression) to be able to develop his psychic abilities. He is now a clairvoyant].

Alice: see above.

Anne: see above.

Betty: see above.

Christine: 'And that's [unethical New Age practice] to me is not being, that's not healing, that's not healing. And [tarot] readings are meant to be healings'.

Daniel: 'Taking you out of your own reality and trying to move you into a higher reality'.

Elizabeth: 'I'm always trying to shift my perception', 'So I use that [yoga sutras] as both an explanatory system and also as a technique for altering awareness and healing people and things like that'.

Fred: 'Growing within yourself. You are God'.

Harry: see the analysis of his case study below.

James: 'Reiki is a process, is the modality of healing which heals on every level. Not just the physical, but also mental, spiritual and emotional levels. Essentially there was an awful lot of healing that needed to be done and of course it's a life long process anyway because I've come to realise that what we're all trying to do is get back to God'.

Jane: 'And the fact that I was going to become enlightened somehow despite that I still managed to persevere and kept doing it [meditation]'.

Jennifer: 'And that ritual would normally be for healing [...]', 'It [exercise in alchemy] was always an exercise and a process in self development. I suppose, an exploration and purification'. [See her also below.]

Judith: 'So our form of enlightenment is merely understanding yourself so well as to be able to change yourself as you choose. [...] there is no one true way. There's no one true enlightenment either'.

Julia: '[...] the notion that there was a spirituality within every human being, or God if you like within every person'. [This quote also connects the integral self with monism; indeed, if God is everywhere and if we are god(esse)s, we are thus connected to the universe and we also can develop ourselves into a god(ess)]'.

Julian: 'I think if you know how to empower, if you use it [magic] to empower yourself to do good for others and to do good in the world generally, I think it's a great thing'. [The term empower is used in Julian's discourse as a synonym of psychic development.]

Marc: no indication was found.

Marilyn: 'We are potentially gods in our own right', 'I don't know where we're supposed to go, except completion or masterhood [in a spiritual sense]'. [See also her comments below.]

Martina: 'Sue said to me, do you know how strong your psychic abilities are? And I said no. And she said you need to develop them', [which she did. See her also above and in the introduction of this book].

Michele: see comments on Paul.

Ned: 'I know for a fact that it's possible to become divine', 'We're not really our own self, we're not as we seem, but we're much better. The eternal, immortal youth, which can be achieved'.

Paul refers to 'the next stage in evolution' which is connected to the expression of the Age of Aquarius as it will be presented in Chapter 6. In Paul's understanding, a flow of energy will come down to earth and will develop its inhabitants spiritually.

Peter: 'I guess some people have reached various levels, abilities, but I think humanity is yet to sort of break into the area. I think that we have spiritual abilities'. '[...] I think that people quite often without actually pursuing it, being on a spiritual journey, and that they actually are developing themselves'.

Phillip: 'Everybody in their life has the capability of becoming a clairvoyant or a psychic healer'.

Robert: see above.

Robyn: 'Yeah, empowering yourself. You are God, [...] as long as you do it with integrity and compassion'.

Roger: 'You'll never reach perfection, but you know you'll always be restless and frustrated. As long as you're growing. As long as you're not staying still, stagnating. You know, you've got to be growing'.

Sandra: 'And I've done lots of workshops like that in self development. And half the time when you do these workshops you're doing self development at the same time. [...] So with all these studies, my spiritual self has changed'.

Sarah: 'I believe in developing myself as best as I can'

Steve: 'There's that sort of idea and the idea of saying thou art goddess or thou art god and all that sorts of stuff'. 'You can be more who you are and with God or the divine or the other'.

Sue: 'When I've reached enlightenment [...]'.

Susie: 'And so when I look to spiritual healing I look to heal myself to be able to continue to work in that way'.

Tom: 'I couldn't state exactly what was going on, but I was conscious of a certain enlightenment. Call it whatever you like. And I became positive. I became a better person'. 'So everybody's psychic. Everybody is of their own psychic. Depends if they want to use it. That's their choice'.

Veronica: 'Hopefully we evolve [in a spiritual sense]'.

William: see above.

Thirty-four (97 per cent) of my participants gave me the indication of a belief in what I call the human potential ethic. However, the accounts on this ethic reveal a spectrum. As already seen in Chapter 2, at one extreme, potential is sought through balance, or a healing process, and on the other, it is through development of psychic abilities or engaging a process of complete transcendence of the former self. Inspired by B. Campbell (1978) and his analysis of cults as already seen in Chapter 2 on the networking paradigm, this spectrum could be clarified defining one side as the quest for an instrumental development and on the other side, a search for illuminational development. By illumination I refer to a quest for a direct inner personal experience of the divine within, or for a greater individual potential. In this sense, the search for the human potential ethic is an end in itself. On the other hand, instrumental development refers to some techniques an individual uses to better himself or herself, and to become more effective and efficient in worldly pursuits. In this sense, the instrumental search for the human potential ethic is a means to external ends.

From the indications of my interviewees above, a list of the major indicators of the human potential ethic is presented below. This list is divided according to the illuminational and instrumental criteria.

Instrumental Search for the Human Potential Ethic

- Healing; give a boost of energy to the body for it to heal; healing forces heal people's emotions.
- A balance in body and mind.

Illuminational Search for the Human Potential Ethic

- We evolve (in spiritual sense).
- We have spiritual abilities that need to be discovered.
- To grow, to perfect the spirit; completion of mastery.
- To become enlightened; to be part of the whole.
- It is possible to become divine; we are essentially God manifesting ourselves; we try to get back to God; we are potential gods.
- You expand your consciousness.

Other Indicators Ambiguously Located on this Spectrum

- My spiritual self has changed.
- Self-development; personal development.
- Development of insight into oneself, development of psychic abilities.
- More intuitive, more sensitive.
- Empowering yourself with integrity and compassion.
- Altering awareness.
- To move to a higher reality.

Before leaving this section, Anne presents an interesting case. She searched for many years how to develop her human potential ethic and has now lost her dreams of 'exotic' development:

Anne: 'I've realised that, I'd look at people and think oh they're so spiritual, they must be doing something different to me and they must have some special secret and it must be because they're nuns or priests or because they live in the mountains or something. And when I've gone and seen what they actually did it was like they're just normal people. But they're paying attention to what they're doing and they're very good at being what they are. And they're doing these really normal things and they're not worried about it. They're not saying hey I've got to be something. They're just being themself. And they're cooking and they're cleaning and they're doing their gardening or whatever. I think I sort of came to the conclusion after a while that that stuff was spiritual. That the point was not to try and be a great spiritual person, but it was to try and be yourself and that that was very spiritual. So that took several years to get to, in an hour of your tape'.

Spiritual Knowledge

The following phrases and expressions used by respondents have been read as indicating a search for spiritual knowledge:

Julian expressed his desire to gain more knowledge as such:

Julian: 'I'd like to know a bit more about the Asian systems, about Taoism [...] A bit more about the Chinese medical system even'.

Interviewer: 'Is there a reason for this?'

Julian: I guess I just feel that it's, it would probe me with more information and more of a balance.

Phillip on the amount of knowledge to learn:

Phillip: The only person that is special is the one that wants to attain the knowledge. This is really what it all boils down to.

Interviewer: To attain the knowledge?

Phillip: Yeah. There's so much knowledge out there for a human being to learn where your man-made religions keep that knowledge down.

Sandra and her eclectic touch on knowledge(s):

I'm a Gemini, which whether that means anything to you. But I like to spin surfaces a lot of things and find out things. If I'm interested I'll take it further. Which is good and bad. It gives me lots of ground knowledge in a lot of things. But also I've got to come to accept that whatever it is I'm looking for is in here. All your answers are inside. You've got every answer you need to everything.

Sometimes the concept of knowledge is referred to as wisdom, that is an active knowledge that is fully understood and lived by the spiritual seeker. As Christine said:

> You need to understand the knowledge that you have rather than just have the knowledge and without the wisdom to understand it, give it out, it's not healthy.

A non-exhaustive list of the indicators of spiritual knowledge given by each of the interviewee follows (a difference in the understanding of spiritual knowledge will be also observed):

Alan: see the analysis of his case study below.

Albert: '[...] we're not something that's separate from spirit, from guidance and knowledge and wisdom that we're being offered. we're actually intertwined with it'.

Alice: 'Crystals and tarot, they're just tools to help us to get to know what's inside of us anyway', '[...] finding the truth within ourselves'. [This sort of spiritual knowledge is different from the extracts already presented from other informants. Alice refers to a knowledge that is inside us, whereas the other extracts refer to an outside knowledge. Suffice is to say for the moment that there are two levels of knowledge and this will be the topic of the next chapter].

Anne: 'Because when you sort of sit down, you say I'm going to have a [tarot cards] reading, you're agreeing that you want to know more about yourself and that you don't want to lie to yourself'.

Betty: 'Self knowledge is really important'.

Christine: 'There's another world that exists inside us that no one can see. But if you have that knowingness and you have that ability, you can understand things in life'. [See also above].

Daniel: 'Self knowledge. Knowing who you really are. Not being caught up in a false identity'.

Elizabeth: 'And of course the place I started looking was within that group of people and those kinds of knowledge systems that they had', 'So I teach it [astrology]. And I feel that's my contribution to passing the knowledge on'.

Fred: For him organised religion such as Christianity and Hinduism have hidden what he refers to as the 'real text' and manipulated it to control people. He thus searched for the spiritual 'teachings' without the religious 'rules'. This refusal to take the teaching of structured religions led him to search for the 'real text', i.e. in this sense the knowledge kept hidden by those institutions.

Harry: see the analysis of his case study below.

James: 'Nobody can tell you what you have to do. You've got to find that within yourself'. [This refers to a search for a knowledge within.]

Jane: no indication was found.

Jennifer: see below.

Judith: 'Teachers are people who will help you find in yourself your own strengths and expand on them', [in this sense, teachers are not giving a body of knowledge, but they help their students to know themselves].

Julia: '[...] try and listen to your intuition. What feels right for you. And it's not an easy thing to do. It's not an easy path to find. But you just have to believe in yourself and do what you need to do. To discover it'. [By this, Julia refers to a contact within us that has to be made ('listen to your intuition'), there is a knowledge of the self that comes out and thus allows this discovery of oneself].

Julian: 'I think it's very important to know your heart', [heart being in this sense the self. See also above].

Marc: 'To me spirituality is heart knowledge based. It's intuitive. It's emotional'.

Marilyn: see her account in the next chapter where her understanding of the two kinds of spiritual knowledges mentioned above will lead Chapter 5.

Martina: 'I think finding self is much better, because that's what we're looking for'.

Michele: 'Okay we had the intuitive feeling something is there, but until you read the book you really didn't know which way to go'. [She refers to a book that has given her theknowledge she was seeking for].

Ned: 'Our minds are forever, can forever increase in knowledge and wisdom'.

Paul: see his wife (Michele) with whom he agrees.

Peter: no indication was found.

Phillip: see above.

Robert: 'One of the benefits of meditation is that we get in touch with ourselves', [and this develops some psychic abilities. From this Robert claims that 'we become better in thesense that we know ourselves better'].

Robyn: 'We've got to look within'. 'And the greatest lesson that we ever learn is to be on this earth to learn'. [She is a channeller and gives some psychic counselling in which she 'empowers [people] to look at themselves truthfully, honestly, objectively. Away from their opinions and their ego. They stand back. See themselves in the true life'; through her practice, she thus tries to make her patient/customer know themselves.]

Roger: 'It's like astrology. There's so much to these things. Astrology, numerology. The more you study the more you realise you don't really know'. [See also the last point in Robyn's, a point with which he agrees.]

Sandra: see above.

Sarah: 'I love knowledge. I love learning. I find spirituality a challenge I guess', 'I'm trying to remember this something about be true to yourself or know yourself'.

Steve: see below.

Sue: 'There's an infinitely vast body of knowledge that is associated with astrology', 'Astrology helps you figure out yourself, yeah, why you're doing what you're doing and what might be some of your destructive habits or the positive things you can contribute'.

Susie: '[...] then it's a matter of knowing, just accepting that you can try something and walk away from it. So that you don't have to participate in things that you don't want to and that there's lots of people out there that you can go and get different experiences from, and it's up to you to decide whether if feels good or feels bad'.

Tom: see below.

Veronica: 'I think all of life is one conscious thing and we're like a little splinter that's here to learn something [...]'

William: 'There's a great need to explore the other side of yourself or your collective self which you've ignored for a long time'.

Thirty-three (94%) of my informants gave some indication of what I call spiritual knowledge.

Indications for spiritual knowledge are listed below under the sub-headings of knowledge of the self and of 'external' knowledge. We will come back to this difference in Chapter 5.

Spiritual Knowledge of the self

- All answers are inside.
- To know what's inside us.
- Truth, trust within ourself.
- Discovering my true self; self-knowledge is really important; finding the self.

'External' Spiritual Knowledge

- To pass the knowledge.
- Learning many systems for more information, more balance.

Unknown kind of Spiritual Knowledge

- Our minds can forever increase in knowledge and wisdom; to attain knowledge.
- Exploring the other side of yourself or your collective self; there is another world inside us.

The Triad

The elements of the triad were not dissociated in the interviews. Often they were deeply interrelated in the discourse of my informants. Here are a few accounts that link the elements of the triad:

The connection between spiritual knowledge and the human potential ethic can be found in:

Julian on magic explains the 'power' (human potential ethic) that allows him to 'know things' (spiritual knowledge):

> A lot of people do magic to have power over other people. Which is when it becomes black magic. I wasn't really into that, but in spite of that the sense of power and the sense that you knew things that other, that was seductive this sense of power, and plus the fact that you knew things that other people didn't know or didn't want to know even made you feel a bit superior.

Judith on enlightenment (human potential ethic) and the 'understanding of oneself' (spiritual knowledge):

> Our [her neopagan group] form of enlightenment is merely understanding yourself so well as to be able to change yourself as you choose.

Harry and his understanding of growth that changes our 'knowledge':

> Part of growing up and becoming mature, becoming enlightened, is to realise the forces that have been working within us all along. So I don't think enlightenment changes, or a spiritual growth. I don't believe they change our nature in any way at all. I think they change our consciousness. Change our knowledge. We see more of ourselves. We see more of the world.

Steve on power and understanding (spiritual knowledge):

> Power is a great idea you have because the more power you have the more understanding you have over yourself. Because basically power is understanding you know.

All three elements of the triad are deeply interconnected in some interviews, such as that of Tom, Marilyn and Jennifer.

Tom: 'Knowledge dispels fear, doesn't it? If you know something how can you be afraid of it? Right. Your attitude and knowledge. But you can walk away with that knowledge and that's fine. But now if you sat down and deliberated about what happened to give you that knowledge you go beyond knowledge to wisdom [i.e. spiritual knowledge]. What's wisdom? Power'.

Interviewer: 'What kind of power?'

Tom: 'An energy within yourself of being the wiser for understanding. Widening your perception as to what happened [i.e. the human potential ethic]. So if you take wisdom, that is power. Power is energy. Energy unto energy. Like unto like [i.e. monism]'.

Marilyn: 'But behavioural stuff and mind and power and all the rest of it is very important to understand when you're trying to sort out your spiritual path, your spiritual development [i.e. the human potential ethic] if you like and your finding of yourself [i.e. spiritual knowledge]. It depends which self you're trying to look for. See the spiritual self is the higher self really you're looking for. As I see it the aim is to connect your vehicles which is your physical body and your emotions and your mind with your higher, your soul level, and bring them altogether, work the holistic [i.e. monism]. That's holistic, not a whole collection of therapies. It's the whole person'.

Jennifer on astrology:

I came to that kind of astrology [archetypal or psychological astrology] because it's not about prediction. It's more about self understanding [i.e. spiritual knowledge] and working with energies [i.e. monism] and potential [i.e. the human potential ethic].

Before estimating the amount of the respondents whose testimonies indicate that their perceptions and preoccupations accord with the elements of this triad, it is worth exploring two case studies, that exemplify a self-conscious linkage of the three elements at the heart of a person's spirituality.

Harry

Harry considers himself a perennial philosopher and completed a Ph.D. Our conversation was a great learning experience for me and here is the way the elements of the triad are interrelated in his interview. Some extracts have already been used to describe how the triad is interpreted by my respondents, and I will repeat them for clarity.

Harry dedicated a good part of the interview to the discussion of scientific experiments, subjectivity and objectivity. He argued that '*the subject becomes one in the experience with the object*'. This fusion between the subject and object (i.e. a recollection of opposites) led to his interpretation of monism with Quantum mechanics:

Quantum mechanics is breaking down this distantiation [in which] the subject is separate from the object and the observer is independent of the observed. Quantum mechanics is potentially used for things like where everything's connected to everything else. That's true, that's good.

Mechanistic science was splitting the world into opposites, but now the new physics is re-associating every opposite and gives a support to a monistic theology. A bit further on his discussion on the new physics, he indicates the notion of energy which is a key element for distinguishing monism:

> The presence and activity of some accountable creative presence energy, dynamism, whatever, individuality, god, soul, something. And that presence will be found to permeate all areas of human interest and activity, and to unite everything.

Harry, while explaining his ideas on energy and monism was often using the term unity and I asked him to shed some light on this term:

> Plato described the highest form as the form of the one or the good. The one unity, the one is the principle of unity. What comes from the one, all that comes from the one is unity. The one is nothing other than unity [...] Nothing exists apart from ultimate unity.

And to grasp this ultimate unity, is 'to go beyond that still. To, words fail me, to become the one [...] Well to be part of it, to be part of the whole', this leads us to the notion of the human potential ethic, this idea of developing the self to perceive the ultimate reality. This is also expressed in Harry'S view in these extracts:

> Because I could not think of anything better to aim for in enlightenment. It's the best goal there is. [...] The highest enlightenment, and I say this advisedly, is to become God.

Later, he spoke about the spiritual development and the problems involved in this:

> We just do it [spiritual development] spontaneously up to a point where our spiritual development becomes arrested. It reaches a point where it ceases. If we wish to develop beyond that point then we can't really rely on just spontaneous good luck.

This involves an agency process which consists in reaching spiritual knowledge. Part of developing oneself for Harry, therefore consists in attaining a certain level of knowledge:

> Part of growing up and becoming mature, becoming enlightened, is to realise the forces that have been working within us all along. So I don't think enlightenment changes or a spiritual growth. I don't believe they change our nature in any way at all. I think they change our consciousness. Change our knowledge. We see more of ourselves. We see more of the world.

And for him, 'To know and to be are the same', which leads us to the idea of another kind of knowledge, that of self-knowledge:

> which in the philosophical tradition, that's what wisdom is. Wisdom is self knowledge. The classical sense of philosophy as the search for wisdom, the love of wisdom.

Harry has just offered us his way of linking the elements of the triad in his words and understanding. Alan offers another way and a different vocabulary.

Alan

Alan is a sales assistant in a 'New Age' shop. He likes reading, travelling and meditating. Meditation is the only spiritual practice that is worth following; others, like astrology and tarot cards, are of no interest for him. I asked Alan about his spiritual path and he answered that:

> there are many different paths, spiritually dominant. And to paraphrase somebody else again, have no thoughts of my own. All of these paths eventually lead to the same summit. They all lead to the same spot. But that spot is, I don't know what to call that. [...] It's a kind of place where you have a contact, a kind of relationship between yourself and the universe. You don't feel isolated any more.

This 'spot' expresses the idea of monism, a 'spot' where every path is united and the searcher becomes one with the universe. Later in the interview, he described me one mystical experience that had confirmed him his perception of monism:

> I looked out to the trees outside the window and the sun was shining on them. All of a sudden it was as if the mother of all nature came to me [...] And she said something. I'll never forget the exact words, she said Alan we love you very much. You do what you think is right and no matter what you do we will still love you. And to me it's very interesting because when she said 'we' that applies a kind of pantheistic god in group.

And in this 'we' (which makes a connection between monism and the human potential ethic), human beings can also be integrated: 'That we are essentially God manifesting ourselves and to be alive and to be conscious it's an absolute incredible thing'.

Continuing on this line on the human potential ethic, Alan practises meditation and it 'does seem to help move to a different kind of mental structure', and this allows someone to reach the end of a spiritual path, to merge in unity (monism), in 'we'. Later in the interview, he said that he is:

> very interested in developing some kind of psychic ability. I don't think I have any at the moment. And I'm not even sure that it really exists.

However, meditation helps people to get in tune with the deeper self which explains why Alan's notion of knowledge is deeply inscribed in the self. For him, there is no system of knowledge that detains the truth because *'we will never get absolute truth of anything beyond ourselves'*. Still, this understanding of self knowledge was not clear until he spoke about the New Age territory that has:

> opened up the way of looking at our reasons. And it was probably started by this, it died off for a long time, I don't know why. That way of looking at ourselves [...] And so I think the direction of it is for self understanding. For people to understand why they're here and what they're doing with their lives.

In these two cases, different words and understandings were used. They are idiosyncratic as many of my informants were.

Table 4.1 indicates the amount of respondents who use phrases which indicate their worldview, identity and preoccupations which correspond to elements of the triad considered separately. On the basis of my classifications, 31 (88 per cent) informants, like Harry and Alan, displayed world view and orientations integrating the three elements of the triad, as presented in Table 4.2.

Table 4.1 Informants' belief in perennism

Informants who gave evidence of a belief in (n=35): n respondents	
Monism	32 (91%)
Integral Self	34 (97%)
Gnosis	33 (94%)

Table 4.2 Informants' belief in the perennist triad

Beliefs corresponding to the 'perennial' triad (n=35) n respondents	
Yes	31 (88%)
No	1 (3%)
Indications were too ambiguous	3 (9%)

Three (9 per cent) of my respondents used categories that were too ambiguous to match with the complete triad. Peter avoided categories that could be connected to monism or spiritual knowledge. This may have been due to a mistake on my part. Before interviewing him, I gave him a copy of my theoretical work on this triad (the only case in my field work) and he was therefore aware of what he may have rejected as my presuppositions. Another participant was raised as an Anglican and now goes to Catholic masses. His language indicates a quest for the human potential ethic and spiritual knowledge but there are no traces of monism in his discourse. The third interviewee is Marc who is a parapsychologist and who dedicated his interview mainly to criticising the conservative attitudes of some scientists and clergy. His language indicates some insight of beliefs in Gnosis, and maybe the human potential ethic (it is not clear) but not of monism.

One person, Jane, a Zen Buddhist active in the New Age/Cultic milieu, did not fit at all with the complete triad. She was born in Iran and now lives in Melbourne. Even if she is open to some alternative practices other than Zen Buddhism (e.g. I Ching), she does not believe in spiritual knowledge. For her, Zen Buddhism is more experimental: there is no need to learn a lot. By this, she means that there is no need to seek any form of knowledge to practice her spirituality. Also, she never emphasised a knowledge of the self in her interview. However, she believes in a sense of connectedness (monism) and wants to become enlightened (human potential ethic).

For a Sociological Appropriation

I propose that perennism, outlined above as perennial philosophy, may serve as an ideal type conceptualisation of the spirituality variously referred to as New Age or mystical-esoteric nebulae. I have chosen 'perennism' (based on the Latin root) rather than 'perennialism' (based on the English word) because 'perennialism' is often used as a synonym for perennial philosophy in Anglo-Saxon culture(s) (see Faivre 1992; 1994 and Heelas 1996). In the light of my small sample, 'Perennism' appears to be a more empirically informed and theoretically derived concept than 'New Age'.

I suggest that the notions of monism, the human potential ethic and spiritual knowledge, serve as significant interrelated elements that specify a fundamental paradigm of an extraordinary array of contemporary spiritual actors. And, on the basis of my immersion in the world of those actors, I believe that the inner logic of perennism, as elaborated by Huxley and others, corresponds to central tendencies of beliefs and praxes, evident in accounts by the insider practitioners I have interviewed.

Coleman (1994) (an insider writer) uses perennial philosophy to describe New Age. York (1995, 46) mentions an insider, Tarcher, who compares the core of New Age thought with Huxley's Perennial Philosophy. Ted Peters (1991, 56) (an outsider writer) also draws some parallels between the two. I take these convergences as some measure of validation of my own description of perennism and analysis of it as an ideal typification of the spiritualities commonly, but as we have seen unhelpfully, labelled 'New Age'.

The triune definition of perennism I have been heading towards may now be stated in the following terms: *Perennism is a spirituality which interprets the world as Monistic and whose actors are attempting to develop their Human Potential Ethic by seeking Spiritual Knowledge.*

From this definition, I consider a spiritual actor to be perennist (rather than 'New Ager') only if the three elements are found in their discourse. So far, 31 (89 per cent) of my interviewees are thus perennist, 1 is not and 3 might be but are not clearly so on the basis of their interviews.

If I have changed Huxley's definition of perennial philosophy into that of perennism, it is because I want to distance myself explicitly from at least one theological tenet of his faith – that perennial philosophy is the common core of all religions past and present. My claim about perennism, a tool of understanding, is only that it is a representation of the common core of the spirituality of the contemporary networks I have investigated in Melbourne.

How representative is this case? Isn't it possible that the findings are unique to the particular circumstances of this Australian case? To answer these questions, it appears worth while to compare my finding with that of Heelas and Hill.

Heelas (1996) characterises 'New Age' as a 'self-religiosity'; however, this element is only the 'Human Potential Ethic' part of the triad discovered above and is, according to my approach, unidimensional of the vast 'New Age' panorama. Furthermore, the notion of self-religiosity could refer to Christian mysticism and even, to a certain extent, to the Overman philosophy of Nietzsche. Chryssides (1999, 278), Corrywright (2003), Ivakhiv (2003) and York (2004) also claim that the term 'Self Religion' is not without its problems. Also, because this characteristic is one-dimensional, it does not offer an avenue to differentiate 'New Age' from esotericism as we will explore in the next chapter.

Another point is the prediction of the relevance of 'New Age' Spiritualities in Western Societies by Hill (2004). He summarises Westley (1978) and Campbell's (1978) works and suggests the following detailed inventory as a way of typifying the characteristic features of 'New Age' Spiritualities:

- Individualism
- Idealisation of human personality
- Tolerance
- Syncretism
- Monism
- Empowerment of individuals

From this, Hill argues that 'New Age' is not new because of the recurrence of these six elements in earlier alternative spiritualities. I will argue the contrary in the next chapter with the help of a unique – or a seventh for Hill – element specific of 'New Age', that is knowledge of the self. This specific type of knowledge, even if not new among esoteric philosophies, is new in the everyday life practice of my participants.[1] His points on 'individualism', 'idealisation of human personality' and 'empowerment of individuals' are merged into the 'human potential ethic's component of perennism. However, Hill's point on 'tolerance' and 'syncretism' are not included in my definition of perennism, and, in the light of my informants, should be incorporated. Perennism thus becomes a syncretic and tolerant spirituality.

Claiming that my small sample is statistically representative of the whole population would lead this research on a dangerous path, even if other works seem to correlate my finding. However, this research follows Weber's non positive approach combining explanation with understanding (Ringer 1997). For this reason, the definition of perennism has to be understood as an ideal-type, that is a mental construction which incorporates the essential, not the average, properties of a particular phenomenon. This ideal-type is a methodological concept which facilitates the understanding and explanation of this so-called 'New Age' phenomena. Perennism, is thus a mental construction in the light of 35 informants, and is not a statistically relevant description of reality. This methodological concept will now be used to discover more intricate facets of these alternative spiritualities.

Note

1   It should also be pointed out that in terms of religious content, I argue elsewhere (Possamai 2005) that there has been nothing new invented since at least the mid 1960s. I refer to this as the stasis of religion.

Chapter 5

The Spiritual Knowledges

In the former chapter, two ideal-types of spiritual knowledge were discovered: one which focuses on the self and the other on a more external knowledge. This dichotomy needs to be explored and for this purpose I will go over the history of esotericism up to the emergence of what is called 'New Age' (or what I would rather call now perennism). Through this exploration, I will argue that perennism, as it came out of my sample, is an innovative religion in the sense that it focuses on the self; however, in terms of content, there is nothing new (see Possamai 2005, Chapter 7). As argued in this book, our postmodern times are not only facing a stasis of culture but also a stasis of religion in terms of religious content. However, before going through this argument, it is first important to clarify the knowledge element found in my interviews for this will serve as an Ariadne's thread in this chapter. The case of Marilyn leads us to the thread.

Marilyn and Spiritual Knowledges

Marilyn was 75 years old when I interviewed her in 1997. We talked for a whole afternoon and her life story in alternative spiritualities is rich in anedoctes. However, I will only present Marilyn according to the meaning she can give to this difference between these two spiritual knowledges.

Her mother was deeply involved in spiritualism, anthroposophy, and also in the Theosophical Society:

> At the age of 11, I was initiated into spiritualism, which is talking with people who are dead, so called dead. [...] Then when I was in my late 19s or 20s, so during the war, this was in England, [...] I followed her into [those groups] because I was interested, and she talked about it a lot. [...] I went to meetings and lectures and things and was part of it [...]. In those days things were said in very long-winded ways. Time has speeded up you see and we learn things much more quickly. We have to say things more quickly. I do a workshop now in about five hours, it used to take the whole weekend. And I get exactly the same stuff over, but they don't need all the kafuffle. They don't need all the explanations. They have the nitty gritty and you get straight in there, you do it and you've got it. It's all speeded up.

Up to this point, it is clear in Marilyn's interview that she describes the spirituality of the past as a quest for knowledge, what she associates as '*kafuffle*'. Later in the interview, she described what she understood to be the meditation work and continued to undermine this notion of knowledge. She declared:

[In those times] You did do meditation I suppose, but it was a strange sort of meditation, [...]
it was mainly knowledge then. But since the 60's, with the music, the Beatles and all of it,
and the flower power and all of that stuff, they started living it really. [...] So it all got stirred,
mixed in a pot. It was good. It burst those rational shoulds and shouldn't's of the church, and
got to do what you're told [...]. And so yes it was knowledge. But since then it's been more
I think, there is more experiential stuff around.

She thus favours a spiritual approach based on experience (nowadays) rather than on
knowledge (in the past). How do we make sense of Marilyn's distinction between
knowledge and experience? When I asked Marilyn for advice on how to follow a
spiritual path, she answered:

well it's one thing to get the ratio of knowledge versus experience into some sort of balance.
Don't go just for knowledge. To do things that help you become aware of who you are, as
a soul, as a being.

This last sentence makes it clear that what Marilyn refers to as knowledge is a more
'external' knowledge, such as theories and/or macrohistories presented in groups
such as the Theosophical Society, the Anthroposophical Society and Guénonism (see
below); and the experience refers to self-knowledge, i.e. an experience that helps
'you become aware of who you are'.

Marilyn drew the most explicit difference between those two kinds of knowledge.
Unfortunately, there were only two interviewees old and experienced enough to have lived
this change and express it. Tom is 60 years old and refers to the old days that were, as he said:

very regimented. That's why I spent 2 hours solid in darkness. And that to me is discipline.
You go to groups nowadays, there's no discipline. How can you learn properly if you don't
have the discipline to do it?

Unfortunately, he takes us too far afield from this notion of spiritual knowledge that
we are trying to clarify.

However, even people who have not lived this assumed transition explicitly reject
the reduction of their alternative spirituality to specific, externally supplied knowledge,
just as Marilyn does. Robert, who is a psychic counsellor, refuses to give to his
customers/patients a fixed set of values, or his version of knowledge. Rather, he
adapts himself according to the context:

People don't want absolute values. They don't want to know what's the right think to do.
They want to know what's the right thing in terms of their values. So you shift your ground
for each one [...]. So we say is there any absolute values? No. It's all relative to the individual
who comes.

Steve has been involved in many initiatory organisations, and he also criticises strongly
the idea of what he calls 'universal knowledge':

It's not uncommon for a third degree witch (witch is the highest thing in most witchcraft
systems), to say that she can solve all your problems because she has access to universal
knowledge. Absurdities like this are common.

He continues this idea by connecting it with the ephemerality of some groups:

> People are in one group and they go to another group, another group, another group, another group. It's very very very very common. And there's lots of groups around too and everyone's claiming hidden knowledge and all this sort of rubbish.

For the purpose of this book, I will refer to Steve's 'universal knowledge' and Marilyn's 'knowledge' as macro knowledge, i.e. a universal knowledge gained from sources external to the self, and to Marilyn's 'experience' as knowledge of the self, i.e. a knowledge gained in individual experience mainly.

It would be too complex at this stage to define theoretically the boundaries between 'external' (or macro) knowledge (i.e. doctrine, etc.) versus 'internal' (or of the self) knowledge (i.e. intuitive, etc.). However, it is the purpose of this chapter to sociologically analyse why my informants draw a difference in their interviews. Just over half of my interviewees (19; 57 per cent) favour the knowledge of the self only against four (11 per cent) people exclusively interested in macro knowledge. Seven (20 per cent) informants did speak about them in equal terms, 3 (9 per cent) believed in spiritual knowledge but did not offer any information on its sub-types, and 2 (6 per cent) of them did not give any indication on spiritual knowledge at all. Because of these results, the aim of this section is to understand these different orientations to Macro Knowledge and the Knowledge of the Self in my sample.

Julian represents the seven interviewees who consider that the two types of Knowledges are deeply interrelated:

> In magic you talk about the microcosm and the macrocosm. The macrocosm is anything out there and the microcosm is what's within. I think some systems that you look, you know they contemplate their navel and look within, that's all they do, and some systems look out. I think what you need to do is both. You need to explore the options that are out there.

When René Guénon (1958, 81) argues that 'the Knower, Known and Knowledge are truly one only' (i.e. macro and self knowledges are one, as expressed by seven respondents) he makes mainly a metaphysical claim. What interests me as a sociologist is the way macro and self knowledges are perceived and pursued in everyday life by my interviewees. As an example, members of the Theosophical Society, at least in the last century, were studying first the theory and macrohistory of Blavatsky's writings to only gain afterwards the knowledge of the self. Today, as found in my fieldwork, the emphasis (i.e. 57 per cent) seems to be mainly on learning the knowledge of the self while the macro knowledge is minimally addressed.

I cannot argue from my small synchronic sample that the majority preference for the knowledge of the self indicates a significant development in alternative spiritualities over time. However, I have found in the literature two indications of just this transformation as discovered in my fieldwork. Champion (1995, 242) shows that indeed a shift of this kind occurred and that in the family of alternative spiritualities, now, there is more focus on experiential techniques, i.e. techniques that focus on a direct knowledge of the self rather than on a taught knowledge. She dates the change in focus from the 1960s. Also, Heelas (1996) perceives that there has been a shift in the historical development of the 'New Age' from an emphasis on writing and reading to practising spiritual disciplines. He (1996, 47) notices that Gurdjieff was the person (out of all the 'New Age' precursors) who has done the most to emphasise transformational techniques conducted by the individual at work on the self. Indeed, for Gurdjieff (1984, 29), there is only self-initiation. However, if he was born c. 1877 and died in 1949, his ideas only began to spread from the 1950s onwards through the publication of his writings and the testimonies of his pupils (Salzmann 1987, 139-140). Sutcliffe (2003a, 117) discovered that a totally reconceptualisation of the 'New Age' emerged in the 1970s underlining the change of view of Peter Caddy, from the Findhorn Foundation, as no longer an other-wordly view but as 'a humanistic project of spiritual growth and self-realisation in the here-and-now'.

There is also literature on the abstract dichotomy between modernity/postmodernity that could make sense of this shift (i.e. to explain why those engaged in spiritual quests should increasingly favour the knowledge of the self over macro knowledge). Here are two significant pieces of research:

The loss of attraction for forms of universal Reason, which can lead to a Macro form of Knowledge, can be found in Roseneau (1992, 127-133). She shows us how, in the later twentieth century, critiques of modern reason and macro knowledge(s), often seen as linked under the rubric of postmodernity, have diffused through Western society. Included in these critiques is a questioning of universalist thinking and a rejection of what was understood as totalitarian and oppressive tendency of instrumental reason.

Still in this field of study, Lipovetsky (1993) offers an understanding of the growth of preference for the knowledge of the self. He refers to a second revolution of individualism that occurred in late modernity (what others would call postmodernity)[1] and which is characterised by narcissism. In this revolution, knowledge is still important, but it is that of oneself. Those caught up in these changes mainly focus their attention on themselves and do not invest themselves in 'macro identities' as much as in the past. They focus on constructing their own identity, their own personality, and on generating their own knowledge.

On the basis of my fieldwork and of these accounts, it can be argued that a shift towards the self happened in what is called postmodernity (or late modernity). This focus on the self has, of course, been present before, but mainly in philosophies. What is significant is that this focus on the self seems to have significantly become part of the everyday life since the 1970s (Lipovetsky 1993), and could have changed people's approaches to alternative spiritualities.

These modern/postmodern factors, which will be further explored in Chapters 8 and 9, could also have affected what is called esotericism; this is presented below.

Esotericism Unveiled

In numerous studies, the concept of esotericism – and also that of occultism and Gnosticism – is used in many different ways that confuse. Almost all esotericists, i.e. people practising esotericism, use the concept of esotericism as a label for their teachings. Riffard (1990) provides an interesting analysis of the word in its various interpretations by different groups. For example, Gnosticism called esotericism gnosis; for Pythagoreanism esotericism was synonymous with philosophy (*o.c.*: 97);

esotericism was magic for the Iranian Mazdeism (*o.c.*: 113); in 1883 the word was consecrated for the public in a book by A.P. Sinnet, *Esoteric Buddhism*, but the term was then used to express the doctrine of the Theosophical Society (Riffard, 1990: 78-79). For Foster Bailey (1974: 10) from the Arcane school, esotericism is the secret knowledge found in the work of the founder of the Theosophical Society, Helena Petrovna Blavatsky. For other esotericists, such as René Guénon, Blavatsky is a charlatan and does not know anything about esotericism. The word esotericism has thus a diversity of denotations. It is also so often strongly valorised in a variety of esoteric groups that it has been appropriated by them to establish their credentials with their peers and their public.

Tiryakian (1974, 265) claims that:

> [...] a crucial aspect of esoteric knowledge is that it is a secret knowledge of the reality of things, of hidden truths, handed down, frequently orally and not at all at once, to a relatively small number of persons who are typically ritually initiated by those already holding this knowledge.

And as Riffard (1990) confirms: 'who says esotericism says discipline of the arcana. The criterion of esotericism mainly taken into account, the most visible characteristic, the affirmation the most often renewed among the esotericists, indeed, is the cult of the secret'.

Even if the term esotericism is a multi-dimensional term and is hard to grasp (Faivre and Hanegraaff 1998), for the sake of my argument, I will follow the secrecy dimension of esotericism even if according to Faivre (1994), there is a danger of reductionism if following this path. However, the notion of secret can have different understandings as it is found in Simmel (1991); these are: secret as a form of protection; secret as giving a sense of power for the one maintaining it; and, secret as a sociological finality in itself, i.e. a doctrine will be kept secret for people who want to find it, mainly to force them to gain the experience of this knowledge. This research takes into account that the choice of the definition of esotericism might determine the results of the analysis below, but unfortunately, the scope of this book does not allow further discussion (see Possamai 2002).

There is no need to explore the complexity, the origin and history of esotericism. What is significant for this book is the moment when esotericism became caught up in the modernisation process – say from the 1850s onwards. During that period, the idea and practices of secrecy as presented above progressively decayed; and this, as I will claim below, might itself have in the long term contributed to the shift from macro knowledge to the knowledge of the self. Esotericists, from groups such as Spiritualism, the Theosophical Society, Modern Occultism and Traditional Esotericism (or Guénonism), by the nineteenth century wanted to deliver their 'knowledge' in a clear language to the general public and promoted democracy in their groups. They wanted transparency (as opposed to secrecy). And this is now being detailed in the analysis of these major modern groups:

Spiritualism

Contacts with entities from the noumenal world are not a new phenomenon in the history of esotericism. Shamans experience a trance and speak with astral 'people';

mediums let their body be possessed by a spiritual entity and become transmitters of the supernatural. Before spiritualism, this was called nekyomancy, necromancy or divination by consultation with the dead. What really makes the difference with the appearance of modern spiritualism in 1848 is that suddenly people no longer need psychic power or long training to communicate with the noumenal world. Everybody is now considered able to contact the spirit of the dead and there is no longer a need for the presence of an intermediary. A whole life spent climbing the levels of an initiatory society is no longer required in order to experience the noumenal world. What is important in Spiritualism is that it has democratised esotericism by offering access to the noumenal world to everyone who desires it (C. Wilson 1971).

The birth of modern spiritualism and its democratisation process started with the Fox sisters who discovered a way of communicating with the spirit of a dead person through mysterious raps and knocks. They began their career as spirit mediums through newspaper journalism and in public and toured throughout America. Their manifestations created an intense interest and controversy and was the starting point of the modern Spiritualist movement.

Léon Rivail (1804-1869), under the Breton pseudonym of Alain Kardec, tried to unify and codify Spiritualism to make it a religion 'tinted with sentimentalism and rationalism' (Faivre 1992, 86). Having positivist beliefs, without being an orthodox positivist, he employed 'the scientific method of observation, comparison and evaluation' (Negrâo 1987, 259) to systematise Spiritualism.

He was among the first (if not the first) to reintroduce the theory of reincarnation in the West since its condemnation in AD 533 by the Fathers of the Church, but he reintroduced it with the law of constant progress, i.e. blended with a significant 'spiritual appropriation of Darwinism' (Ellwood in Lewis and Melton 1992, 66 and Cottom 1991, 42).

After Kardec's work, the large family of Spiritualism divided into two main tendencies. One (often referred to as Spiritism) followed his work, e.g. the Brazilian Spiritist Federation created in 1874, a federation which is far from unifying every Brazilian group.[2] The other refused his systematisation and turned to predecessors of the movement, like Swedenborg for example, to rationalise Spiritualism with a Christian faith.

In the nineteenth century, the Theosophical Society (Blavatsky 1972a, 27-33) and Occultism (see below) criticised this movement because of the reductionism of its vision of the noumenal world. Spiritualism as they represent it only contacts the spirits of the dead, while they believe in the presence of other kinds of spirits such as elementals, astral bodies, angels, demons. In this sense, Spiritualism is perceived as a vulgar form of necromancy.

The Theosophical Society

Helena Petrovna Blavatsky (1831-1891) and Henry Steel Olcott (1832-1907) created the Theosophical Society in New York in 1875. It was established as a centre dedicated to studying paranormal phenomena, and gradually became a cult movement (in the sense used by Stark and Bainbridge 1985, 29-30).

Blavatsky wrote her first book *Isis Unveiled* [1877] in which feminine power is assessed through the myth of Isis. Through this myth, the Theosophical Society wanted to restore power to feminine religion. The Theosophical Society's introduction of the myth of Isis into its canon (Lantier 1970, 147-150), and Spiritualism's espousal of woman's rights (in Lewis, Melton et al. 1992, 65), were first attacked, not by the scientific world, but by other movements of the same esoteric culture: Occultism[3] and Traditional Esotericism. The latter was unable to accept the idea of men and women confronting the noumenal world equally.

When Blavatsky and Olcott came to India where they were welcomed by some non-orthodox Hindus, they founded in Adyar (Madras) the world centre of the Theosophical Society. Later, Blavatsky came back to America and wrote what would become the manifesto of the Theosophical Society: *The Secret Doctrine*. She developed a new cosmogony and cosmology based on seven planes of reality. With this book, she introduced Eastern ideas into esotericism (York 1995, 33-34) but adapted them to a Western ethos.

She also synthesised a new eschatology which was based on evolutionism and the theory of reincarnation. Blavatsky did not reject Darwinism but insisted that it had omitted the spiritual side of evolutionism in favour of materialism. Inspired by an evolutionistic discourse, she adapted and Westernised the concept of reincarnation by syncretising it with the concept of spiritual progress. As Theodore Roszak (1976, 118) puts it:

> Her [Blavatsky's] effort, unlike that of the Christian fundamentalists, was not to reject Darwin's work, but to insist that it had, by its focus on the purely physical, wholly omitted the mental, creative, and visionary life of the human race.

Blavatsky's (1972b, 9) polemic in favour of her syncretism is exemplified in this passage:

> If the Pythagorean metempsychosis should be thoroughly explained and compared with the modern theory of evolution, it would be found to supply every 'missing link' in the chain of the latter. But who of our scientists would consent to lose his [sic] precious time over the vagaries of the ancients?

In the East, reincarnation is not only progressive, i.e. allowing the possibility of a better embodiment in the next life, but can also be regressive. In the West, the cultural transaction between evolutionism and the theory of reincarnation allowed only for progressive reincarnation: progress on a symbolic spiritual ladder, until the final theomorphic stage. Reincarnation is not, in this sense, a fate from which humans may have to be liberated as it is in the East, but a factor of progress.

Thus the theory of progressive reincarnation explains how utopia is attained: one day the whole of humankind will have developed its divine spark and built a world similar to that of Adam and Eve before their fall. However, this time, according to the members of the Theosophical Society, is still far away. Serious spiritual progress still needs to be achieved over thousands, maybe millions of years.

Bernard Shaw, who had an affair with Annie Besant (see below), describes this soteriology in *Back to Methuselah* under the terms of 'Creative Evolution' which, for him, was 'already a religion, and is now unmistakably the religion of the twentieth century' (Shaw quoted by Green 1992, 154). Ferguson (1981, 52) uses instead the concept of 'Collective Evolution' in her New Age book of the 1980s.

When Blavatsky and Olcott died, Annie Besant (1847-1933), a former socialist and feminist activist, became the leader of the movement and presented a young Indian, Krishnamurti (1895-1986), as the 'vehicle for the coming of the World-Teacher' and the proclaimer of the new universal religion. This announcement provoked much dissidence within the movement. For example, the Austrian Rudolf Steiner decided to come back to a more Christian conception, reintegrated the ideas of the Rosicrucians in his doctrine, and founded the Anthroposophical movement in 1913. Many others, because of this claim about Krishnamurti, or on the basis of their own ideas and affinities, left the movement to create their own.

Inspired by the idea of democracy, the Theosophical Society was more an open school than an initiatory group (apart from some inner groups within the society). It refused any kind of hierarchy or grades, even if it had leaders. There was no longer the relation between master and pupil but the shape of a spiritual school in which people came for lectures and conferences. Lantier (1970, 278) published an extract of a lecture given by a member of the Theosophical Society who wrote that the Brahmans, the priests of Memphis, of Eleusis, of Orphism and the Esseniens had admitted to their mysteries only men of a high class. The lecture declared that the Theosophical Society was against this notion of *mystagōgos* (the priest who leads the candidate during an initiation). He continued, underlining the 'openness' of the Theosophical Society to everyone. Like Spiritualism, it wanted people to have free access to the knowledge of the noumenal world without the service of an intermediary elite.

The Theosophical Society and Spiritualism were the two movements that not only democratised themselves, but also gave the opportunity for women to experience esotericism:

> The anti-establishment flavour of the material is reminiscent of Spiritualism, whose uncompromisingly individualistic proponents denounced the authority of churches over believers, of governments over citizens, of doctors over patients, of masters over slaves, and, most of all, of men over women (Riordan in Lewis et al. 1992, 111).

If before esotericists had been mainly male and seldom had let women participate in their rituals, in modernity, the latter had the opportunity to express themselves religiously. Because of the feminine freedom of expression in these two esoteric movements (and also for other reasons), others, with phallocratic tendencies, denigrated both of them.

Occultism

Eliphas Lévi, the pseudonym of Alphonse-Louis Constant (1810-1875) created a movement to fight against materialism in France and named it Occultism. He was also a romantic, a communist, and had been ordained to the diaconate.

After the XVIIIth century, the study of the Kabala was losing its vitality outside the Jewish community. Eliphas Lévi reintroduced this mysticism to his contemporaries. If the Theosophical Society was mainly based on Westernised Eastern doctrines, Occultism was strongly influenced by the Kabala.

Another important figure of early Occultism is Papus, the *nom de plume* of Gérard Encausse (1865-1916). He is considered as the 'Balzac of Occultism' because he left two hundred and sixty titles. He was a physician and an initiate of numerous occult groups. He believed in the cure of the body through the treatment of the aura. Patients queued for hours in front of his consulting room. He even received a medal of honour from the *Assistance publique* of France. He was also the spiritual teacher of Nicholas II in St. Petersburg.

This movement attracted people of apparently diverse personalities who did not condemn scientific progress or modernity but who integrated science in their teachings against materialism. They planned to elucidate all the mysteries lying in the esoteric traditions and wanted to unveil all the secrets. Many new initiatory orders were created from this movement, e.g. the Golden Dawn by Samuel Mathers, an order almost strictly for men.

Occultism kept intact the concept of initiatory groups but published many books in 'clear' (or non-cryptic) language unveiling all the information that was formerly kept secret. Just like other esoteric groups in the XIXth century, occultists aspired to be scientific. So just as modern science attempted to explain the secrets of the empirical world using a logical method, Occultism attempted by open scientific inquiry to unlock the secrets of the non-empirical world – though with adaptations deemed suitable. It combined logical and alogical method.

Traditional Esotericism or Guénonism

René Guénon (1886-1951) was first a disciple of Papus but later broke with his teaching. He rejected modernity and its visions of progress (accepted and integrated in the other three movements) and even conceived of modernity as the ultimate degree of degeneracy (Riffard 1990, 858). He wrote books against the Theosophical Society (Guénon 1922) and Spiritualism. He was also hostile to the mushrooming initiatory organisations of the Occultist movement. Guénon rejected all the traditions coming from Western esotericism. He was a purist, a sort of fundamentalist esotericist.

He believed in a great primordial tradition that was once revealed at the beginning of the universe, and was transmitted through diverse traditions. Rejecting the Theosophical Society's eschatology, for Guénon the only salvation was to find the 'great' knowledge that was once given to humankind. He believed that the knowledge could be discovered in the great religions which changed the original message, so that it could be found only by an archaeology of religious knowledge. As a contemporary enthusiast puts it:

> He bestowed [...] upon traditional concepts and symbols their essential meanings lost for the most part in the West since the Renaissance. He also presented to the West for the first time the essential teachings of the Eastern traditions in an authentic manner, and his presentation was accepted by the living authorities of those traditions (Nasr 1987, 128).

For Guénon, esotericism was layered palimpsest and what he searched for was the original text, the basis of all the palimpsests. Guénon left for Cairo in search of Sufi texts in 1930. He became a naturalised Egyptian and changed his name into Sheik Abdel Wahêd Yahia. This Traditionalist religiophilosopher did not establish a school, but he left a review: *Etudes traditionnelles*. He created a wave of thinking which is, according to Riffard (1990, 858) nowadays represented by J. Evola, F. Schuon, G. Vallin, Â.K. Coomarasâmy and S.H. Nasr.

Esotericism Simplified

Through the years, and more specifically during so-called postmodernity – say from the 1970s onwards – we can posit that the process changed from this idea of sharing the doctrines (as found in the four groups above) into that of (over) simplifying them. As an example, I compare the book by the 19th century Occultist Papus (1994), *The Tarot of the Bohemians*, which even if it supposedly answers the secret of Tarot Cards, underscores macro knowledge (e.g. cabbala) and, is difficult to understand for the non-initiated; whereas a kind of do-your-Tarot-cards-reading-yourself-in-five-minutes book is faster to grasp by focussing on easy and quick information about the cards, and without entering into any theoretical underpinnings (c/f. a knowledge of the self).

If the tendency in the 'Esotericism Unveiled' phase was to reveal the secrets and to present purported macro knowledge(s): the tendency in what Riffard (1991) calls 'Esotericism Simplified' is to simplify what was already revealed a century ago and encourage the practitioner to develop his or her knowledge. It is necessary to point out that even if this is a major tendency, there are spiritual practitioners who engage in very profound spiritual research (or in search of universal principles). However, what is emphasised is that the simplification of esotericism has given the opportunity for everyone to have access to this, sometimes commercially prepared, knowledge (see Possamai 2005).

Esoteric knowledge seems to be no longer secret. Even if there still exist initiatory societies with diverse rites of initiation, those rites are also found in the literature. For Trevelyan (1984) there is no more need to access what he calls the 'secret wisdom' in groups, because the access for individuals is now facilitated. Schlegel (1995, 110) writes about the French esotericist, Raymond Abellio, who declared that our time would be synonymous with the end of esotericism. Every spiritual technique (e.g. astrology and numerology) is now easy to find and to learn and there is no need to belong to any secret group. Secrecy being the key element of 'traditional' esotericism (according to the definition adopted above), it can be argued that since modernity, secrecy has been opened up, and is now (in post modernity, or late modernity) on the shelves of New Age bookshops and, even on the Internet.

As Bauman (1997, 180) notices, transcendence was once the privilege of an aristocracy of culture such as saints, hermits, mystics, ascetic monks or dervishes. Now, this transcendence is in every individual's reach and this could explain my participants' favour for the knowledge of the self over macro knowledge.

This taste for the knowledge of the self seems to reflect a new tendency in esotericism, and it is a paradox to notice that the divulgation of macro knowledge may have caused not a wider interest in macro knowledge, but in the longer term, the knowledge of the self. We may even wonder if macro knowledge was mainly valorised because it was kept secret; perhaps, what endures is the mystery, not the explanation.

Through this analysis between macro knowledge and the knowledge of the self, and because of this focus on the knowledge of the self rather than on macro knowledge as in – supposedly – previous spiritualities, it is thus possible to argue that the spirituality under investigation is, on the level of its everyday life practices, but not in terms of its content (see Possamai 2005), an innovative form of esotericism.

Notes

1   For Lipovetsky, the first revolution of individualism happened with modernity, but this individualism was mainly restricted to the economic sphere and to some avant-gardes movements.
2   See Ireland (1991) for accounts of some interesting mixtures of African spiritualities with Kardec's spiritism.
3   On the other hand, Blavatsky (1972a, 25-27) was against this movement because of its perceived selfish race for power.

Chapter 6

A Sociological Chart of the
Age of Aquarius

While chapters 1, 2, 3, and 4 attempted to find a common denominator for my informants, Chapter 5 aimed at differentiating different types of perception on spiritual knowledge. Chapters 6, 7, and 8 aim at underlying the diversity of these spiritual actors within perennism. This chapter deals with those who follow the etymology of the term 'New Age', that is, the age of Aquarius.

The Age of Aquarius as the New Age

Some of my interviewees believe in a new age to come, the Age of Aquarius. For some of these 'Aquarians', there is also a Critical Mass to attain in which an Aquarian Christ will emerge. These ideas of the Age of Aquarius, the critical mass and the Aquarian Christ will be introduced with the case study of the married couple, Paul and Michele, who are involved in a network that focuses on the coming of Maitreya, one of the Aquarian 'Christs'.

After visiting many New Age festivals, I wanted to focus on some networks that I was told were meditating on, and hoping to usher in, a new age to come. I contacted the representatives of one such network, asked them if I could come to one of their sessions, and they warmly invited me. The session took place in a public library and the first hour was dedicated to watching a video tape which revealed evidence of the coming of Maitreya, the second Christ (see below). During the second hour, about twenty people, including myself, sat on a chair and started to meditate. We were not told of any techniques to follow, we were just asked to sit and to concentrate. This was supposed to develop a flow of energy that would contribute to the coming of the Age of Aquarius. I thus meditated and did not know what I was supposed to do or think and closed my eyes for an hour. It was only a few weeks later, when I managed to arrange a conversation with Paul and Michele, that I finally understood what I was supposed to be achieving through this meditation. We were, through meditation, building a critical mass for the coming of the Age of Aquarius and of the second Christ (Maitreya).[1] The case study of Paul and Michele (presented in the form of a dialogue) will clarify what was involved.

Paul: '[A zodiacal] cycle [...] broken into 12 is roughly 2,150 years. And during this period, our solar system comes into a proximity of a particular constellation. And a spiritual field if you like of that constellation begins to affect the planet. So as the solar system moves from one spiritual field into another spiritual field the energies of that field affect all the kingdoms on the planet. [For] each of the ages a teacher comes along [...] to inaugurate the new age. To inaugurate is to give the teachings to the next age. Now if nobody comes in, the energy's still pouring because it's the energy of these constellations. [...] And these stages are designed. It's hard to grasp. But each stage, each system, is designed in such a way, like it goes around and around to promote the next stage in evolution. On the whole solar system. On the whole planet. On each planet, on each kingdom, on each level. It's kind of hard to grasp. But that's how it is thought. So by the energy of the constellation of Pisces, Jesus came 2000 years ago. Through Jesus the Pisces was inaugurated'.

Michele: 'The Age of Pisces'.

Paul: 'The Age of Pisces was inaugurated [i.e. the start of Christianity]. It took disciples a pretty good what 3, 4, 500 years until it become more or less spread.[...] Nevertheless, people responded to the teaching not because the teaching sounds good, but because there was plenty of energy first. And they say well we need change. What do we do? What do we actually need to do? And then they began to relate to the new teaching'.

Michele: 'The teachings begin to make sense as the energy changes'.

Paul: 'As the people change within, the teachings begin to make sense. So that's why, even if we didn't do anything, if Maitreya [the Aquarian Christ] did not come out by himself, [if] he just simply gives somebody a book or whatever, [...] things will still happen. It will just take a lot longer'.

Interviewer: 'Like 5 or 6 centuries or something?'

Paul: 'That's right. Evolution will take its course and will just take longer. All of these measures accelerate'.

Interviewer: 'But through this meditation, you can accelerate it?'

Michele: 'Yes'.

Paul: 'Because what happens, we build up much quicker. We build up a lot more energy which stimulates this change, as the change is accelerated. That change which comes with the new age is accelerated. [...] Anyway, at the moment Maitreya is waiting. He's watching humanity and he's waiting for the best opportunity. He's watching humanity. He's also watching an objective situation. [...] So he has to look for an objective opportunity where people are, well the prevalent situation is the most beneficial for his emergence'.

In this interview extract, Paul and Michele refer to the Age of Aquarius (and the Zodiacal Ages), the critical mass (this building of energy that can accelerate the coming of the Age) and a new Christ to come (Maitreya). It is important to underline that the precise beliefs of Paul and Michele are not held by every believer in the Age of Aquarius. In the following sections, I will draw out a common genealogy from the different interpretations and then outline the differences in more detail.

New Age as the Age of Aquarius: Its Genesis

Paul Le Cour and Atlantis

In 1930, Paul Le Cour (1871-1954), a French astrologer, set up *Atlantis*, a journal that was to be the channel of expression of the concept of the Age of Aquarius which would dawn in the world in AD 2169. In 1924, Le Cour (1995, 171) declared that he had received his first inspiration about the Age of Aquarius and started to write about it in the very first issues of *Atlantis*.

Astrology has many branches and schools with a wide variety of astrological theories. One of them (which deals with nations and people) is called mundane astrology by Cavendish (1972), or religious astrology by Le Cour (1995). Just as a chart can be drawn for an individual, so too for a society. Following Le Cour, some modern astrologers claim that the sun changes its zodiacal sign every 2160 years, according to the astrological law of the precession of equinoxes. This migration into another zodiac is supposed to create important modifications on earth; and just such a profound alteration is about to happen in the third millennium. The sun is leaving the zodiac of Pisces and will gradually enter the zodiac of Aquarius, affecting the behaviour and attitudes of every living creature.

Based on this interpretation of the Scripture of the stars, some astrologers deconstruct 'Grand Narrative' history and reconstruct it according to an astrological ethos. The process is simply a tendentious account of the past which enhances the sagacity of astrologers. Here is a summary of this 'Aquarian' account:

In the IXth and X[th] century BC the world was passing through the Age of Leo, the ruler of the sun. This Age was therefore marked by sun worshipping. Then followed the Age of Cancer, a water sign that was the cause of the Great Flood. Because Cancer is ruled by the moon, this Age was also characterised by moon cults and worship of female divinities. The Age of Gemini, 6000 to 4000 BC, saw the invention of writing, because Gemini's ruler, Mercury, is the planet of communication. The Age of Taurus brought the worship of the bull, of the Golden Calf and also the construction of pyramids, ziggurats and other important constructions because Taurus is, in astrology, the fixed Earth sign. The bull is a central figure in Mithraism in which the bull-slaying scene (tauroctony) is central in all of its sanctuaries (Mithraeum). The Age of Aries brought ram worship. During this period, Abram changed his name into Abraham – which means 'coming from the ram' or 'son of the ram' (Le Cour 1994, 103). Then came the Age of Pisces and the consequence of its appearance at the vernal equinox was the growth of Christianity. The fish became a secret sign by which Christians recognised one another in the midst of hostile non-believers. This symbol appeared in the early Christian world until the end of the IVth century. Also, many of the apostles were fishermen. Furthermore, according to Le Cour (1995, 115-116) the Greek word, Ichthus (meaning fish) was supposed to signify Jesus. His interpretation is based on the notarikon of ICHTHUS, meaning 'Iesous Christos Theos Uios Soter', 'Jesus Christ God, saviour of men [sic]'.

This Christian Age, for counter-Christian perennists, was supposed to stress unselfishness and service to others, but because Pisces is a watery sign, the Piscean Age is interpreted as being one of 'watery confusion and emotionalism' (Cavendish 1977, 235). For Christian perennists like Le Cour though, it was only one step on the ladder of spiritual evolution away from the imminent level of the Age of Aquarius.

Because of the sun's appearance during the vernal equinox in the zodiac of Aquarius, humankind will be influenced in attitude and behaviour under the Aquarian 'totem'. Aquarians in astrology are, in astrology's own positive interpretation, brilliant and inventive and also persistent and determined. They are greatly concerned to help others, pouring themselves out on the world. It is therefore deduced from this identity that the paradigmatic characteristics of the world in the Aquarian Age will be orderliness, constructiveness and intelligence.

For Le Cour, the 'totem' of Aquarius corresponds with the myth of Ganymede who, in the classical myth, is a beautiful Trojan youth. Because of his 'Adonisian' like appearance, he was abducted to Olympus by Zeus who made of him the cupbearer of the gods. The young god is symbolised by a horn pouring water, i.e. the Horn of abundance being full of fruits; this also represents a spiritual treasure. The action of Ganymede, the Water Carrier in the Aquarian symbol, symbolises the pouring of spiritual knowledge and a peaceful paradigm on the earth at the Age of Aquarius. It is therefore hoped, through this positive projection, that this Age will be a time of international harmony.

However, despite his role as a populariser, Le Cour did not invent the Age of Aquarius so much as reinvent and expand its significance. This can be seen on the basis of a short excursus on astrology.

Excursus on Astrology

The concept of the Ages of the Zodiac has to be attributed to Hipparchus (129 BC) (Riffard 1990, 894). This theory, apparently, was ostracised with the advent of Christendom. In 365, Valens persecuted astrologers. In 408, the law of Theodosius II condemned their ideas (Riffard 1990, 966). Astrological discourse became common again during the Renaissance and the concept of the precession of the equinoxes reappeared during the Enlightenment to, but paradoxically, severely compromise astrology.[2]

In the XVIIIth century, according to Alexandrian (1994, 182), the Encyclopaedist philosophers discredited astrology with so much force in their rhetorical discourse that it would have seemed, at this time, that it would be impossible for astrology to emerge again with credibility. Those 'Voltairian' philosophers rediscovered the concept of the precession of the equinoxes and used it to prove that traditional astrology could not be valid because the constellations of the zodiac trade places every 2160 years. Gilbert-Charles Legendre, in his *Traité de l'opinion* (1741), spoke ironically of the fact that astrologers attributed all the virtues of the bull (advanced two thousand years before) to the contemporary ram. Voltaire used the same argument in the article '*Astrologie*' from his *Dictionnaire philosophique*. What he did not know was that some astrologers themselves had already analysed the difference between the real zodiac – which should be called constellation – and the '*imaginaire du firmament*' (to use Voltaire's vocabulary). But at the time, the astrologers appeared to have no rejoinder to the attacks of the Enlightenment philosophers.

J.A. Dulaure (1974, first published in 1805) used the same idea of the precession of the equinoxes for his thesis on the cult of the phallus. He analysed the representation of the bull and the ram in the religion and mysteries of pre-Christianity, and hypothesised that those astrological signs were used as symbols of the fecundating of the world. Because in spring, during the vernal equinox, the sun was in the constellation of the bull and later in that of the ram, peasants gave a zoomorphic and/or a zoo-anthropomorphic aspect (e.g. Apis, Pan, Sylvan, Satyr, Priapus) to the symbolism used in their myths, in their agricultural praxes and in their spring festivals. For Dulaure, these signs of the zodiac were so much identified with the regenerating actions of the sun that it was no longer the aster that was worshipped, but an embodiment of the two signs of the Zodiac (e.g. Pan), and in this situation an ithyphallic god. The author continued with the progressive amnesia of those symbols which have survived history and Christianity to become totally irrelevant (in a logocentric sense) in the XIXth century and its beloved secularisation.

Many years after the intellectual exile of astrology, it was revived in America by Alan Leo (1860-1917), a member of the Theosophical Society who legitimised, in the eyes of his contemporaries, the reading of the stars. He was the most successful publicist for astrology, and the first astrologer to be professionally well organised. He managed, through the Theosophical Society, to survive and prosper, although he was arrested and tried for fortune telling under the Witchcraft Act of 1736. The infrastructure built by the Theosophical Society (for example: national societies and multiple branches, journals in many languages, lectures and informal discussions with influential people) allowed the infiltration of astrology into modernity and popularised it. In France, astrology was revitalised through the work of Jules Eveno, known as Julevno (1845-1915). Le Cour built on the foundation of this revival when he renovated the idea of the Age of Aquarius.

In the same period, Levi Dowling (1844-1911) published *The Aquarian Gospel of Jesus*, in 1907, which narrated the travels of Jesus between his twelfth birthday and the beginning of his teaching career around the age of thirty. This book could serve as evidence that the idea of the Age of Aquarius was clearly stated before Paul Le Cour. However, Levi Dowling did not use the explicit metaphors of the Age of Aquarius though he often mentioned the word 'Age'. Only a few lines refer to a coming Age:

> And then the man who bears the pitcher will march forth across an arc of heaven; the sign and signet of the Son of Man will stand forth in the eastern sky. The wise will then lift up their heads and know that the redemption of the earth is near (Levi 1964, 10).

Explicit reference to the coming of the Age of Aquarius appears only in the introduction of the book by Eva S. Dowling written in the mid-twentieth century. She legitimises her interpretation with a reference to a manuscript by Levi, which has never been published, and which, I believe, is apocryphal. Ferguson (1981, 288) claims that the original book itself was not written until much later in the XXth century.

Le Cour was not the first to avow the coming of the Age of Aquarius, but might have been the first to systematise and conceptualise in detail this idea in its religious sense. He analysed history, produced an 'Aquarian' narrative and projected hope and peace on to the next millennium. In these senses, he was a strong carrier of the eschatology of the Age of Aquarius.

Alice Bailey

A key figure in the popularisation of the Age of Aquarius in the Anglo-Saxon world is Alice Ann Bailey (1880-1949). She was a disciple of Blavatsky and was asked to leave the Theosophical Society in 1920 because she had been accused of stealing manuscripts from Leadbeater. In 1923, Bailey created the Arcane School to teach meditation and to develop spiritual powers. In 1932, probably influenced by Krishnamurti's case (see Chapter 5 on the Theosophical Society), she declared that Christ would come a second time to prepare humankind for the New Age.

She wrote in her autobiography (Bailey 1976, 230-231) that she had received a message from a Tibetan Master through channelling while she was in Ascona (in the canton of Ticino, Switzerland) in 1932. The message sent to Bailey was about the coming of a world civilisation whose qualities would 'be primarily a spirit of inclusiveness, a potent desire selflessly to serve one's fellowmen plus a definite sense of spiritual guidance, emanating from the inner side of life' (ibid., 231-232).

The advent of this new civilisation is lent credibility by its association with the imminent Aquarian Age. It is in Bailey's work that the concept of New Age – in its contemporary and religious sense – is introduced as a synonym for the Age of Aquarius[3]. Bailey (1972, 74) even started to create groups of people before the second World War to prepare and welcome the Age of Aquarius, the New Age.

We may doubt that the equation of the new world civilisation, the Age of Aquarius and New Age was put into Bailey's mind by a Tibetan. She was clearly influenced by the theories of the mundane (or 'religious') astrologers that started to emerge a few years earlier.[4] As I see it, Bailey interpreted the Age of Aquarius as the upper rung of human spiritual evolution, and accelerated the prophetic message of Blavatsky with the help of the theories of mundane astrology.

Bailey also drew on Christian messianic belief. She taught that if the Christ came and started the Age of Pisces, by analogy, a Christ-Aquarius would come soon to open this New Age and to deliver his or her holy teachings. It is therefore important for her to welcome his or her coming fittingly.

Paul Le Cour and the Return of Christ

In 1936, Le Cour (1995, 28) proclaimed that the coming of the Age of Aquarius would be ushered in by the return of Christ. The concept of the return of Christ is recurrent in history and therefore it is impossible to assert that Bailey influenced Le Cour, even if he claimed to realise the second Coming after she did. But Le Cour's conception of Christ's return was different.

Le Cour was a Christian and did not perceive the coming of the Age of Aquarius as a new and universal religion, but as a reform of Christianity (Le Cour 1995, 156-157). He considered the Christian religion to be the only true traditional religion, and argued that the eclipse of Christianity under modernity and its *laïcité* in France was only momentary because its positive transformation would be immanent with the coming of the Age of Aquarius.

The French astrologer did not base his discourse on the theory of reincarnation (being a Christian), but on Paracletism (Le Cour 1995, 35-36), the coming of the Holy Spirit, the Paraclete. Paracletism points the reign of the Holy Spirit, the third reign in

Christian history, the first being that of the Father during the period of the Old Testament and the second being that of the son during the time of the New Testament.

There are, according to Le Cour, three main cycles based on the Holy Trinity: the principle of the Father (the age of Virgo, Leo, Cancer and Gemini), the principle of the Son (Taurus, Aries, Pisces, Aquarius) and the principle of the Holy Spirit (Capricorn, Sagittarius, Scorpio and Libra) (Le Cour 1995, 84). Each Age is a progress in humanity and humans have to expect more after the Age of Aquarius, around the year AD 4320 with the Age of Capricorn and the first coming of the Paraclete.

The Critical Mass

Aquarians, or what could also be called Aquarian perennists, work for the coming of the Age of Aquarius. They are not involved in political or social action, but they believe that in order to change the world into a better one, they first have to transform themselves. As the perennist Trevelyan (1984, 160) states, 'change man and you change society. Try to change society without the inner change in man, and confusion will be the sole result'. There is the belief that people have to work spiritually on themselves for the Age of Aquarius not only just to dawn, but to happen in earnest.

The extension of this belief in individual work to the collective is found in the notion of the 'critical mass':

> According to the critical mass theory, if enough people believe strongly in something, suddenly the idea will become true for everyone. This theory assumes that a reciprocity exists between one's individual consciousness and the collective or higher consciousness. [...] if a number of people – enough people to form a critical mass – concentrate on something, we may pass a threshold. Passing this threshold will have a spiritual and then a social impact on the whole world (Peters 1991, 77).

This theory is backed up by various sub-theories, e.g. the butterfly effect, a theory borrowed from quantum physics. If a perennist develops his or her human potential ethic, he or she will provoke what the quantum physicists call a butterfly effect, i.e. that a very small difference in the initial state of a physical system can make a significant difference to the same state at some time later.[5] It means that if one spiritual actor is enlightened, he or she will show the way to other people, and try to make them also become theomorphic. Another theory is that of the hundredth monkey written by Lyall Watson in *Lifetide* (Peters 1991, 77). In 1952, on a small Japanese island, scientists gave potatoes to monkeys to stop them from raiding farmer's gardens. One of the animals learned to wash the potatoes before eating them and taught her companions the technique. By 1958, the number of monkeys washing potatoes had been estimated at 100 and had attained a critical mass. Suddenly 'knowledge began passing instantaneously from monkey mind to monkey mind' (ibid.) and on a neighbouring island, other monkeys began to wash their potatoes. This critical mass, it was claimed, had crossed a threshold that advanced the whole of collective consciousness, and this concept of threshold could be applied to the human race. This theory is empirically contested, but this is not the focus of this section. Another variant of the critical mass theory is that propagated by Transcendental Meditation (TM). If one per cent of the world population become meditators, a critical mass would be attained and would establish peace on earth, according to TM teachers.

For perennists who are waiting for the coming of the Age of Aquarius in the very near future, it is important to ensure that the dawning will have full effect. There will be a burst of new energies but for the planet to receive and deploy the energies in earnest, it is important to prepare the 'recipients' through work towards the critical mass. For those who believe that the Age of Aquarius will come too late for them to live it, work on critical mass can fast forward the advent of the Age (an idea already used in its original version by Le Cour (1995) and also followed by Paul and Michele who have introduced this chapter). For those spiritual actors, it is important to change themselves quickly, and this, in turn, can transform the human consciousness within a single generation.

This idea of speeding up is reflected in an advertisement found in specialist magazines: 'Spend 50 years meditating in a cave, or try Synchronicity High-tech meditation. Both open you to radically expanded states of meditative awareness. One takes a lot less time'. This product is sold by Master Charles, a high-tech guru, who declares that 'we are Americans [...] if we can create fast food, can we not create fast enlightenment?' (Ziguras 1994, 24).

For other perennists who expect the Age of Aquarius in the far future and who do not attempt to accelerate the process through a critical mass, the global process of metamorphosis cannot be achieved in one lifetime. Hope for these believers lies in the theory of reincarnation for non-Christians (though not exclusively so) or the theory of the Paraclete for Christian perennists (see above).

These examples show the diversity of opinions regarding the Age of Aquarius.[6] Diversity is also found in the interpretation of critical mass theory. I have noticed a significant difference of opinion among my informants. The term critical mass includes two major variations that are not noted in the literature; while they both aim for change, their methods for, and conceptions of change, differ: one method is based on meditation and aims at a change in consciousness and spirit, the other one is based on social action and aims at a change in the social paradigm.

The work for a Critical Mass by Meditation (CMM) refers to the belief that externally supplied energy may be harnessed by a certain mass of people meditating, or being transformed into integral selves, and this will change the world as explained above. As my informant Marilyn declares:

> One of the principles around at the moment, the way we will save this planet and humanity is a thing called critical mass, which you've probably heard of, with the 100 monkey story. [...]. And the principle is that when any one or small group of a species gets an awareness, at a certain point in their numbers, [...] it will suddenly become available to all the rest. Without them knowing it. And they will suddenly all start doing it.

Roger said:

> If enough people are aligning spiritually, it will cause an effect, a resonance. A resonant effect, yes. And that's what happens. The more and more people...

The work for Critical Mass through Social Action (CMSA) does not refer to an unconscious shift brought by meditation but more to a paradigmatic shift in social life. It follows the description by Marilyn Ferguson (1981) of the Aquarian Conspiracy; is a qualitative change in everyday life. This can happen by a networking of many networks aimed at social transformation. It is called a conspiracy by Ferguson, and it is for her a revolution of a new style. It aims at changing the consciousness of a critical number of people to provoke a renewal of the society as a whole. However, the changes have first to happen inside individuals which in turn will operate change in a larger scale. The aim is to provoke a 'paradigm shift' in social structures and practices in the sense used by Thomas Kuhn. The interviewee Julia presents her view of critical mass brought by social action:

> Western culture's becoming more and more alienated from a spiritual approach and a caring approach. But on the other hand you've got all these small community groups springing up all over the place that are quite strong and quite active and quite committed. And they're a substitute in a sense for what we lack in the Western culture at large. And I think those small community groups or spiritual groups or whatever they are, are really having a huge effect on people's lives, because without them we'd all be stranded. [...] Just general community groups where people will get together and try and work on a certain problem. Like the Save the Albert Park Group. Or there's a group that I belong to called the Buddhist Peace Fellowship and we talk about different social issues and things that are of a concern to people. Like the closing of Fairlea Prison. The exploitation of animals to make drugs. So it's a sharing of knowledge and it's happening on a small scale in a sense. You know we're not using the World Wide Web. We're talking to each other. And I'll talk to you and you'll go and talk to someone else and so on and so forth. I think that that sort of knowledge is not even really recognised largely in mainstream culture, but I think it's critical. It's a critical way of exchanging knowledge, and I think it's a lot more influential than we would think it is on the surface. Just handing someone a brochure about someone. It's like that concept, I don't know who coined it now, but a butterfly flaps its wings in Guatemala or somewhere [...]. And there's a tidal wave in Tokyo or something. And I think there's some truth to that. Just on a community level. You just spread the word. But it involves caring and it involves making an effort. And you can't just sit in front of the TV and say isn't that terrible and then do nothing. Even if it's just having a conversation with someone or handing a brochure that you've got in the mail to someone who might be interested, or telling someone about a conference or a workshop, or something that's coming up about an issue that they're concerned about. It involves caring and taking action. And I think that there are people doing that all over the place. Grouping together a common interest.

CMA refers to an action in the 'collective unconscious' (to use Jung). It works on universal energies coming from above which, if well channelled and tamed, will speed up the coming of the Age of Aquarius and render it fully effective. On the other hand, CMSA works through building on social change under way in everyday life, especially in a variety of social movements. It operates by the increment of small actions. Work in and on one's community affects other communities, and from this, a snowball effect (or a butterfly effect) takes shape little by little.

Table 6.1 Informants' teleologies

Teleology (n=35)	n respondents
CMM + A. of A.	13 (37%)
	Positive: 7 (54%)
	Different: 4 (30%)
	No information: 2 (16%)
CMSA, no A. of A.	8 (23%)
CMM, no A. of A.	1 (3%)
Change in far future	1 (3%)
Neo-pagan	4 (12%)
No eschatology	5 (14%)
No information	3 (8%)

Abbreviations: Age of Aquarius (A. of A.); Critical Mass by Meditation (CMM); and Critical Mass through Social Action (CMSA).

As presented in Table 6.1, 13 (37 per cent) of my informants believe in the connection between the extramundane critical mass and the Age of Aquarius. As Julian declared:

> I do believe in critical mass. As far as coming from the creator or the god, from heaven as well, well I think this is all, there is a plan I believe. I don't believe in fixed faith. I think we all have a choice, but at the same time there is a plan and that things are going according to plan.

Or Alice on the same topic: 'Well as above so below. You know it's happened in the stars and now it's happening down on earth'.

Or Paul on the strong symbiosis between the extramundane critical mass and the Age of Aquarius:

> Because what happens, we build up much quicker. We build up a lot more energy which stimulates this change, as the change is accelerated. That change which comes with the New Age is accelerated. [...] Because the more people do transmission [meditation] the more energy is released this way, the faster the changes will accelerate.

The one person who underlined CMM without the Age of Aquarius appears from her language to believe in pure agency. Those who believe in the CMSA (8) do not believe in the Age of Aquarius. There is therefore a strong correlation between belief in CMM and the Age of Aquarius. However, among the people who combine CMM and the Age of Aquarius, there are 7 who argue that this change will be positive, and 4 who think it will be only a change, not necessarily for better or worse. As Daniel, one of the latter category, stated on the Age of Aquarius:

> And so yeah I mean in some ways the new world order is enhancing the negative aspects of the Age of Aquarius. Which is not good. The positive aspect of Aquarius is finding God in each other and from that perspective. But the cold impersonal, you know everybody's a

number, everybody is, dehumanisation is another danger. That we're not humans any more with problems. We are reduced to machines or numbers, whatever. So this age, you know, will have its negative and positive sides.

On the Critical Mass

I do believe in critical mass. That if enough people, say, learn to perceive something in a positive way, that even, without even having to talk or communicate with other people, they will start to be drawn into that. But I also do believe that every positive, I don't know if you want to use the word positive, but every truth contains its equal and opposite. And that also has to be worked into the formula. In other words, if you create let's say, if you do an enormous amount of conscious positive affirmations and everybody does a lot of these positive affirmations and it's not done in a genuine way, in an unconscious way, negative affirmations will start to arise. To challenge that. Because this hasn't gone far enough and deep within it. So the shadow comes up and says but what about this and it goes, can't answer it.

Suffice is to say for the moment that there are two different types of beliefs in the Age of Aquarius and in the critical mass theory (a positive and a neutral interpretation), and this difference reflects a difference in the types of religious/spiritual actors. Until more information is presented in Chapters 7 and 8 this problem will be left aside. The types of neo-paganism and those who deny the critical mass and the Age of Aquarius (no eschatology), will also be discussed in the forthcoming chapters. 'Orthodox' spiritualists who believe in change, but only in a distant future, have already been identified in Chapter 5.

The Second Coming

In the course of my field work, I met Ned who claimed to be the new Christ, or rather to be part of the new Christ consciousness. My interview with Ned is probably one I will never forget. When I first spoke with him over the phone, and he declared that he was the new Christ, I was quite anxious to meet him. And, as most probably the reader is doing, I smiled in anticipation. However, when Ned started to tell his story of a difficult life, I lost my smile. He admitted that he was schizophrenic. Every day he had to go to the hospital and stay overnight. He was only allowed to come home in the morning. Each night, doctors gave him drugs and he felt sad about this practice. He claimed that through meditation he could control his illness, but he found this impossible while being drugged. Telling more about his story will take us too far afield. His account, too far from representing the alternative scene, provides an interesting case study about a specific belief system, even if it is part of the story of someone with a serious mental illness; other more representative cases will follow. The extracts from his interview below, taken outside the interview context, will probably trivialise his narration. Following the approach detailed in the introduction, I do not try to explain his mystico-pneumatic experience, but just report it, using his own categories as far as possible:

When I was 21 my mother took me to the Royal Melbourne Hospital and the doctor there said I was schizophrenic [...].

He was asked to sit down at a desk and he wrote:

the first words that came were I'm Jesus Christ and Hitler. Gee I must be schizophrenic you know. The nurse came up and gave me a sheet of paper to sign myself in as schizophrenic. I said all right, I signed it.

This happened in 1972, then February the 6th, 7th, 8th, 9th and 10th of '74, [...] the holy Christ mind descended completely and I knew that the Being and I were one.

After this experience, he realised that when he first wrote that he was Christ and Hitler, it meant that he could choose to follow the right hand path or the left. God or evil.

After 1974, he completely identified with Christ. Until the end of the 1970s, he could not make sense of his experience with Christ until he came across a book written by Alice Bailey who referred to the second coming of the Christ in energy form, an energy that would spread among people as Christ consciousness. From this reading, he rationalised his experience as being part of the Christ consciousness. This consciousness has to be understood as a flow of energy coming from above, and in his understanding, more than one person will receive the flow. This was the case of his now deceased partner who believed to be the living Christ in female form.

For some, like Paul and Michele whom we met at the start of this chapter, Maitreya is the embodiment of this new energy that will bring the Aquarian Christ. These two informants belong to the Australian Meditation Network which is an offshoot of Alice Bailey's Good Will. The only difference between these two groups is that the latter rejected the announcement from the introducer of Maitreya. However, according to Michele:

I think now the events in the world are showing that what's really happening, they're [groups of Good Will] quickly changing their tune. We know quite a few Good Will groups who fully accept it. You know they fully accept our story.

Another version of the Aquarian Christ is offered by Marilyn, the informant who introduced Chapter 5. In the late 1970s, Marilyn met Peter Caddy (the founder of the Findhorn Community in Scotland, see Sutcliffe (2003a) for more information) in England. She referred to his wife at that time, whom Marilyn said:

became what she called, she thought she was the feminine Christ. She thought she was the embodiment of Christ this time, the second coming you see [...]. She went on this, she was mentally out of balance.

Marilyn does not think that the Christ energy can be carried by one body, as she said:

the second coming of the Christ energy is here right now, is coming in. It's not coming through any one person like it did the first time, through the master Jesus. But it's coming through anybody who loves, through the heart. So it's coming through people.

As she emphasised later in the interview:

> the second coming is through everyone, through anyone. And it's not going to be through a person. There isn't going to be. There'll be some anti-Christ who'll say all the right words and some of these cult leaders I'd say are anti-Christs. [...] They'll say all the right things. So we've got to be very careful not to follow.

Marilyn has another conception of the second coming which differs from that of the above informants. Paul and Michele subscribe to critical mass theory so as to prepare, and to fast forward, the second coming which will happen with certainty and in the form of a person. In Marilyn's understanding, that second coming is already beginning, is a collective phenomenon, and the time of its completion is uncertain: 'so that when a certain number of people have this awareness, for instance, the Christ energy, the second coming is now.

In this understanding, the second coming of the Christ energy is uncertain and will be possible only if a critical mass succeeds. And if it succeeds?

> Only people who are living the loving, enough percentage, will be able to cope with the new energies coming in. Anybody else who's hooked in greed and destruction and hatred and these extremes will spin out. They won't be able to cope with the energy. It'll fizz and they'll kill themselves off one way or another you see. Which they're doing in motor cars, alcohol, drugs. You name it you know. And there's no judgement in it. Either you will be able to go with new age or not. But the new energies will come into consciousness through the critical mass. And it is said that there are 144,000. Whether that's an actual number or a figurative number, I don't know. We'll never know.

And after, when the second coming of Christ will happen:

> I think one almost one morning we'll all wake up and suddenly there won't be any fear of planet earth. [...] We are going to have a planet earth and a humanity without fear.

This Christ of second coming is not considered the son of God but rather a form of energy that will be spread among everyone (or the elect) on earth. For others, as we have seen, this new energy will be embodied in a person who is called Maitreya. Even in my small sample, there are various interpretations of the Aquarian parousia, and more might be expected in a larger sample.[7]

In my sample, 6 (17 per cent) participants were concerned about the return of the Christ. And all of them equated this return with the Age of Aquarius and CMM. Except for one, all view this coming positively. It is also striking to note that 46 per cent of those who believe in the Age of Aquarius and CMM also believe in the second coming of the Christ.

Notes

1　See Sutcliffe (2003a, Chapter 7) for a similar and more extended ethnography at Findhorn.
2　See Johnson and Payne's (2004) detailed analysis on the various relationships between astrology and Christianity.
3　Occhigrosso (1994, 471) observes that the phrase 'New Age', in purely etymological terms, began to appear before the First World War as the title of a Freemasonic publication and of a weekly newspaper in London published by the British literary critic, A.R. Orage. Even if Orage was involved in the Theosophical Society, the New Age, by 1911, mainly 'had become a leading socialist commentator, appreciated for its literary and journalistic quality outside socialist circles ' (Roger Lipsey quoted by L. Welch (1982, 17). In 1926, Orage resigned from his position as an editor and from his active participation in social reform in order to find God (ibid., 69). For this purpose, he got involved in the teaching of Gurdjieff and participated actively in his school. However, as underlined by Webb (1989, 206), the editor printed in the first editions of his journal that this journal was aimed at the creation of a race of progressively intelligent beings. This connects more to a Nietzchean perspective (strongly followed by Orage between 1907 and 1917 (Webb 1980, 209)). If the word New Age in this journal corresponds to an eschatology (which is not explicit), it will be to that of creative evolution (Shaw subsidised 500 pounds to the journal) or that of the Theosophical Society (Lewis Wallacw, a member of this Society, was also involved in this subsidy). If New Age it would be (in the far future), it is not connected to that of the Age of Aquarius which is imminent and different. Also, it might be tempting to correlate Swendenborg's New Church with the New Age, but as Mayer (1998) points out, Swendenborg indeed hoped for something new and believed in progress, but he did not connect these perspectives with astrological consideration.
4　It should be noted that Sutcliffe (2003a) makes reference to two astrological books written in English in the 1920s with a reference to the 'Aquarian Age' in their title. Based on this information, it becomes blurred as to from where exactly Bailey was influenced.
5　From the theory that a butterfly flapping its wings in one part of the world might ultimately cause a hurricane in another part of the world.
6　See Sutcliffe (2003a) for an analysis of some of these opinions expressed in the Findhorn community.
7　Paschkes-Bell (2004, 321) underlines that 'the term "the Cosmic Christ" proclaims power that transcends the human, while the term "Christ consciousness" expresses human participation in that power.

Chapter 7

Neo-Paganism and Presentist Perennism

Neo-Paganism

Five of my interviewees distinguished themselves from the rest by a specific religious practice: they perform more structured rituals. If previous respondents tended to practice rituals, they tended to be centred on meditation and be loosely structured, e.g. the triangle meditation. As we will see, these five informants tend to follow rituals that have been established by nineteenth century Occultist groups. Contrary to the other informants, these five actors spoke about their rituals as strongly being a part of their spiritual life. Julian is one of the five:

Julian first started to become interested in alternative spiritualities when he arrived at university. He became involved in a born again Christian movement as well as in an Occultist group that was performing magical rituals. Experiencing various tensions, he left both groups and stopped being involved in alternative spiritualities for a few years. Now that he is back into it, he is studying astrology and would like to resume magical rituals but with people he can trust:

> The people who started it [his magical group] out they supposedly, I mean I can't prove this had been initiated in the past up to a certain level. Once you get to a certain level you're supposedly able to start your own group. I only took the first level of initiation [...].

They followed the rituals of the Occultist group, the Golden Dawn (see Chapter 5), 'and you would call up the four archangels and you'd ask for their protection and their help and developing stuff like that'. Those rituals used to take two hours:

> it was like very heavy. We swore quite serious oaths, you know, which looking back now, I guess I have a different view of them now. I think it was all a bit unnecessary. But I mean a lot of what we did is available in some of the books I've got anyway. So oaths of secrecy seemed a bit silly.

The other four practising more rigid rituals claim to be neo-pagan and their beliefs and orientations fit the perennist type. However, their vocabulary differs greatly from other perennists whose voices were heard in Chapter 6: there is a strong emphasis on (more structured) rituals, initiation, goddess and worship of the goddess. Jennifer is one of the four.

Jennifer is a feminist spiritualist who does not like the rigid structure and the levels of initiation of some neo-pagan organisations (which she calls Wicca):

> The first group that I was in was a group of all women and we would meet weekly and have a circle and do a ritual in the circle. And that ritual would normally be for healing or something like that.

She later went into a Wiccan group, 'and some of the people were really suss and there was a lot of power games going on. I'm sure that's not all wiccans'. However, 'Wicca is fine for some people. It's fine. If they can work with that structure. I just can't work in that structure'. She is now involved in women's spirituality (a neo-pagan spirituality for women only) and she often goes to meetings where she engages in rituals with other members. However, some rituals are for herself and performed by herself:

> I've got certain basic rituals that I use and certain basic acknowledgments that I always make. And I try to be really mindful when I make them. Not matter of fact or habitual, but are mindful. And I meditate in my room.

Steve is also against any rigid structure in groups and is now involved in a networking form of neo-paganism, the Church of All Worlds: 'I've done rituals for years. You know for far too long. [...] the last 10 years, yeah I've been basically in occult groups'.

Tensions occurred in those groups, some people wanted to gain more power within the group and too much politics was involved for Steve, politics that was taking too much time away from the rituals of magic. So, he decided to leave:

> And quite frankly, I did less magic in OTO [an occultist group] land than I actually did on my own [...]. So I've always found you get more magic from working by yourself than you do with groups.

He is now into neo-paganism, but for him, there is not much difference between occultist groups and neo-pagan groups:

> by neo-pagan terms, [I mean] that's the whole group, the whole scene from magic, Satanism, Wicca, OTO, Golden Dawn, all that stuff [...]. I call them neo-pagan or late 19th century occult revival groups.

When I asked him if there was some difference between rituals performed in occultist groups, he answered that:

> the pagan movement is [...[quite different. It's totally unregulated. Like the magical pagan scenes are the same, although they'll pretend that they're not. Basically, in the long run and in substance [the techniques from occultist groups and neo-pagan groups are the same], in detail no. A lot of pagans find magic too complicated to learn. So they do it simply. They try and simplify it.

However, for Steve, rites can be changed and adapted without necessarily being simplified:

And it [a specific ritual] had the thing called cakes of life. And in it you were meant to put in menstrual blood. [...] We never made decent cakes of life. So in the end we ended up buying [...] croissants from the shop and that because you know we just couldn't cook them. You're meant to burn the blood first and all this sort of stuff, for health reasons and all this stuff. It tasted like a cough lolly. It was disgusting.

Steve also calls himself an urban shaman. That appears to be what P. Johnson (1995) refers to as neo-shamanism, a form of shamanism characteristic of modern Western societies (if shamanism preserves traditional knowledge, neo-shamanism emphasises mobility and individual choice).

Judith was searching for an initiator in neo-paganism for many years. She never found her 'teacher' and became one herself:

Wicca to me is a practising Pagan [that is engaging in Pagan using rituals]. It's this difference between a Catholic and a Catholic priest. So if you are a Pagan you are a Catholic. If you are a Wiccan you are a Catholic priest or a sister. That is the way I define it. That's not necessarily how other people use the words. But Wicca does imply that you are a practising witch.

She also initiated Betty who refused to be affiliated to any groups. She describes other Wiccan groups as very much ritualistic, whereas she sees herself as doing rituals close to meditation:

It is very easy to say that I'm in a coven and I worship. We get together every Tuesday night and we do this ritual and we're worshipping her [the Goddess]. I am a solitary practitioner who tends not to rely on ritual, so I guess I almost see my life as a celebration. I worship her every time [...]. And I guess I would say that I celebrate my relationship with her all the time.

The other three neo-pagans also refer to the Goddess (and this also distinguishes them from the Aquarian perennists seen in the previous chapter). We will return to this notion of Goddess.

None of the four neo-pagans believed in the critical mass or in the Age of Aquarius. Betty does not think that 'the world is going to change. I certainly don't think it's going to change just because of anything in 200 or 300 years'. Except for Steve who is totally disillusioned with any theory or social vision but who still participates in neo-pagan festivals, and ceremonies; they all envision social change but only for the neo-pagan community. Fully understanding that there will be hostility to their aim and rituals, they try to bring alive a neo-pagan lifestyle for themselves and sympathisers. The focus is therefore not on a global change as it is for believers in the Age of Aquarius but more a local communal one. As Jennifer expressed her goals and hopes:

I'm still a member of the women's spiritual community and I'm very committed to it, and I want to live in a women's spiritual community ultimately. That's how I want to live, in a community with women. On a spiritual path. [...] I would love to do it now but it takes a lot of work and it's just not happening. And we're meeting regularly and trying to make it happen. I've been trying to make it happen for years.

Betty also wants to live in a neo-pagan community, but she admits that it is going to be difficult to attain her goal:

> I don't think there's enough community any more. I like the sense of community. That you're trying to build. I mean I don't think it's going to succeed completely because not everyone wants to be Wiccan. And I don't think it's going to succeed because there are too many people.

These neo-pagans performing rituals, I argue, constitute another sub-group of perennists who cannot be encompassed within what is often called 'New Age'. In the next section, I will describe what these rituals (and covens) are and in the following section I will formally compare these neo-pagans to the Aquarians in order to strengthen my claim.

Neo-Pagan Rituals and Covens

Not all neo-pagan groups agree on each ritual. Rituals vary from an elaborate ceremony, to a simple ritual, to a simple meditation accomplished by one neo-pagan. Generally, the common practice is to consecrate a sacred space, symbolised by a 'circle', and then worship the Goddesses and/or Gods within it. Magic can also be performed within the same circle which can be drawn in city apartments, in suburban backyards and in country places.

Certain tools are used for these rituals, such as an athame, i.e. a ceremonial knife for casting a circle. Also part of the ritual is the altar which denotes the Aristotelian Elements: Earth, Air, Fire and Water. A pentagram or pentacle is also often used to symbolise Earth, whereas a thurible (or censer) represents Air, a candle or small pot of fire, Fire and a chalice of water, Water. Often the witch will own his or her Book of Shadows, which is the witch's handwritten book of spells and magical information.

These tools (and others not mentioned) are part of a complete symbolic system which provides the neo-pagan with a 'map' for entry into other psychic realms and reach another state of consciousness.

Within the sacred circle, two main activities occur: 1. the solar celebration; and 2. the practice of magic which coincides with the phases of the moon.

1. Wiccans and some other neo-pagans celebrate eight major festivals or sabbats each year; these are religious ceremony deriving from ancient European festivals celebrating seasonal or pastoral changes. They are also called solar celebrations, and are symbolised as the 'Wheel of the Year'.

Dates taken traditionally from the North Hemisphere can be thought of not being adequate to the South Hemisphere. Some neo-pagan groups will keep the original dates, and others will adapt them to the Australian context (Hume 1999). Table 7.1 presents a list of these celebrations with the dates for the South and North hemispheres, as well as the different names of these events.

Table 7.1 Solar Celebrations – Sabbats

Nth Hemisphere	Sth Hemisphere	Exoteric Name	Esoteric Name
October 31	April 30	November Eve	Samhain
December 21	June 21	Winter Solstice	Yule
February 2	August 1	February Eve	Imbolc (Oimelc) or Brigid
March 21	September 21	Vernal Equinox	Ostara
April 30	October 31	May Eve	Beltaine
June 21	December 21	Summer Solstice	Litha or Midsummer
August 1	February 2	August Eve	Lughnasadh or Lammas
September 21	March 21	Autumnal Equinox	Mabon or Harvest Home

The two most important sabbats are Samhain (the neo-pagan new Year's eve: a night in which the barriers between the worlds of life and death are uncertain and in which the ancestors are supposed to walk among the living) and Beltaine (a fertility festival, i.e. the birth of summer).

2. There are also lunar celebrations which are called esbats, and are held thirteen times per year, during the full moon. Magic is often practised during that time for psychic healing sessions, for focusing and directing energy to achieve some results, and for developing the spirituality of its practitioners.

At the end of the Sabbat and Esbat, people usually share food and drinks, exchange story-tellings, bless the Goddess and/or God, and open the circle, allowing the space not to be consecrated any longer.

As illustrated by the case studies above portraying a negative attitude towards structure, not everyone is part of a coven. These covens are usually based on the teachings of Gardner and Sanders (see below), and one of its main rituals is the casting of the circle as illustrated by Jayakar (quoted by Jayran in Harvey et. al. 1996, 209):

> She faces East, saying 'I call the power of Air, and intelligence', lighting the yellow candle. She then faces front and South, saying 'I call the power of Fire, and of the will', lighting the red candle. She then faces West, saying 'I call the power of Water, and of emotions', lighting the blue candle. She then turns behind her to the North, saying 'I call the power of Earth, and of the body', lighting the green candle. She raises her wand to point upwards saying 'The circle is cast. I am between the worlds, beyond the bounds of time, where night and day, birth and death, joy and sorrow, meet as one'.

Covens are organised to celebrate the different pagan celebrations, to perform magic and to exchange knowledge on the Craft. It is usually a group of witches who practice worship together. All covens are totally autonomous and are lead by a High Priest and High Priestess, and are traditionally convened at full moon. It does not have a financial burden: all members contribute towards the purchase of magical equipment and food, and also bring their own tools. Money is not usually solicited from their members. Its organisation is based on the initiatory forms of modern occultism: there are three levels of initiations.

The first initiation invites the neophyte to enter the inner-circle of the coven. He or she learns the basis of witchcraft such as casting the circle, setting up the altar, and other basic principles.

For the second initiation, the novice reaches a higher knowledge of the Craft and is expected to be able to teach a first-degree novice. Before reaching the third level, Wiccans need to choose a neo-pagan of the opposite sex with whom they will form a partnership, which can be symbolic or actual.

For the third degree, it is expected to master the knowledge of the Craft, i.e. understanding perfectly the different symbols and tools which provide the third degree neo-pagan with a 'map' for entry into other psychic realms, and being able to reach another state of consciousness. This level also involves the Great Rite or sacred marriage. This can be enacted by a couple (formed during the second level) as an act of (physical or symbolic) ritual sex. The couple takes on the role of the Goddess and God and performs a sexual union (physical or symbolic) with the deity.

As a New South Wales witch revealed to Lynne Hume (1997, 135):

> My Great Rite was, for me, a most holy and sacred experience. It all has to do with will, intent, and the correct use of energy. It has to do with the flow and use of energy. Physicality is only a very small part. Sex, as sacred sex, creates a lot of energy but is very misunderstood. What occurs in the Great Rite is the person's engaging in sex become the God and the Goddess – if it is done properly. You have to think that inside the person is the God/Goddess. You don't see it as being unfaithful to your own partner or as having merely physical sex. There is a great misuse of the Great Rite, depending on the integrity of the coven.

In those covens, there are often a Craft High Priest and High Priestess who have reached the third degree and who lead the coven.

Aquarians and Neo-Paganism

Before resolving the questions relating to the extent of difference between Aquarians (i.e. those who believe in a cosmic change in the near future, as detailed in Chapter 6) and neo-pagans, it will be helpful to identify the neo-pagans more clearly, especially in terms of their difference from pagans. As Christian Bouchet (1997) notes, the pagan movement itself has to be separated in two categories: the denominationalist, i.e. people who refer to a specific god in a clearly defined pantheon connected to a specific ethnic group, whereas the non-denominationalist refers to a non-specific god and is not connected to a specific ethnic group. Neo-paganism has to be understood as a non-denominationalist group that first appeared in the 1940s (see below). As soon as a pagan system is taken outside its ethnic sphere, it becomes neo-paganism, or what is also called Wicca.

Differences in Aquarian and Neo-Pagan Discourses

As seen in the previous chapter, 'New Age', being in its origin synonymous with the Age of Aquarius, involves the belief in the changing of the world into a better one in the near future (between 'now' and 2160). However, the word 'New Age', being a meronymy, is often used to include neo-paganism. Paul Heelas (1996) and Samuel

(1996, 374) for examples, believe that neo-paganism belongs to the New Age paradigm, that 'of self-oriented religion rejecting a contaminated ego for a Higher Self which represents a realm of perfection'. But there are indications that we are faced with two quite different spiritualities here.

Many Aquarian perennists do not consider themselves neo-pagan, and likewise, not all neo-pagan groups identify with what is called New Age. All neo-pagans are part of a nature religion whereas not all Aquarians share the same belief about nature (Ivakhiv 2003, 94). As York (2004, 372) writes:

> Paganism itself subscribes to an immanent understanding of the godhead that allows – or even centralizes – the natural world as manifest sacrality. New Age, on the other hand, descends from a competing theological perspective, namely, a Gnostic/Theosophical tradition that views nature as an obscuring obstacle to hidden spiritual truth. The physical world becomes, accordingly, either an illusion or at least something of secondary and lesser importance. From a strictly sociological perspective, New Age and Neo-Paganism are simply rival theologies – each part of long-standing and legitimate spiritual traditions.

Neo-pagans are mainly interested in practising religions of the pre-Christian era, whether as a survival or a revival. They are mainly focused on the atavistic pagan religions and are generally not interested in post-pagan religions (with the possible exception of Hinduism). Whereas Aquarian Perennism is self-styled as an *awakening* in the future, neo-paganism thinks of itself more as a *re-awakening* of riches of the rituals and beliefs of the past (York 1995). Indeed, neo-pagans believe they are practising an ancient folk religion and focus on the past; the past, however, is not romanticised but serves mainly as a source of inspiration to be selectively drawn on. Furthermore, they are not particularly interested in a New Age in the future (Aidan Kelly in Lewis and Melton 1992, 138). These are general trends in the Weberian sense that help us to form these two ideal-types of religious activities. There are of course social actors who do not fit perfectly well – in an academic sense – in these ideal-types. As Kemp (2004, 169) underlines from his knowledge of the field in the UK, there are self-describing neo-pagans who expect a new age and there are self-describing 'New Agers' who perform rituals of the occult type.

> In general, Neo-paganism may be summed up as comprising an animistic, pantheistic, and pluralistic religious orientation that is non-doctrinaire but employs traditional pagan metaphors (myths, foci, and rituals) or modern reconstructions of them as a means of celebrating a this-worldly emphasis either on a solitary basis or with others of a like mind. It stresses self-responsibility, self-development, individual exegesis, and full freedom of self-determination, the experience of ritual and ecstasy, and an ecological preoccupation with the well-being of the planet regarded as a living entity. The interconnectedness of all life forms and the habitat is a central belief. Other concerns include tolerance, respect for diversity, healing, and the use of non-malevolent forms of 'magic'. Its ethics are pragmatic and grounded in the concept of honour (York 1995, 136).

I have found the points presented in Table 7.1 clarify the distinctions between Aquarian perennism and neo-paganism made by York (1995) and these will be compared with the findings from the four neo-pagans who introduced this section. The number in brackets refers to the page number of York (1995):

Table 7.2 Aquarian perennism versus neo-paganism

	Aquarian perennism	Neo-paganism
1	'Pursues a transcendent (2) metaphysical reality'	'Seeks an immanent locus of deity' (2)
2	'Innovation – Awakening' (2).	'Links to the past - Re-Awakening' (2)
3	'Global transformation' and a 'new planetary culture' (162-163).	No search for global transformation *per se* (162-163).
4	'Self-indulgence and excess personal growth focus' (162-163)	More community oriented (162-163)
5	Self development drawing on inner experience and potential (231).	Self-empowerment harnessing external power (231).
6	—	Nature based religion (200)
7	—	Goddess worship (200)
8	—	Ceremony and rituals (230)

In Table 7.2, points 1, 2 and 3, on the Aquarian perennist side, refer to the Age of Aquarius and its expected global transformation; on the neo-pagan side, as seen by my participants: these points refer to the desire of establishing a neo-pagan community. Point 4 refers to the human potential ethic of Aquarians, and to a community orientation for neo-paganism. However, neo-pagans, being perennist in my sample, appear also to be focussed on growth (cf. the human potential ethic element of perennism). Points 6, 7 and 8 refer to a set of words that neo-pagans use and that were presented by my participants above. However, an important remark has to be made about the Goddess worship (point 7). The goddess (the personification of nature) is witchcraft's central concept. She is used as a metaphor of nature. 'She is in the world, of the world, the very being of the world' (Luhrmann 1994, 49). She is, in other words, a powerful metaphor for monism, an element of perennism. Further to this line on perennism, Luhrmann (*ibid.*, 53) argues that in neo-paganism every woman can be a goddess, and every man can be a god; and this correlates with the conceptualisation of the human potential ethic:

> The Goddess is dissolution. The very nature of the concept entails the interconnectedness of all things. We are not separate from the world, magicians say. We are of the world, not autonomous individuals but connected wholes, connected with webs, meanings, vulnerabilities that shared yield greater strength (*ibid.*, 101).

Thus neo-pagans distinguish themselves from other perennist sub-groups by using the term Goddess as a powerful metaphor for monism.

Difference between Aquarian and Neo-Pagan Genealogies

If Aquarian perennism comes from the Theosophical Society's stream of thought (see Chapter 6), neo-paganism must also be located in relation to modern occultism (as defined in Chapter 5). Among contemporary neo-pagans, as in the case of Julian with whom we opened the chapter, cabbalistic magic, high magic and occultism appear together with neo-paganism as defined above. This association has caused dissension: however the link with occultism has always been there (Hume 1995, 6). T.M. Luhrmann (1994, 41-44) traces the roots of neo-paganism in the Hermetic Order of the Golden Dawn, an initiatory society founded in 1887. This group belonged to what I have described in Chapter 5 as Occultism. The Hermetic order fragmented and one of the new groups, formed in 1922 by Dion Fortune, was called the Society of the Inner Light. This society influenced new groups coming out of the Occultist stream, but they were not yet identifiably neo-pagan. Luhrmann (1993, 1994) calls the groups influenced by Dion Fortune, the Western Mysteries groups and see themselves as the continuation of the mystery traditions of the West, e.g. Eleusis, Mithraism, Druidism,... According to Luhrmann, the groups demand far more intellectual engagement than witchcraft (which 'comes from the guts and loins', see below) does. The practitioners of Western Mysteries are grouped in fraternities or lodges, tend to be Christian, and often work on cabbalistic principles. They appear to be a contemporary form of modern Occultism.

Further fragmentations of occultism, from the 1940s, saw the emergence of exactly the sort of neo-paganism described by Bouchet above. Gerald Gardner, who had met Aleister Crowley (from two occultist groups: the Golden Dawn and the O.T.O.), published fictitious ethnography of contemporary witches mainly in the late 1940s and the 1950s. He claimed to have been initiated and had revitalised Witchcraft (i.e. neo-paganism) in the Western world. For Gardner, witches had ancient knowledge and powers handed down through generations. This invention of tradition was claimed to be a revival of ancient nature religions. Witchcraft was organised in covens run by women called 'high priestesses' who presided over rites of initiation for new members of the coven.

At this stage, it is possible to elaborate the difference between Wiccans, neo-pagans and witches. Most witches are pagans, but not all pagans are witches. It could be argued that a Witch is a neo-pagan who practises one or more varieties of magic on top of honouring Nature, whereas a neo-pagan who is not a witch, sees Nature as sacred but does not attempt to practice magic(k) to the same extent. Wiccans are witches, but not all witches are Wiccan. A Wiccan would be someone mainly following Gardnerianism or Alexandrianism (i.e. the system elaborated by Alex Sanders). Unfortunately, there is no certainty of the definitions of those terms because of the wide variety of interpretations among neo-pagans. As Hume (1997, 66-67) underlines from a pagan newsletter, 'Ask four witches to tell you what the Craft is about, and you'll get four different opinions'.

Inside the neo-pagan movement which for Lynne Hume (1995) addresses the modern concerns of ecology and feminism, there is also the Feminist Spirituality Movement (also called Feminist witchcraft and Female Divinity by Wendy Griffin (1995)). Its adherents and interpreters may be witches and/or goddess worshippers. This movement focuses on women's nature and women's experiences of the sacred. It characterises dominant forms of organisation of society as phallocracy, and urges other modes be adopted. They mainly look for models in societies where interrelatedness is interpreted as being the primary value, as supposed of Palaeolithic and Neolithic societies. For example, Eisler (1990) uses Cretia (before the Aryan invasion which has, according to her, slain the people worshipping the goddesses peacefully) as the epitome of a perfect society, which she calls a gylany. But eyes are not turned exclusively to the past: the movement also searches for a new model of society that remedies the supposed spiritual lack of Western society. For example, Green (1992, 237) explains how a native American, Paula Gunn Allen, sees (or generalises) her roots, and these roots are the ones (some) female spiritualists would also like to share:

> Indian tribal-styles, for instance, are never patriarchal; indeed, they are usually gynocratic. They are thus charged with the dream that inspires many dissidents from the white culture; and though the latter must beware of simply imitating this other culture, they cannot but be fascinated by it. Being women-centred, the American Indians are sexually free, and often honour homosexuals. One often finds, in the tribes, nurturing, pacifist, and passive men and decisive, self-defining women.

There is the assumption that the emergence of the feminine principle – the Goddess – will foster an alternative kind of political system, particularly if global emphasis is on interconnectedness rather than on hierarchy; indeed, for Gordon (1995) there can be 'inextricable links between politics and spirituality, particularly feminist politics'. If neo-paganism celebrates the god (the male embodiment of monism, also called the Horned god) and the goddess, feminist spirituality focuses its ritual exclusively on the goddess and participants are only women. The Feminist Spirituality Movement covers many groups with different ideals and not all of them consist of homosexuals and radicalist separatists. However, the Feminist Spirituality Movement has its counter-part, the Radical Faerie Movement (Rodgers 1995) which is a distinctly gay spirituality.

All of these varieties of neo-pagan spirituality, we have seen, have at least genealogical links to modern occultism. It is this lineage and its effects on belief and practice that further distinguish neo-pagans from Aquarians.

Presentist Perennism

> 'I see the Past, Present and Future existing all at once, before me.'
> William Blake (quoted by Davies 1995, 72)

At issue among perennists is orientation to history. As we have seen, Aquarians deconstruct history in terms of Zodiacal ages and orientate themselves to the future, while neo-pagans orientate themselves to the past and attempt to reconstruct a pre-Christian lifestyle. In this section still, a third sub-perennist type will be introduced, that of presentist perennism. This is the perennist group which has no concern with the past, no vision of a succession of age: it is perennism which focuses exclusively on the present.

Several of my informants were anxious to dissociate themselves from Aquarian history at least. Harry is one of them:

> The Age of Aquarius, [...] it seems to be some kind of technical term to explain an astrological period. I don't know enough about astrology. There seems to be a fair amount of dispute and discussion amongst the astrologers as to exactly when it's going to happen. [...]. I believe in symbols. I believe in metaphors. I believe in metaphors and metaphysics is what

I believe in. I don't believe in facts. I don't believe in history. I don't believe in those things.

Sarah finds a certain arrogance in Aquarian history. I asked her what she thought about the Age of Aquarius and she answered:

> *Sarah*: 'I think it's arrogant to think that things get better as we go along and progress. We don't progress. It's cyclic [...]. I think we're all heading for another kind of spiritual time. But we could lose it and we probably will. Things seem to be cyclic. You get so far and then you go back and as I said there's nothing we've got that I don't think that people have had before at certain times and in different cultures. Egyptian culture, Mao culture. It may be expressed in different ways, maybe not. I don't know, is there a word for being time centric?'

> *Interviewer*: 'Time centric?'

> *Sarah*: 'Rather than ego centric. Yeah well I think we do. [...] Well you know how you can be ethnocentric and think that your culture's got it the best? [...] Yeah we can suffer from being time centric, but I don't know if there's a word for it'.

Sue uses astrology among other means as a psychological tool to understand herself, to reach self knowledge. Since she has mastered this discipline, she has started to do meditation. She teaches astrology and also draws charts. Often, people ask her about their future, however, she says:

> I've often found it difficult to understand people who are obsessed with knowing their future. Because surely, I mean you've got to live in the present. This is what I try to do with meditation.

Later in the interview, knowing I was interviewing a professional astrologer, I asked her about the Age of Aquarius, and she explained what it was about. But at a certain stage in the interview, I asked her if this change would be better for her. Her answer made it clear that she is not an Aquarian of the kind described in Chapter 6:

> I don't know. I haven't thought about that much actually. I mean I think that's probably what New Ageism is all about. You know, en masse. I'm very non-global in the way I think often.

Harry, Sarah and Sue, sceptical of historical knowledge, despairing of historical progress or critical of orientation to the future, all live mainly in the present. They provide us with a key to understanding presentist perennism as outlined below.

Some of my interviewees express interest in the age of Aquarius, neo-paganism or feminist spirituality, but they do not expect the whole world to change as they follow their interests. At most, they hope for small changes in local places. They do not think of bringing a past world into the present. They are mainly concerned with developing their divine spark but often in an altruistic way, helping others, hoping to build a better world without transforming it radically. Even if they see cycles in history, they focus on the present, trying not to be 'time centric'. I call these presentist perennists, a term which emphasises the focus on the present.

In some ways, they are like the neo-pagans who are also concerned with the local, and in a sense, they concentrate their ritual activity on the present. But neo-pagans still valorise history (or 'invented' history) and wish to reach back into history to restore ancient lifestyles. This is where they differ from presentist perennists.

A dichotomy raised by Gilbert Durand (1996, 166) and inspired by Paracelsus (an esotericist) can shed some light on these presentist perennists. Time is multiple and can be classified under two forms, the objective time (*Wachsendzeit*) and the subjective time (*Krafzeit*). The *Wachsendzeit* is the time followed by clocks, astronomy and meteorology. This time is universal in a mechanical world and can be measured objectively, whereas the *Krafzeit* is locally placed in every human being. It is the destiny of each one of us and it is for some the time fixed by God. Further philosophical discussion of this distinction is not the objective of this section. However, the dichotomy helps us distinguish presentist perennists from Aquarians and neo-pagans. New Agers and neo-pagans by positively valorising the future or the past include in their *Zeitgeist* an objective universal time. However, presentist perennists deal with the time of their destiny, their subjective time, their *Krafzeit* and do not feel a strong concern about universal time. In my sample, five of my participants express disinterest in prevision of the future. Another four accept that there will be a change but they think it will only be different (not a golden age). Those informants, I argue, focus their spirituality mainly around subjective time. There is no use in speculating about the past or the future, but only on their subjective time; now.

Harry was very explicit about this notion of time in his interview and uses the term 'eternity' to explain *Krafzeit*, and 'empirical perception' and 'time' for *Wachsendzeit*. Because his reasoning is quite complex, I extend here his belief and the way he lives it:

> In Hinduism they have the Buddas of 3 times. Past, present and future. Which indicates an eternal reality. A transcendent reality. Reality that transcends time. [...] Time is the moving image of eternity. [...] It's an image. It's not the original. And it's moving, changing all the time. Whereas eternity doesn't change. Eternity's always the same.

Harry gave an example of this by explaining the problem of looking at a mountain from every side at the same time:

> One could think of it [eternity as opposed to time] in terms of a mountain. Let's say a mountain. And from a physical point of view we can only ever see one side of the mountain at any time. [...] And [...] the front side of it obscures the back side of it. So we walk around, taking photographs. And we put all those photographs together and we string it all out and then we make a movie. And we show, here's the mountain, here's the reality. And we show the movie. But it's an image and it takes a certain length of time to traverse, to encircle that, to display the whole of reality. [...] The mountain itself is there constantly. All the time. At any time. It takes no time to display its whole self. It only takes time for us to see them. So the reality of the mountain [in subjective time] transcends. It transcends difference. But our grasp of it [in objective time], where it spheres, is, well it's empirical. We rely on the empirical perceptions. Then empirical perceptions take time. So all we can see with our empirical senses are the temple of appearances of things.

With this example, Harry explains that it is necessary to get out of the empirical world and its objective time. Thus, for him, it is necessary to be:

established in reality [and in subjective time], we must open ourselves to unity. To enlightenment, to God, to the ultimate reality. There is no, okay the ordinary empirical world of space and [objective] time, the sense of people live here. But I don't mean it to be mean at all. [To live in subjective time] is the experience of oneself being an intrinsic part of the whole of reality. And just seeing not a mass of individual details [like the different sides of the mountain].

I asked him if he was living this experience in his everyday life, he answered, 'All the time. All the time, I live in it'.

This notion of subjective time (or eternity) is not new in itself. It even goes back to Plotinus for whom time represented a prison for human beings (Davies 1995, 24). It is time as experienced by mystics in their peak experiences, and is also described by Eliade (1959) as the myth of 'eternal return', a transcending time that surpasses birth and death. However, these are expressions of subjective time in which the subject escapes the everyday mundanity. For presentist perennists, subjective time is inner-worldly and lends significance to the everyday. Presentist perennism might be a very new development in perennism in Western societies, since groups like the Theosophical Society and Spiritualism embraced the notion of progress, in the sense that they appropriate a 'divine' time in their everyday life and try to live it. Theories of postmodernity will be able to explore this claim in the next chapter.

Chapter 8

Three Perennist Spiritualities

The Three Perennist Sub-Types Back Together

Table 8.1 Informants' affiliations

Affiliation	n respondents
Presentist perennist	17 (48%)
Aquarian perennist	9 (25%)
Neo Pagan	4 (12%)
Creative Evolutionist	1 (3%)
Insufficient information	4 (12%)

Table 8.1 shows my sample distributed according to the different perennist groups discovered in the previous chapters. I have included in the neo-pagan category those who declare themselves as neo-pagan and who practice neo-pagan rituals and ceremonies. As Aquarians, I have included people who believe in, and interpret, the Age of Aquarius and CMM (Critical Mass by Meditation) as a positive change. As presentist perennists, I have inserted people

- who do not believe in the Age of Aquarius and CMM, and
- who act to contribute to a CMSA (Critical Mass through Social Action). (There are no eschatological references in their interviews and they mainly focus their social action on the local and on the present) or,
- who believe in the Age of Aquarius and in CMM but who see these only as change that is neither total nor necessarily positive.

The category of 'creative evolutionist' (see Chapter 5) refers to those who reject the Age of Aquarius, and the idea of fast-forwarding toward a better world. Unfortunately, I did not have enough significant information for four (12%) informants to clearly indicate their ideal-type category.

The types of contemporary perennism, I have argued, are to be distinguished in terms of genealogy and in terms of continuity versus discontinuity with the traditions from which they have emerged.

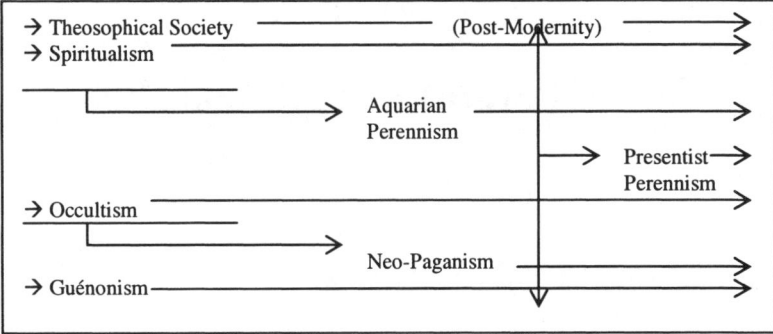

Figure 8.1 Perennist genealogies

Figure 8.1 presents the four modern esoteric movements which are still active in contemporary Western societies. The Theosophical Society (and Spiritualism to a certain extent) has engendered Aquarian perennism, while Occultism has inspired neo-paganism. These two perennist groups were formed in the 1930s and 1940s: they were not an outgrowth of the 1960s counter-culture movements.

Presentist perennists are not connected to a specific esoteric movement but, I argue, have grown out of a cultural shift in industrial societies. Post-industrial societies are defined partly in terms of deep cultural changes occurring within them. These include declining belief in the idea of progress, radical individualism, and fluidity of movement between sub-cultures. Presentist perennism, even though it borrows eclectively from earlier esotericism, is to be understood as an expression, in the field of spirituality of emergent post-industrial or post-modern culture.

The characteristics of these three perennist spiritualities are summarised in Table 8.2.

Table 8.2 Characteristics of the three perennist sub-types

	Aquarian perennism	**Neo-paganism**	**Presentist perennism**
Eschatology	Age of Aquarius and CMM (universal)	Re-enactment of pagan lifestyle (local)	None or CMSA.
Perception of time	Objective	Objective	Subjective
Specificities	Some wait for the Aquarian parousia	Focus on rituals, ceremonies and the Goddess	

There are perhaps other perennist spiritualities. The Rainbow Warriors described by Buenfil (1991) may represent another type. These warriors mix beliefs in the coming of the Age of Aquarius with neo-pagan perspectives and focus more on a deep ecological spirituality. Their Age of Aquarius is the 'ecotopia millennium'. Is this a spirituality blending the ideal-types of Aquarian perennism and neo-paganism? Or is it a new type of spirituality more focused on ecology than any of the other types? In this book I can raise only the questions, and concentrate on the three ideal-types of perennism found in my sample.

As stated previously, these are ideal-types in the Weberian sense and that they illustrate broad characterisations and not clear-cut categorisations based on a clear sense of identity or convincing statistical discoveries. This typology is neither true nor false. It is rather more or less useful. There are social actors, especially of the postmodern types (Melucci 1996; Elliot 2001), who do not fit perfectly well with these ideal-types. It is evident that some spiritual actors would have some characteristics that match with 2 or 3 types at the same time. In this, identities are always fluid and cut across types. This has been studied at length in Possamai (2005) where I observe the ways social actors construct their spiritual identities through popular culture. As an example, I found on a chat room on Jediism (the religion inspired from the *Star Wars* series), a neo-pagan who wished to redraw her boundary:

Wiccan Jedi

> Hi everyone! I recently found out about Jediism, read, and Re-read the website and decided that i love Jediism 😊 I am actually Wiccan, but as Jediist's morals are excellent as well, i decided to merge the two belief systems so i'm a kind of Jedi Witch.

Modernity/Postmodernity

As already argued, the genesis of Aquarian perennist and neo-pagan sub-groups could be the outcome of incremental shifts inside modern esoteric movements. In the case of presentist perennism, broad culture changes external to esotericism appear to have ushered in a clear break with the past. I will argue that the presentist perennism sub-group has been engendered by the advent of postmodernity. In this section, I will attempt to describe that phenomenon.

For this purpose, I first detail two forms of rationality in the development of modernity, as formulated by Castoriadis (1992), and consider their involvement in postmodernity. Through this, the increasing validation (or collusion) of perennism in postmodern society will be revealed. In the second sub-section, I use Weber's notion of elective affinity and define some affinities between perennism and postmodernity. This will allow further differentiation of the perennist sub-types.

Remembering Weber's (1968) subtle analysis of elective affinities between the spirit of capitalism and ascetic Puritanism, it would be foolish and doctrinaire to posit perennism as a result of postmodern causes. Further, influenced by postmodernity's own critiques of certainty and grand narratives (e.g. Bauman 1997, 24), I limit myself to the tracing of affinities only.

I understand the terms modernity and postmodernity as ideal-types, or rather heuristic tools, which serve as a guide to understanding the interaction of broad cultural changes in Western societies with perennism, and I hope to avoid reification of them.

Perennism and Postmodernity

As posited in Chapter 1 and detailed in Chapter 9, perennism is part of a consumer culture which sells spiritual services and objects. However, this consumption culture is for some pushed to the extreme of profit making as an end in itself; this is criticised by 14 (40%) of my respondents who perceive the term 'New Age' as representing a shady business (as seen in Chapter 3). Let us see if the theoretical dichotomy between modernity and postmodernity can help us explore this perennist consumer culture. We will first start with Castoriadis and his analysis of the modernity/postmodernity dichotomy.

Castoriadis (1992, 18) defines modernity (1750-1950):

> by the fight, but also the mutual contamination and entanglement of these two imaginary significations: autonomy and unlimited expansion of 'rational mastery'. They coexist ambiguously under the common roof of 'Reason'.

1. 'Rational mastery' is understood by the author as the living logic of capitalism. It is 'embodied in quantification and lead[s] to the fetishisation of 'growth' per se' (ibid.) and its maximisation process treats other values such as human nature and traditions instrumentally. 'Everything is called before the Tribunal of (productive) Reason and must prove its right to exist on the basis of the criterion of the unlimited expansion of "rational mastery" (ibid., 19).
2. 'Reason', on the other hand, is the critique of traditional and religious forces that held sway before the Enlightenment. This 'reason' cleared the way for social and individual autonomy, i.e. 'the affirmation of the possibility and the right for individuals and the collectivity to find in themselves (or to produce) the principle ordering their lives' (ibid.).

For Castoriadis, these two 'reasons' shared 'the imaginary of Progress' and its technical-materialist utopia, and were in opposition and tension with one another. This conflict was the means of the dynamic development of Western society and the expansion of capitalism.

Now, modernity is perceived as being in a crisis state. It is no longer a vehicle of ultimate meanings: the teleology of material progress proposed two centuries ago and increasingly accepted as common sense, has lost its plausibility. Out of this loss, a negation of modernity has appeared: post-modernism, 'both as an effective historical trend and as a theory' (ibid., 22).

Castoriadis uses the work of Johann Arnason to summarise the theoretical or philosophical tenets of the present trend which undermines 'modern reason'.

- The rejection of the global vision of history as progress or liberation.
- The rejection of the idea of a uniform and universal reason.
- The rejection of the strict differentiation of cultural spheres on the basis of a single underlying principle of rationality or functionality.

However, even if modernity's dream has faded, the belief in 'rational mastery' is still alive and is no longer in tension with 'Reason':

But in as far as this development of capitalism has been decisively conditioned by the simultaneous development of the project of social and individual autonomy, modernity *is* finished. Capitalism developing whilst forced to face a continuous struggle against the status quo, on the floor of the factory as well as in the sphere of ideas or of art, and capitalism expanding without any effective internal opposition, are two different social-historical animals (ibid., 23).

What might have been the implications and affinities of untrammelled 'rational mastery' in perennist culture? As in mainstream society, the two rationalities are found in perennism, but in different ways.

1. 'Reason' has not decayed in perennism: on the contrary, perennists still seek and find rational development, but of a particular type. As Andrew Ross (1991, 73) notes:

> New Age [or perennism] is a response, if you like, to the so-called Enlightenment 'project of modernity' that was, and still is, bound up with the imperatives of growth and development. In principle, New Age [or perennism] proposes a continuation of this project, but in the name of a different human rationality.

These 'imperatives of growth and development' may interrelate in two ways with perennism. a) In perennism in general, this 'imperative' is found in the notion of the quest for the human potential ethic; b) In Aquarian perennism, the 'imperative' is expressed in the historical vision of the Age of Aquarius. The modern ideology of growth is found permeating perennism, but most deeply embedded and expressed in Aquarian cosmology.

2. The so-called untrammelled 'rational mastery' of postmodernity also colludes with perennism. Lyon (1993, 122) refers to a shift from production to consumer capitalism as a distinguishing feature of postmodernity and notes that the religious supermarkets of perennism are expressions of the shift. Heelas (1993, 106) claims that perennism's case with the newest form of capitalism shows it to be:

> bound up with modernity but in an apparently different fashion. In tandem with the triumphalist capitalism which developed during the 1980s, increasing numbers of avowed New Agers have become active in the world of big business.

This side of postmodernity will be explored at length in the following chapter.

Elective Affinities with Postmodernity

If the two types of reason may be found expressed in perennism in general, the sub-types are quite differently orientated and related to modernity and postmodernity. Aquarian perennism, as suggested, expresses a modern ethos (the notion of progress is found in the Aquarian eschatology as we have seen). Neo-paganism, on the other hand, is anti-modern (it valorises pre-Christian spiritualities and proposes a re-enactment of pagan life-style). It is presentist perennism that is most obviously a postmodern spirituality.

However, while presentist perennism is most directly and tightly linked to postmodernity, the latter, we will see, has affected all types of perennism. We may think of perennism as linked to a constellation of factors constituting postmodernity which has prepared the way for popular acceptance of perennism.

The analysis of this constellation proceeds on three levels. The micro level focusses on the postmodern attitudes of individuals. The second is the macro level of broad structural conditions impregnating at the individual level. In between is the meso level, including the many movements and cultures that have re-inforced and diffused perennist beliefs. Explaining this level, I will be guided by my informants who variously describe science fiction, the sixties counter-culture, the Jungian movement and the popularisation of ideas of quantum physics as their mode of entrance to perennism. There are certainly other modes of entrance but they were not discovered in my sample.

It is important to note that the affinity between perennism and postmodernity might not be exclusive. However, studying other groups with the same affinity would take us too far afield.

Individual Level

The Individuation of Decision

As already seen in Chapter 1, my informants are individualists and choose their religion *à la carte*. However, this independence of decision goes even further as they reject any form of external authority.

Are my informants alone in their individualism and rejection of external authority? Or are they part of a general trend? If so, does that trend represent a deep cultural change? Many contemporary analysts would answer the first of these questions negatively and the other two in the affirmative. In this individualism and location of authority in the self, my informants would appear to express the culture of postmodernity.

Traces of postmodernist critique of reason (Roseneau 1992, 127-133) and rejection of external authority can be found in the counter-culture of the 1960s, according to Theodore Roszak (1969, 262-263). Roszak argues that there was a parallel between the Protestant fight against the theocracy of the Roman Catholics, and the battle of young adults of the 1960s against the priests of Scientism (the technocrats). They saw in them a new kind of corruption and denied scientists their legitimacy and their symbolic power. As Kellehear (1996, 97) notes, a wider critique of roles and statuses in modern society was involved in this: 'The belief in the value neutrality of science is long gone, together with unconditional reliance on the local doctor, lawyer, teacher, and parson'.

The academic world would no longer be perceived as seeking truth but rather as a machine to produce partisan and factionalised technical explanations. There would be a growing scepticism toward institutional authority. The 'given', the 'traditional' answers supplied by what Voyé (in Roof et al. 1995), inspired by Lyotard, calls the bearers of 'Grand Narratives', would be questioned or ignored. Many of the educated young would no longer accept the 'set menu' of canonical knowledge, but would choose 'à la carte' ideas and feelings which will form their subjective paradigm (as seen in Dobbelaere and Voyé 1990).

These trends influenced wide circles of the young and affected the social relations in everyday life. This was the socio-cultural world in which popular perennism was born and of which it became a part.

The 'individuation of decision' in that postmodern culture appears linked obviously to the shift from macro knowledge to the knowledge of the self documented in Chapter 5.

The Post-Modern Individual

Postmodernity has been defined not only in terms of cultural traits but in terms of a broad personality profile. Roseneau (1992, 53-54) describes the postmodern individual (an ideal-type portrait), and, from this description, significant parallels can be drawn with perennists, and with presentist perennists in particular:

> The post-modern individual is relaxed and flexible, oriented toward feelings and emotions, interiorization, and holding a 'be-yourself' attitude. S/he is an active human being constituting his/her own social reality, pursuing a personal quest for meaning but making no truth claims for what results.

This profile expresses in other words the characteristics of perennist technical mystics (Chapter 1). Roseneau continues on the postmodern individual:

> S/he looks to fantasy, humour, the culture of desire, and immediate gratification. Preferring the temporary over the permanent, s/he is contented with a 'live and let live' (in the present) attitude.

Here again we find a fair characterisation of the attitude of presentist perennists corresponding to the profile presented in Chapter 7. But again, all of my perennist informants would appear to correspond to Rosenau's elaboration of the postmodern personality:

> More comfortable with the spontaneous than the planned, the post-modern individual is also fascinated with tradition, the antiquated (the past in general), the exotic, the sacred, the unusual, and the place of the local rather than the general or the universal.

Nevertheless, among the types of perennists, the presentist perennists appear most nearly identical to Roseneau's postmodern individual.

Structural Level

The advent of the postmodern individual, as a frequently found type, cannot be understood except by reference to the Welfare State. It provided freedom, motivation and resources for the constructors and constituents of postmodernity. In a way, it freed humankind from social bonds:

The Welfare State appeared to render superfluous all traditional forms of support for the individual, thus liberating him. Consequently, the individual became the centre of the modern project and its meaning. However, contextual conditions did change, and with them, both 'mood' and values. Of course, the individual is still central and pretends not to wish to be enclosed in constraining groups: from 'ascription' groups he transferred to elected networks (Dobbelaere and Voyé 1990, S9).

Further, the Welfare State changed educational patterns and (in the context of booming economies) stimulated many young postwar adults to be more responsive to new ideas than their parents (Beckford and Levasseur 1986, 33). The more educated young were less committed to life-long engagement such as marriage and work than their parents: their spending power was greater; they were keen to experiment with new lifestyles and discover new cultures (ibid., 34). Susan Brown (in Lewis and Melton eds. 1992) identifies this generation as the baby boomers. This was the first generation to be affected by television and feel the impact of mass communication. It is not difficult to suggest elective affinities between the experiences of freedom, the loosing of social structures, the increasing range of options of the baby boomers and what we have described as the culture of postmodernity. Then, nesting within that culture, as we have seen, is the spirituality of popular perennism.

Cultural Level

At this level, I will explore affinities between a variety of cultural phenomena and the emergence of perennism. In particular, I will explore cultural developments that my informants themselves associate with their involvement in perennism.

Popular Culture

In Possamai (2005), I write about the interrelation between religion and popular culture. Different cases are explored. For examples, the Church of All Worlds is a neo-pagan group formed in 1967 in the USA which found its inspiration from the Science Fiction novel, *Stranger and a Strange Land*, written by Robert Heinlein, and the *Star Trek* television series. *Star Trek* and the *X-Files* were also a source of inspiration for the infamous Heaven's Gate group. The Church of Satan was founded in 1966 in San Francisco and uses as part of its rituals the weird fiction of H.P. Lovecraft. Neo-pagan individuals also use fictional characters, such as *Buffy the Vampire Slayer*, for their practising magic. The *Star Wars* movies have led to the creation of an Internet Spirituality; Jediism. The same applied to the *Matrix* trilogy and Matrixism. Inspired by the theory of Baudrillard, I developed in this book the descriptor of hyper-real religion; that is a simulacrum of a religion partly created out of popular culture which provides inspiration for believers at a metaphorical level. People involved in perennism find great inspiration from popular culture, and while New Age is not a hyper-religion such as Jediism and Matrixism, it nevertheless borrows extensively from popular culture.

The impact that popular culture had on new spiritualities started in the 60s and 70s. During that time, Theodore Roszak (1975, 23-24) discovered in science-fiction, acid rock, and sword-and-sorcery, an array of 'romances enjoying close to the mainstream level an almost reverential respect as doors of extraordinary perception'. They all depict heroes and/or anti-heroes meeting supernatural characters or travelling in fantasy worlds, or, at an extreme, changing into supernatural creatures.

In our own day, a visit to the Internet at the 'Gothic' and 'Vampyres' reveal large numbers wanting to become vampires, to become part of the other world. Even if the vampire has been popular since the nineteenth century, 'it has never had as pervasive an appeal in American popular culture as it has had in the past decade' (Schopp 1997, 232). For Auerbach (1995, 155), the character of the vampire is revised in the 1970s and aroused a longing for personal transformation. During this period, vampires were 'more frightened than frightening' and became 'at their worst, edifying, Superman-like rescuers'. Some Gothic witches even have a strong affinity with vampires (Hume 1997, 55). The vampire can be attractive to fans because of its embodiment of power, and can be a source of inspiration for perennists.

Truzzi (1974) already noted 30 years ago increasing comfort with the paranormal in popular culture, e.g. the phenomenon of teenagers spending the night in supposedly haunted houses to see ghosts. Truzzi reflected on the character of the witch, which if once negatively stigmatised, is now viewed as glamorous among the middle-class young. 'Glamorous' horror literature also invades children's literature. Monsters and ghosts are no longer exclusively described to scare but also to entertain the young readers. Arguably, literature makes it possible (imaginatively) for the reader to tame the supernatural.

> While numerous scholar-writers have documented the plight of modern separation persuasively for learned audiences, it is film which has articulated the message for those Aristotle called 'untrained thinkers'. In particular, space science fiction and fantasy make cosmic connection in mythic form (Rushing 1985, 188).

Rushing continues with a list of movies like *Star Wars* (in which the Jedi knight follows the human potential ethic and the force reflects monism), the *Star Trek* series, *E.T.* on whom he focuses his article, and others. I chose to describe *2001, A Space Odyssey* to illustrate the affinity between certain popular films with perennism. This film is, for D. Williams (1984), essentially a 'religious' film.

In the last sequence of the movie, Kubrick (the director) stirs emotions, subconscious and mythological yearnings in the viewer (Agel 1970, 161). In less than five minutes, he has the hero older, and older, but then reborn as a baby floating in the stars. Here was a dissertation in time popularly presented and consumed, a graphic communication of the notion of subjective time exactly conceived in presentist perennism. Further, the newborn who floats among celestial bodies, the star-child, not only reveals a new humankind of a high mental and spiritual development, but the music by Richard Strauss also denotes the coming of a new knowledge that will be shared (the descent of the mountain by Zarathustra). This new humankind (cf. the human potential ethic), the coming of a new spiritual knowledge and the correspondence between the child and the stars (monism), present a powerful symbolic synthesis of the triad of perennism.

There have always been works of art supporting and rendering plausible a perennist discourse (see e.g. Faivre 1992, Henderson 1987). However, what is important and new, is that these works are constituents of popular culture (a culture highly valorised in postmodernity, e.g. Feartherstone (1991)), and thus contemporary mainstream culture.

The Counter-Culture Movements

Fights for the minority; new social movements (feminism, ecology, student manifestations for peace in Vietnam); the children of flowers singing peace, love, universal harmony: these were signs of a massive protestation against the materialism, racism and aggressiveness of Western societies, but also against both the religious wars *and* the secularisation which have disenchanted the world (Vernette 1992, 47).

These counter-culture manifestations had their 'prophets' like Gary Snyder, Kerouac, Ginsberg (all from the beatniks) and its Mecca like Esalen in California where diverse mid-century influentials like Allan Watts, Arnold Toynbee, Carl Rogers, Paul Tillich, Carlos Castaneda, J.B. Rhine, Abraham Maslow spent time. Another Mecca was in Findhorn (Scotland) which offered for ecological mystics a vision of mother earth as a living entity, Gaia.

Theodore Roszak (1969, 125) claims that:

[a]n eclectic taste for mystic, occult, and magical phenomena has been a marked characteristic of our postwar youth culture since the days of the beatniks.

Not only did this counter-culture find an interest in perennism, but it also opened the doors to the path to reach the human potential ethic and monism through the use of psychedelic drugs. For Drury (1985, 215), Aldous Huxley (in the avant-garde of those movements) is perhaps the author to whom the debate about the validity of the drugs and mysticism nexus can be appropriately traced. Huxley walked through William Blake's *Doors of Perception* (1979) and recounted in an anthropological mode his experience in the artificial paradise of Nerval and Baudelaire which he associated with a development of consciousness.

Huxley first promoted mescaline as a safer means of self-transcendence than alcohol or the legal forms of drugs. When he wrote 'The Drugs That Shape Men's Minds' for the *Saturday Evening Post* in 1958, he had experienced LSD and was persuaded that the ultimate significance of the psychedelic drugs was religious. David Reid (1992, 211) quotes Huxley who writes:

That men and women can, by physical and chemical means, transcend themselves in a genuinely spiritual way is something which, to the squeamish idealist, seems rather shocking. But after all, the drug or the physical exercise is not the cause of the spiritual experience: it is only the occasion...

From this started the 'psychedelic revolution' which focused on the cause of the spiritual experience and not on the occasion. This 'revolution' can be summarised by this syllogism:

change the prevailing mode of consciousness and you change the world; the use of dope ex opere operato changes the prevailing mode of consciousness; therefore, universalize the use of dope and you change the world (Roszak 1969, 168).

For the insider Buenfil (1991, 15-17), the use of psychedelic and psychotropic substances has allowed 'millions' of people to experience other (non)realities. The author, even if he warns about the danger of exploring the inner space without preparation, states that 'psychonauts' can explore some of the deepest mysteries.

Drury (1985, 215-222) gives his account of experiencing LSD and comes to the conclusion that there are less dangerous ways to reach a higher state of consciousness. He dedicates a large part of his book to Castaneda's shaman, and claims its powerful, but not necessarily helpful effects. He claims that people can learn instead techniques which he calls Western shamanism. He presents the Qabalah and the Tarot which he considers as the yoga of the West and a more secure path for reaching a higher state of consciousness than with LSD.

The Eastern religions have had more to say about levels of consciousness than Christianity or orthodox Islam, and thus it is not surprising to notice the parallel development of interest in psychedelic and in oriental thought in the early 1960s; these streams mutually reinforced each other (Drury 1985, 91).

But this re-importation of Eastern spiritualities was different from the previous import into modernity. To illustrate this, we may explore the case of Allan Watts. He is considered as a guru of the counter-culture movement. He was first an Anglican priest, later became a specialist of Eastern religions and promoted Zen Buddhism. As seen in earlier chapters, Eastern religions which could be re-worked to express an evolutionist eschatology (see the Theosophical Society) or drawn on for some part of the universal truth that had been retained out of revelation in cosmogonic time (see Guénonism), took a quite different task. Watts propounded a theory of subjective time which he called eternity (instead of objective time which he called, simply, time). As he wrote (1998, 4), 'Time is a hallucination. There is only today. There never will be anything except today'. This truth, and the means for living it, he claimed, were found in Eastern spiritualities.

There are then strong affinities with the counter-culture of the 1960s and the perennism of the 1980s and 1990s, especially presentist perennism with the views of Allan Watts. They should not be overdrawn or stated as causal propositions. Even without the counter culture, perennism was emerging from the shadows of secrecy, but perhaps at a slower pace than it has since done. The counter-culture movements are not the seed of perennism (e.g. Melton 1992, 5), but rather a catalyst which allow the popularisation of perennism in mainstream culture by transferring it from inherited secrecy to full transparency and accessibility. As Lewis and Melton (1992, 252) realise, the 'occult explosion' of the late sixties has made the 'occult' more 'respectable'.

Again, it is presentist perennism especially that has close ties to counter-culture movements. Yet these movements include also an Aquarian perennist discourse (e.g., as in the Age of Aquarius songs) and an affinity with pagan values (e.g. Buenfil 1991).

(Some) Psychoanalytical Movements

Richard Noll (1996, 188) argues that Jung considered psychoanalysis to be the new religion of modernity. Noll even attempts to show that Jung was a charismatic leader and that he had managed to form a cult around his persona:

> The Jungian movement [...] resembles a twenty-century version of an ancient Hellenistic
> mystery cult, which was a pagan form of personal religion that also entailed the paying of
> fees for transformative experiences (ibid., 292).

Even if Jung and what is called 'New Age' should be dissociated (Tacey 1998; 2001),
the Jungian concepts of collective unconscious (monism), of individuation (the human
potential ethic) and the self knowledge research of the patient through the analysis of
her or his dreams (spiritual knowledge) show this movement's affinities with
perennism. Further, insofar as followers of Jung focus on individual fulfilment in the
present, there may be an especial affinity with presentist perennism.

Similarly, affinities, or even continuities can be established between the Human
Potential Movement, Transpersonal psychology and presentist perennism. While Kay
Alexander (in Lewis and Melton eds. 1992, 36-46) sees them at the roots of what I
call perennism, I see them developing a new sub-type of spirituality: presentist
perennism. The Human Potential Movement and Transpersonal psychology started
in the early sixties emerging out of the works by Abraham Maslow, Carl Rodgers and
Fritz Perls (the founder of Gestalt therapy). Heelas (1996, 53 and 57) notices that as
the 1960s progressed, the Human Potential Movement became more spiritually
orientated; it shifted from its neo-Freudian background to Eastern spiritualities. Some
elaboration of these psychological therapies focus on the present and display affinities
with presentist perennism. On the other hand, Ken Wilber, for example, is a
Transpersonal psychologist committed to the eschatology elaborated by the
Theosophical Society (see Wilber 1981, 1996).

These movements, by focusing on the therapeutic practices and by using some
perennist resources, have not only developed the validity of perennism in mainstream
society but may also have influenced the concern of a majority of my interviewees to
develop self knowledge.

Quantum Physics or the Non-Oiled Mechanical World

Quantum physics eradicates the assumption of a mechanical world. In this new physics,
an electron can be situated at two or more positions at the same instant, and time is
distorted. 'Nothing happens in the past (or the future), everything occurs in the present'
(Talbot 1992, 63). This physics offer for some authors a scientific basis for religious
discourse, but not always for the same religion. For example, Talbot (1992) uses
quantum physics to validate mystical experience according to Eastern spiritualities
(and close to perennism). For him, quantum physics opens the doors to new knowledge
(spiritual knowledge) and is fixed in the present. On the other hand, for Guitton et al.
(1991) the new physics supports a Catholic ethos, beyond which the reality of the
universe cannot be known. This physics, if interpreted in a certain fashion, may also
inform and legitimate a Jungian discourse:

> Corresponding relativities and paradoxes were discovered in the domain of the psyche.
> Here, too, another world dawned on the margin of the world of consciousness, governed by
> new and hitherto unknown laws that are strangely akin to the laws of nuclear physics. The
> parallelism between nuclear physics and the psychology of the collective unconscious was
> often a subject of discussion between Jung and Wolfgang Pauli, the Nobel prize-winner in

physics. The space-time continuum of physics and the collective unconscious can be seen, so to speak, as the outer and inner aspects of one and the same reality behind appearances. (Jaffé Aniela in Jung (ed.), 1978, 302).

The new physics also serves some as a model of an utopian society based on values identified in this thesis as perennist values. For example, Zohar and Marshall (1994) and Capra (1990) reappropriate these scientific discoveries selectively to support their vision of a society based on monism (or holism) and on creative evolution (of the kind associated with the Theosophical Society).

Quantum physics opens new doors on religions and can be interpreted and reappropriated in many ways. However, in certain circumstances, it corroborates a perennist discourse and in some hands is drawn on to lend plausibility to presentist perennism (e.g. Talbot 1992).

The Perennist Trinity

The New Age belongs to modernity in that it is progressivistic (looking for the future) and constructivistic (rather than things having to be continually repeated, they can be changed). (Heelas 1996, 169).

This quote demonstrates the danger of using 'New Age' as a label for rather different phenomena. As seen, the three sub-types of perennism are different and cannot all be understood as progressivistic. New Age, insofar as Heelas's interpretation holds true, should be understood as Aquarian perennism which originated from the Theosophical Society and is indeed a product of modernity. It emerged in the 1930s and propounds an eschatology based on progress. At the same time, neo-paganism appeared from Occultism: neo-paganism is anti-modern and re-enacts pre-Christian lifestyles. While these two ideal-types also have some postmodern characteristics (e.g. the individuation of decision), presentist perennism would be the epitome of a peculiarly postmodern perennism. Arguably, exclusive focus on the present is a distinguishing feature of postmodernity which has nurtured popular presentist perennism.

Jameson's (1984) observation about the postmodern world, that 'we now inhabit the synchronic rather than the diachronic [...]', helps establish the point about the ethos of postmodernity. Bauman's (1997, 89) notion that to live in a postmodern time is to live in a continuous present (a present severed from history) lends further authority to the argument about the characteristics of postmodernity. Maffesoli (1996, 1997) characterises postmodernity in terms of its ethic of the instant and even describes (1996, 100-101) the postmodern focus on the present as intemporal time, an *illus tempus*. This appears to be very close indeed to subjective time as lived by presentist perennists.

Once again, it appears that to be a presentist perennist is to live a spirituality *in* and expression of postmodernity. But the other types of perennism, it should not be forgotten, have also been nurtured by postmodern cultures' individuation of decision and its popularisation of the occult, of Jungian psychoanalysis and the new physics.

Chapter 9

Perennist Reenchantment: The Cultural Logic of Late Capitalism and Communicative Action

Perennist symbols are now produced in mainstream culture, and this invasion of the public sphere through consumer culture in conjunction with postmodernity/postmodernism (as described by Jameson (1984) and Featherstone (1990)) might involve a reenchantment with parts of the world presumed lost to secularisation. This chapter will first address the accessibility of these symbols/commodities. Paradoxically, this chapter will also present some forms of resistance to consumer culture from within these spiritualities using the theories of Habermas as a backdrop.

There is no doubting on the accessibility and widespread diffusion of perennism – even if its importance may be questioned. Robyn and Roger whom I interviewed together in a 'New Age' shop, testify to accessibility. Robyn is a pensioner and organises 'New Age' festivals. Roger is a palmistry reader and also participates in Robyn's 'New Age' festivals. During the interview, they referred to a difference in spiritualities between the old times and today. Roger and Robyn contrasted old and new in terms of a difference in accessibility of esoteric knowledge:

> *Robyn*: 'I mean if we were doing readings back in the days of the gypsies [many years ago] we'd be burnt at the stake you see. So it's probably taken us that few centuries to get more open'.

> *Roger*: 'That's right. And it used to be a closed circle. Esoteric minority before it become popularised. Accessible to everyone on the street, to all people'.

> *Robyn*: 'Yes, more accepted'.

> *Roger*: 'More classes. Far more accessible now'.

They are themselves active in giving access to the general public these alternative knowledges. Robyn organises 'New Age' festivals in the hope that some perennist ideas will stay in the minds of the people wandering around the displays:

> *Robyn (Rb)*: 'The general people who are searching, even though it's not getting them into the depth of it, but it's obvious that they come to this [New Age festival] because

they're searching for something within themselves. And even though you present it in a light, fantastic way and fantasy and fun, there is a depth I believe'.

Roger (Rg): 'Definite resonance. Going on within the world'.

Rb: 'Yes, within them. And that's why they come along. And we have good you know happy people'.

Rg: 'Good vibes'.

Rb: 'Good vibes yeah. And they go away and even if you say did you have a good day, oh we had a lovely day thank you. But they don't understand the depth of the meaning of what's happened to them. There's something stirring within them. [...] The New Age festivals just get them going and it's up to the person'.

Rg: 'It's a catalyst. It brings it all together'.

Rb: 'Yes. It just made good some spark in them that gets them going'.

Rg: 'Inspiration'.

Rb: 'Yes. That's what I believe'.

Rg: 'Even if for some people it will remain out of their conscious awareness, they won't quite understand, remain unconsciousness, and it gives them some inspiration. Some sort of stimulation'.

Rb: Yes. Something gets into their subconscious there.

Rg: 'That's right'.

The Space of Perennist Symbolism: Consumerism and Re-enchantment

We have seen in Chapter 1 that people consume perennist symbols which predispose and reinforce their alternation into alternative spiritualities. However, we faced the problem that the influence of these consumed symbols was hard to study for the reason that neither interviewee nor observer could pinpoint exactly how the symbols worked in the process from their production to their consumption. This problematic was left open until this chapter which analyses the production of these symbols.

As Robyn and Roger have reminded us, there is a production of symbols in 'New Age' festivals that, according to them, stays in the mind of the religious consumer and may affect his or her beliefs (though the extent of this effect remains unknown).

Alice also organises New Age festivals and thus produces perennist symbols which allow visitors 'to learn, to expand and to find out [...]':

I started running these expos which I hadn't planned to do at the time. So I've been doing them for a few years now. The main reason for setting up this place was that I wanted to learn more about the New Age and I was getting frustrated that I was always missing out and didn't know when expos were on or didn't know where to go. So I decided to set up a place where people could come on a monthly basis, purely for that reason. To learn, to expand and to find out what was going on. So yeah it's been a great learning experience for me.

There are ways to produce perennist symbols other than by only organising 'New Age' festivals. For example, Martina reads Tarot cards at home and in 'New Age' festivals and tries to encourage people in their lives; as she provides encouragement she communicates through and popularises perennist symbols:

Even though I've been searching I've always been motivated about it. So I decided that what was needed [...] was to go out... There was someone who was positive, motivated, spiritually looking, psychic, to give people hope. And that's what I set out to do. I set out to tell people that there was something there for them. And even if it only is to be content, that's something to aim for. I realised how unfocused I'd been for so many years and just letting people take responsibility for me. So that's what I started doing, doing these festivals. Because I felt that I could, make a difference sounds so pompous, but be some encouragement to someone. I started studying again and I did a formal degree in motivational time management. And I realised that there was just, that this was, to motivate people is something that we don't do. And to motivate people with a light at the end of the tunnel, which I'm not saying I create a light at the end of the tunnel, but I could turn anything, not anything, yeah pretty much anything around to be positive. So people have something to aim for and focus for. And then it just grew and I just got to the stage where I just had regular clients and I was doing these festivals and people would come back.

Julian is just as committed to his project of sharing his knowledge and thus spreading perennist values and symbols:

So I feel like down the track my girlfriend and I, if this all works out, that we'll know all our astrology and tarot and all that other stuff, and that we'll be able to start teaching other people. So yeah I feel like we'll teach people and we both like to write as well and I think we might end up writing books, and maybe, so I think, I see my spiritual path largely as I'm in a growth phase at the moment and at a certain point when I've learnt enough that I'm feeling comfortable with what I know and what I believe, that I'll start sharing it. So hopefully to help other people.

Phillip understands the proselytising value of the perennist paraphernalia he sells and spells out the connection between selling his cards, providing encouragement in everyday life and drawing his customers further into perennist belief:

You look at [magical] cards. There's some that sell very well and there's some that don't. I've got a card in there that I've designed, but if you want to create the impossible then this card will help you. And people buy them. People buy them. It's a very good seller actually. But it gives people that moral, well not so much moral, but it gives them that encouragement, because they will believe in it. See this is what again New Age is all about. People are looking for encouragement. Because there's none out there. There's no encouragement out there so they're looking for different ways to encourage. Like they become wealthy to keep the bank manager off their back and all the rest of it. They're looking for encouragement for that sort of thing and that's where it is.

These informants produce perennist symbols (including services and merchandises) which, I argue below, construct a plausibility structure for perennist beliefs. Possibly, the more that is produced, the bigger the effect. How to test this possibility?

Perennist symbols are ubiquitous in a city like Melbourne. Just as churches transmit a credo, 'New Age' shops selling their products also project their symbolic universe. Those objects for sale, books, tarot cards, crystals, CDs, aromatherapy products, ... have long since lost any taint of the demonic and become common products. New Age festivals and Psychic fairs proliferate. In Melbourne, it is possible to go to, at least, two a month, in Town Halls on a Sunday.

Consultants, tarot cards readers, clairvoyants and so on, offer their service not only in specialist shops and fairs, but also in more conventional shops (e.g. craft shops and galleries) and craft markets as well as from private homes. Many conventional book shops and music shops often have a stall specifically for 'New Age' books and recordings. An array of popular journals, magazines and fanzines diffuse perennist symbols. In Australia, the saturation is not as complete as in the US, but US influences on the Australian scene are strong in this (as in other) aspect of popular culture. In the USA, the market for 'New Age' books is estimated to be worth $100 million: there are 100 'New Age' magazines and there are also 'New Age' radio stations (Heelas 1993, 112). If we admit an affinity between those symbols and magic (i.e. a rather collective phenomenon capable of creating a network of meaning and symbolic significance which has direct influence on the daily life of individuals (Eleta 1997, 54)), we can argue as Eleta (1997, 62) that in contemporary society, magic becomes a consumer product. And consumption, in this instance, is an enactment of lifestyle and – adapting Heterington's (1992, 97) findings on the Stonehenge festival to these broader issues – is 'more than just shopping, it is a significant feature that helps to provide the stability while a new lifestyle is being created'.

It is still unclear how many people are influenced by these symbols and/or consumer products. In the case of Australia, for example, while the amount of people reading New Age books or attending New Age workshops has increased rapidly in the 1990s, it has not lead to many identifying themselves as belonging to 'New Age' religions/spiritualities (Hughes 2000). There are other indicators. Indeed, a state wide newspaper noticed in 1996 that Australians buy more self development and spiritual books per head than the US and Britain (Johnson 1997). Australian New Age magazines such as *Conscious Living*, the *Golden Age*, *Southern Crossings*, the *Whole Person* and *Australian Well Being* have healthy distribution rates. The attendance figures for the Mind, Body and Spirit festivals in Sydney have been between 50,000 to 60,000 during the mid 1990s (Johnson 1997). In 2001, the festival was sold, and since then the attendance figures have declined.

In the absence of available official figures, a fair estimate would be that, since 2000, approximately thirteen thousand people now attend each festival. This decline reflects four factors. One is the general saturation of Australian society to the point where information and services related to DIY spirituality is accessible in bookshops, local awareness centers, and on the Internet. Second, many smaller festivals and exhibitions now dot the landscape, and the novelty of Mind-Body-Spirit has long since passed. Neo-pagan and neo-Buddhist networks now flourish independent of this festival. Third, the Mind-Body-Spirit festival has a strong commercial ethos; seekers who prefer a countercultural ethos are unlikely to patronize it. Fourth, the exhibition company that now sponsors Mind-Body-Spirit appears to have repositioned the festival as a more mainstream gathering, but thus far has been unable to generate the same passionate interests in the public, as compared with the mid-1990s (Johnson 2004, 237).

Apart from these urban festivals, Australia also attracts perennists in more rural environments. ConFest, a bi-annual gathering of alternative lifestyle and spiritualities and radical political movements, is one example; held in Australian bush land and often comprising 8000-10,000 people. It has operated since 1976 and was held for the last seven years on the Murray River near Tocumwal and Moama, New South Wales. This biannual event has been host to a wide variety of 'villages' – e.g. 'Spiritual', 'Rainbow Dreaming', 'Spiral', 'Self Development and Therapy', 'Pagan', 'Forest', 'Healing', 'The Labyrinth' – camping and performance zones where hundreds of workshops are conducted - on themes ranging from 'Celtic Chakras' to 'Nuclear Free Futures'. Rooted in the 'counterculture' of the 1960s and '70s, ConFest has its immediate precursor in the 'multispiritual' Rainbow Gathering in the US (see St John 1997; 2001a; 2001b). Also, there is an emergent genre of psychedelic gatherings mixing elements of rave music, shamanism and New Age in the Australian bush. These gatherings are called 'bush parties' and 'doofs' (Tramacchi 2000).

In regards to the representability of neo-paganism in Australia, the case is different. If we take a look at the 1996 and 2001 Australian censuses, neo-pagans have identified themselves under different sub-categories. Some of the neo-pagan sub-categories used for this chapter might be questionable – e.g. Druidism which at times can be more Christian than neo-pagan and Satanism in which Satan is viewed more as a pagan god than as the Christian devil – but is nevertheless used for the purpose of this chapter. It can be noted in Table 9.1 that neo-paganism has increased by 113.7% between 1996 and 2001. People identifying with Wiccan/Witchcraft have increased by 373.5%. On the other hand, Satanism seems to be in decline (-14%).

Table 9.1 Neo-pagan sub-categories as listed in the 1996 and 2001 censuses

Census sub-Categories	1996 Census	2001 Census	96-01 Growth Rate
Nature Religion, nec	1617	2176	34.6
Nature Religion, nfd	117	49	-58.1
Animism	727	763	4.9
Druidism	554	697	25.8
Pantheism	835	1085	29.9
Paganism	4353	10632	144.2
Satanism	2091	1798	-14
Wiccan/Witchcraft	1849	8755	373.5
	Total	**Total**	
	12143	25955	113.7
Percentage of Australian Population	(0.07%)	(0.14%)	

Source: Data from Australian Bureau of Statistics reports.

Whereas there are clear data on the growth of neo-pagans in Australia, the same comment cannot be said about Aquarians. However, to understand the impact of perennism, there is a need to go further than just assessing the membership and group activities. As Bruce (1996, 197) notes, the popularity of 'New Age' cannot be measured by the number of 'New Agers' identifying with constituent groups but rather by the extent to which people are influenced in everyday life by the 'New Age'. Further, Andrew Ross (1991, 21) and and Parkins (2001) realise, though most perennist practices are confined to a minority culture, perennist ethical principles and orientations permeate mainstream culture. He even refers to the Oprah Winfrey Show, an American popular TV talk show (also popular in Australia) which is not avowed perennist, but popularises perennist principles such as 'growth' and 'potential' (i.e. elements referring. to the human potential ethic). The permeation of mainstream culture by perennism is also aided and abetted by training programmes in the business world. Business spends between $3 and $4 billion on training in which perennist orientations and personal development and motivation techniques for achievement of the human potential ethic are employed (Heelas 1993, 112). So it is no surprise that, as Paul Heelas (ibid., 106-107) makes us realise, an increasing number of perennists are active in the business world. In England, hundreds of training organisations sell employees a way of becoming enlightened. Roberts (1994) follows this line of thought and describes an anthropological study at a large international conference of 'New Age' management consultants and trainers. See as another example the works of Salamon (2001) and her research (2005) on the Mandraked economy of the late 1990s which openly relied on fortune-tellers. Heelas claims these training programmes affect alternations to perennism.

Studies by Heelas (1993; 1999), Roberts (1994), Hill (1992), Van Hove (1999) and York (1999) underline a strong correlation between 'New Age', neo-liberal capitalism, and globalised consumer culture which has seen increasing prominence within (post/ late) modern societies. It can be argued that perennism is part of the cultural logic of late capitalism (Possamai (2003; 2005)).[1] This logic has been analysed by Jameson (1991) who claims that there are three periods in the development of capitalism. These are: first, market capitalism, which is characterised by the growth of industrial capital in largely national markets – from about 1700 to 1850; second, monopoly capitalism in the age of imperialism, which coincides with the period when European nation-states developed international markets, exploiting the raw materials and cheap labour of their colonial territories; and third, and most recently (from the 1960s), the phase of late capitalism, which is that of multinational corporations with global market and mass consumption, creating the world space of multinational capital.

Moving towards an analysis of culture in this phase of late capitalism, Jameson argues that, previously, modernist culture could be judged against certain dominant standards – for example, the distinction between high culture and low culture – and might even be oppositional or shocking, whereas postmodernist culture – a culture symptomatic of this 'late' phase of capitalism – is fully commodified and tends to be judged in terms of what gives instant pleasure and makes money. We are living in a culture of the simulacrum in which 'the very memory of use value is effaced' (Jameson 1991, 18).

And no doubt the logic of the simulacrum, with its transformation of older realities into television [and other types of] images, does more than merely replicate the logic of late capitalism; it reinforces and intensifies it. (Jameson 1991, 46).

In Possamai (2005), I argue that perennism is a hyper-consumerist religion. It consumes all types of products and messages across a vast array of religions, and the choice is in the hand of the consumer. Whereas with hypo-consumerist religions such as religious fundamentalism, they are still consumerist but they tend to only consume what is offered from within their own religion; and the choice for the consumption of a product and/or message has to be agreed by a type of authority.

In a variety of ways, perennism appears to constitute a re-invasion of religion in the public sphere (Casanova 1994) through the production and (mainly) consumption of symbols. While it can be argued that perennism does not have the social significance of the church or the sect, and for this reason, following Bruce's (2002) argument, it would be hard to argue that perennism de-secularises the West at a structural level, I would nevertheless suggest that we may be seeing a reenchantment from below.[2]

Weber saw the changes that drove western society from a traditional to a modern context as a process in which the timeless magic of the universe might be removed and kept outside from a tightly closed iron cage. This, according to Weber, might have reduced human perception and experience of the world to a banal parade of predictable actions in a society of arid routines. Many researchers have commented on the fact that there is a collective move away from the over-rationalisation of everyday life to re-enchanted forms of public and personal spaces. Westerners are facing the return of spiritual/magical thinking in their everyday life which produces a sense of the mysterious, the weird and the uncanny. For Tacey (2000), it is a reconnection with nature – e.g. indigenous landscape – which is at the heart of the re-enchantment process; for Maffesoli (1996), it is the identification with our fellow humans practised in culture of festivities where people play with their multiple identities. In this sense, it represents 'the means by which the hidden or unrecognised powers of human consciousness are made explicit for the purpose of transcending the limits of the secular world... To be re-enchanted means to leave behind the structures that bind individuals to the mundane logic of this world and to reclaim the powers that invigorate the manifestations of other realities' (Lee, 2003: 358).

For Mike Featherstone (1991: 67-68) and Maffesoli (1996) a feature of the times in advanced western societies (or in the global village) is an aestheticisation of everyday life. This is a consequence of the rapid flow of signs and images in contemporary society. Among these signs, which are central to the development of consumer culture, are those of popular culture used by some spiritual actors (see Possamai 2005). For Ritzer (1999), the development of consumer culture itself – with its dizzying proliferation of cathedrals of consumption such as shopping malls, electronic shopping centres, superstores, cruise ships, and casinos – is enchanting our world. These actors, arguably, imbue aestheticised sensibility with a sense of mystery, of invisible power that might be harnessed in consumer and popular culture for human use of enchantment.

Resistance

Habermas' (1987; 1991; 1996) work is vast and complex. For this reason, this section will only concentrate on one of his key concepts: that of the colonisation of the lifeworld (*Lebenswelt*). The systematic colonisation of the lifeworld is in reference to the replacement of the mechanisms of social coordination by mechanisms of political and financial accumulation.

I will first deal with his concept of the lifeworld; which can be understood as everyday life, and will come back to his concept of colonisation very shortly. The author sees in this lifeworld a field where culture, personality, meaning and symbols meet and where civil society would more or less be active. This lifeworld would form the basis for communication; that is, communicative action. By these actions, Habermas makes reference to individuals' linguistic interaction such as debates in newspapers and television, conferences and seminars, café discussions, etc. The communicative interactions allow individuals to reach a level of knowledge of the other; that is, an intersubjective recognition. This would enable the establishment of cooperation between individuals which is not based on the maximisation of profit, but that is, on the contrary, aimed to develop debate on questions dealing with the quality of life and to open dialogue with others. Thanks to this, human beings humanise themselves through their interaction with other individuals and, through this, the plurality of values linked to an ethic based on the understanding between movements and groups which makes possible the constant renewal of social consensus.

In contrast to communicative action, instrumental reason operates through the system – the system is the field where we find the instrumental action of multinational corporations and political power. When this instrumental reason spreads in the lifeworld, Habermas makes reference to an effect of colonisation which is growing more and more in this period of late capitalism and thus reduces all expression of communicative action. By this, he argues that methods used for making profit and being more efficient are used extensively for the sake of efficiency, even within civil society. This leads to the fetishisation of growth per se, and its maximisation process treats other values such as human nature and traditions instrumentally. Indeed, the effect of corruption from economic factors on the democratic political process, the obscure mixture between news information and entertainment, the transformation of students into consumers and teachers into producers, and the passive civil engagement of westerners, are but a few examples on the way the colonisation of the lifeworld happens. The lifeworld tends to be reduced while the system is spreading its tentacles. This colonisation of instrumental reason, aiming at the accumulation of profit, reduces more and more the strength of communicative action from the lifeworld. The result of this process is a permanent tension between the lifeworld and the system, which threatens the Enlightenment project.

In regards to religion, this phenomenon that modernist philosophers were trying to get rid of or to privatise, Habermas saw in it an agent of communicative action that was not necessarily taking part in the emancipation project carried by the enlightened philosophers. He also thought, in the 1980s, that religions were agents of legitimation for state intervention in civil society. Now, he admits himself that religions can also be agents of contestation and can offer new ways of being that are not calculative (Habermas 2002: 79). For example, Wallace (2003) uses Habermas' theory to understand Islamic fundamentalism. He demonstrates that the colonisation of the lifeworld can only be in antagonism with religious sensibilities. This antagonism can even exacerbate the conflict with the colonisation forces and even provoke a deep religious reaction. From this, Wallace claims that the fundamentalist branches of Islam are in a structural tension with the system. Since the publication of his *Communicative Action*, Habermas' opinions in regards to religion in general have changed, and his theories have even become a kind of post-metaphysics theology (Rosati, 2003). Unfortunately, exploring this aspect of his theory would take us too far away from the analysis of this book.

If we come back to perennism, it becomes easier to argue that these spiritualities are being colonised by the system, and that they even take part in the process of colonisation. As seen above, a few spiritual actors do not see a problem to have their spirituality taking part in this logic of late capitalism, as long as this symbiosis is not forced too much. Some of their spiritual techniques are even used by global corporations to develop their staff's mental and managerial abilities; abilities which could in consequence make the colonisation work more efficient. It is also of interest to point out a paradox in this process; if these corporations use the techniques borrowed from perennism to develop their 'colonisation' abilities, it can also be hypothetically argued that this process could also 'humanise' the instrumental action used with this colonisation process.

Viewing these spiritualities as part of the logic of late capitalism and thus taking part in the colonisation of the lifeworld, can call into question the sincerity and serious commitment of these practitioners. As Mulcock (2001, 170) observes, these practices of consumerisms and cultural borrowing might evoke the superficial materialism that would come to mind to many outsiders, but this should be viewed instead as a way of life, as part of the daily routines of these perennists, and I would argue, as a new spiritual way of being in this phase of late capitalism; that of being a religious individualist who locates authority in their inner self. Indeed, as Bruce (2002, 90) states:

> One might, like the Protestant reformers, see such commerce as unspiritual, but it is perfectly acceptable to New Agers because it fits with the general consumerist ethos of their world and because it reinforces the autonomy of the consumers. They are not locked into open-ended commitments of reciprocal obligation; they buy the book, tape or training session, and are free to make of if what they will.

If these spiritualities are part of the logic of late capitalism, there are of course variations in their belonging; some are more involved in the logic of late capitalism than others. For example, Ezzy (2001) researched the commodification of witchcraft, and for heuristic purposes, used the term 'Wicca' to refer to the older initiatory tradition of neo-paganism, and 'commodified Witchcraft' to refer to the more recent popularized movement which is fully immersed in the logic of late capitalism and its colonisation of the lifeworld. As he comments,

> Although there is a wide spectrum in between, I characterized commodified Witchcraft as Witchcraft in which the majority of exchanges are commodity exchanges. In contrast, Wicca is characterized by the exchange of both knowledge and goods as gifts, external to the market. These gifts are embedded in familial-like social relationships of mutual and moral

obligations. In contrast, commodified Witchcraft involves the exchange of commodities embedded in social relationships that are dissolved by the exchange, with no ongoing obligations (Ezzy 2001, 42).

Kulchyski (1997) confirms this approach in his study of aboriginal cultural production in the age of postmodernism by arguing that if commodification is the dominant logic in this late capitalist world, it has not achieved anything like the total hegemony of generalized commodity production; there also remain many viable sites for resistance; such as the practice 'by marginal and dominated social groups of deploying cultural texts produced by or for the established order in the interest or with the effect of cultural resistance (Kulchyski 1997). These sites of resistance can also be found in the 'other' wing of New Age, as described by Heelas (1993; 1996), that is not involved in pro-capitalism, is counter-cultural of modernity, and refuses to be involved in capitalist mainstream. Introvigne (2001) also makes reference to the Next-Age which is a movement from within the New Age which aims at moving away from the commercialised aspect of what is commonly known as 'New Age'. Geoffroy (2001) notices in Quebec some concerns with the commercialisation of these spiritualities. We also saw in Chapter 3 how some of my informants were dissociating themselves from the label 'New Age' because of its commodified connotation while they still took part in the cultural logic of late capitalism.

Even if these spiritual actors are individualist and are interested in developing their human potential ethic, some of them also work towards changing the world. As Dawson (1998, 591) notices, the religious groups which offer a message based on an economy of the self are not only focused on changing the members' spiritual and mystical abilities, but they also believe that by changing each individual, a type of global change as seen in a previous chapter can eventuate. Dawson even sees in this an underlying current in our society that favours the growth of globalisation. As seen in Chapter 6, we have two types of perennist actors working on changing the world through a critical mass; one that works towards a Critical Mass by Meditation (CMM) and one that works for a Critical Mass through Social Action (CMSA).

If we come back to Habermas' theories, it becomes apparent that social actors who work towards a CMSA use a kind of communicative action. Even if all these actors belong to the cultural logic of late capitalism, some of them are nevertheless attempting to bring to the fore spiritual issues and a culture of cooperation that are not expected to be found in the process of colonisation of the lifeworld. By being active in various groups, by attempting to improve the quality of life, and by exchanging information, they indeed take part in communicative action.

This type of communicative action is also a form of resistance to the colonisation of the lifeworld, but can we compared it to the new social movements described by Habermas? Bruce (2000, 95) argues that if these social actors have been involved in environmental protest, in anti-capitalist rallies and in developing alternative technologies, the impact has been limited. He (2000, 97) wonders where are 'the New Age schools, nurseries, communes, colleges, ecological houses, women's refuges, practical anti-racism projects and urban renewal programmes?'

[Perennist] exegesis courses did not turn stock traders and bankers into trade-union activists, community workers or subsistence farmers; they just made them happier and more effective stock-traders and bankers... In many instances it does seem proper to impute a degree of hypocrisy to those New Agers who use the language of being 'alternative' and 'counter-cultural' while continuing to enjoy all the material benefits of bureaucratically rational consumerist capitalism (Bruce 2000, 98).

'Classical' new social movements have been in conflict with the system in regards to questions about the quality of life, equal rights, and the right for anyone to have a part in social life. Many of these groups have been involved in a fight against all forms of militarisation, of the destruction of the ecosystem and the erosion of women's rights. These movements are central to the type of communicative action that opposes the colonisation of the lifeworld, whereas alternative spiritualities are more central to the spiritual development of the self; communicative action for these spiritualities are more secondary. We could argue that these new spiritualities are not as active in communicative action as these new social movements. We should of course bear in mind that some of these spiritual actors are also involved in some of these movements, for example neo-pagans in green movements, and would thus be more involved in communicative action outside of their specific spiritual work. Indeed, various research points out that people involve in perennism can also be part of a movement. Kemp (2003) makes reference to the Corporate Social Responsibility movement from which perennists have been at the forefront since the 1970s. This movement tries to influence corporations by attempting to convince these entities to follow what is referered to as Socially Responsible Investment; that is aiming for a 'sustainable development' of a environmentally and socially conscious corporate world. Höllinger (2004) discovers through an extensive survey that even if the most recent wing of 'New Age' legitimates the neo-liberal capitalist work ethic, it still maintains, to a certain degree, a counter-cultural characteristic:

> Contrary to the widespread claim that involvement with spiritual and esoteric methods goes hand in hand with a lack of interest in social and political matters, our studies show that New Age followers read political newspapers and magazines, listen to radio and TV news, and discuss political matters somewhat more frequently than the rest of the population. Furthermore, New Age followers have significantly higher rates of reported participation in political protest activities and solidarity campaigns, they also participate somewhat more frequently in political party activities, such as election campaigns, than those who are not engaged in New Age activities. Thus we can say that the general level of social participation and activism among New Age activists is above the population mean (Höllinger 2004, 304-305)

Even if perennism can be argued to be the epitome of hyper-consumerist religion and borrows on a new lifestyle which is in symbiosis with the cultural logic of late capitalism, it should be noted that there is resistance to the full commodification of these spiritualities by insiders. These insiders who resist this colonisation of the lifeworld are thus active in communicative action, perhaps at a higher level than the population mean. Through communicative action, perennists exchange cultural and material products through their almost continuous affectual networking and thus spread perennist values in everyday life. Perennists are not fixed in a social setting; they are nomads and interact with different sectors of society at large carrying perennist symbols with them.

In particular, some perennists striving for critical mass through social action (CMSA, see Chapter 6) communicate perennist values and orientations by intentional networking. This affinity networking comes close to what Melucci (1996, 114-115) describes as a contemporary movement, i.e. a movement that has a variable density and resembles an amorphous nebula. His picture of contemporary movements could serve as a formal description of the perennist networks:

> Movements in complex societies are hidden networks of groups, meeting points, and circuits of solidarity which differ profoundly from the image of the politically organized actor. [...] One notes the segmented, reticular, and multi-facetted structure of 'movements'. This is a hidden or, more correctly, latent structure; individual cells operate on their own entirely independently of the rest of the movement, although they maintain links to it through the circulation of information and persons. These links become explicit only during the transient periods of collective mobilization over issues which bring the latent network to the surface and allow it to submerge again in the fabric of daily life. The solidarity is cultural in character and *is located in the terrain of symbolic production in the everyday life* (My emphasis).

By selling perennist artefacts, by running workshops and readings, by organising 'New Age' festivals, by encouraging people in therapeutic networks (or simply interacting with them by networking in a perennist social movement in Meluccis' understanding), perennists produce, consume and distribute their symbols of alternative spirituality, and sometimes take part in communicative action. As they do so, and even through their communicative action, they may be establishing legitimacy and plausibility structures for a re-enchanted world.

Notes

1   I also argued in Possamai (2003; 2005) that perennism is part of the cultural logic of late capitalism because of its pastiche approach to borrowing cultural content from indigenous culture, history and popular culture.
2   What Maffesoli (1996: 66) calls a postmodern re-enchantment.

Conclusion

The term 'New Age' has various connotations and provides a name for an array of religious phenomena. Its etymology connotes the age of Aquarius. 'New Age' becomes a mirror which reflects worries, frustrations and pejorative sentiments regarding unethical practices and zany beliefs associated with alternative spiritualities. For this reason alone, researchers exploring the range of alternative spiritualities grouped by the term had best avoid it, just as those involved in those spiritualities do. Unable to work without the term initially, I set out to find whether there was indeed a family of spiritualities reasonably grouped under the term 'New Age', and if there was, to find a new name for the family. To these ends, I found it necessary not only to consult the literature on 'New Age' but in a sense to place the conceptualisation and claims of that literature in jeopardy against the 35 insiders' accounts of their spiritualities.

The first aim, then, of the book was to attempt to find a common descriptor for the diverse orientations, practices and discourses of perennists. A second, complementary aim, was to explore differences within the supposed family and to name and describe those differences.

The Introduction, Chapter 1 and Chapter 2 laid the foundations of the book, defining and justifying methodological approaches and theoretical assumptions. In Chapters 1 and 2, a basic descriptive profile of these spiritual actors and their 'sociality' was compiled.

It was argued that this type of spiritual actor is religiously individualist (or 'new voluntarist'), a technical and an intramundane mystic, sometimes of satirical bent. These actors appear to place the inner self as the arbiter of the spiritual quest. They evolve via affinity networks in (and outside of) the 'cultic milieu'. It was found that they alternate to alternative spirituality by experiencing either mystico-pneumatic or everyday life crises and by consuming perennist symbols.

The problematic of Chapter 3 consisted in determining whether there might be a descriptor that would meaningfully aggregate the eclectic discourse of the 35 spiritual actors interviewed. The triad of monism, the human potential ethic and spiritual knowledge were found and confronted with insiders' accounts in Chapter 4. This confrontation validated the notion of perennism whose definition was:

*Perennism is a syncretic and tolerant spirituality which interprets the world as **Monistic** and whose actors are attempting to develop their **Human Potential Ethic** by seeking **Spiritual Knowledge.***

In Chapter 4, the perennists I had interviewed were found to divide according to their option for one of two types of gnosis. Four (11%) informants opted for a macro form of knowledge whereas 19 (57%) focused their attention on a knowledge of the self obtained by self-reflection on personal experience. This difference was traced back to a shift in esotericism (the putative ancestor of perennism). When esoteric movements entered modernity, they tended to democratise esoteric knowledge, and eradicated the notion of secrecy: they offered open knowledge. This decay of secrecy and its consequence, the accessibility of macro knowledge, appears to have caused, paradoxically, the shift from a preference for macro knowledge to a knowledge of the self. In the course of this investigation, it became clear that perennism is indeed an innovative form of esotericism.

Chapters 6 and 7 were able to specify exactly what sub-types of perennism are hidden behind the meronymy of 'New Age'. In Chapter 6, it was first found that the notion of 'New Age' was coined as a synonym for the age of Aquarius in the 1930s. A dissidence and offshoot of the Theosophical Society spelled out a new eschatology: creative evolution. A distant final age was brought forward by the coming of the Age of Aquarius. I called this belief and its associated spirituality Aquarian perennism. In Chapter 7, I outlined splits in occultism in the 1940s. Emerging from these a new sub-type of perennism was conceived: neo-paganism. Contrary to Aquarian perennism, it rejected the eschaton of the age of Aquarius and urged the re-enactment of pre-Christian values to return, at least locally, to a supposed pagan utopia. A third type was also discovered in Chapter 7, presentist perennism, a type never discussed in the literature. Presentist perennists focused their spirituality on the present in such a way that objective time was no longer relevant. The subjective time experienced by mystics in their peak experience was found by these actors, not in the extramundane, but in their everyday lives. This sub-type did not reject the Aquarian eschatology *per se*, but considered it only as a change among changes, not necessarily better or worse, not the eschaton. No direct filiation between this sub-type and other types of perennist groups appeared to exist, which led to the next Chapter and the study of these sub-groups and their varying degrees of elective affinity with postmodernity.

Chapter 8 summarised the findings from the three former chapters and attempted further differentiation among the three sub-types. Though Aquarian perennism and neo-paganism had some post-modern traits, the former was mainly modern and the latter was anti-modern, whereas presentist perennism was the epitome of postmodernity in its concern for the present. These findings are summarised in Table C.1.

Table C.1 Summary of the differences among perennist sub-types

	Aquarian perennism	Neo-paganism	Presentist perennism
Eschatology	Age of Aquarius and critical mass by meditation (CMM) (universal).	Re-enactment of pagan lifestyle (local).	None or Critical Mass through Social Action (CMSA).
Perception of time	Objective	Objective	Subjective
Specificities	Some wait for the Aquarian parousia.	Focus on rituals, ceremonies and Goddess.	
In connection to modernity (on the level of their cosmological discourses)	Modern	Anti-modern	Post-modern

Chapter 9 analysed the importance of perennism in mainstream culture and its cultural logic of late capitalism. Although perennism is a hyper-consumerist spirituality, it was also found that some spiritual actors resist the full commodification of their spirituality through communicative action. This involvement in the cultural logic of late capitalism, and to a certain extent the different processus of communicative action, have a part to play in the aestheticisation and even of the re-enchantment of everyday life. It was found difficult to gauge the full extent and impact of this entry of perennism into the public mainstream, but it was demonstrated that the means of production and distribution of perennist symbols were functioning such that we might expect rapid increase in influence and impact.

Bibliography

Agel, J. (1970) *The Making of Kubrick's 2001*, Agel Publishing Company, New York.

Alexandrian (1994) *Histoire de la philosophie occulte*, Editions Payot & Rivages, Paris.

Amirou, R. (1989) "Sociability/'Sociality'" *Current Sociology. La sociologie contemporaine* 37 (1), 115-120.

Auerbach, N. (1995) *Our Vampires, Ourselves,* The University of Chicago Press, Chicago and London.

Bailey, A. (1972) *Discipleship in The New Age – Volume I*, Lucis Publishing Company, New York.

Bailey, A. (1976) *Discipleship in The New Age – Volume II*, Lucis Publishing Company, New York.

Bailey, Foster (1974) *Changing Esoteric Values*, Lucis Publishing Company, New York.

Balch, R. and D. Taylor (1978) "Seekers and Saucers: The Role of the Cultic Milieu in Joining a UFO Cult" in James T. Richardson (ed.), *Conversion Carrers. In and Out of the New Religions*, Sage Contemporary Social Science Issues (47), 43-64.

Bastide, R. (1996) *Les problèmes de la vie mystique*, Quadrige/ Presses Universitaires de France, Paris.

Bauman, Z. (1997) *Postmodernity and its Discontents*, Polity Press, Cambridge, UK.

Bauman, Z. (1998) "Postmodern religion?" in Paul Heelas et al. (eds) *Religion, Modernity and Postmodernity*, Blackwell Publishers, Oxford, UK.

Beck, U. (1992) *The Risk Society,* Sage, London.

Beckford, J. and M. Levasseur (1986) "New religious movements in Western Europe" in Beckford, J. (ed.), *New Religious Movements and Rapid Social Change*, Sage Publications/Unesco, 29-54.

Bendle, M. (2003) "Reflexive Spirituality and Metanoia in High Modernity" *Australian Religion Studies Review* 16 (1): 6-23.

Beyer, P. (1991) "Privatization and the Public Influence of Religion in Global Society" in Mike Featherstone (ed.), *Global Culture. Nationalism, Globalization and Modernity. A Theory, Culture & Society special issue*, Sage Publication, London, 373-395.

Blavastky, H.P. (1972a) *The Key to Theosophy, Being A Clear Exposition, in the Form of Question and Answer of the Ethics, Science, and Philosophy for the Study of which the Theosophical Society Has Been Founded*, Theosophical University Press, Pasadena, California.

Blavastky, H.P. (1972b) *Isis Unveiled. A Master Key to the Mysteries of Ancient and Modern Science and Theology. Vol. I – Science*, Theosophical /University Press, Pasadena, California.

Bloch, J. (1998) *New Spirituality, Self and Belonging: How New Age and Neo-Pagans Talk about Themselves*, Praeger, Westport.

Bouchet, C. (1997) "Pour une typologie du paganisme contemporain", *Murmures d'Irem* (6), 40-44.

Brown, C. (1992) "A Revisionist Approach to Religious Change" in Steve Bruce (ed.), *Religion and Modernization: Sociologists and Historians Debate the Secularization Thesis*, Clarendon Press, Oxford, 31-58.

Bruce, S. (1996) *Religion in The Modern World, From Cathedrals to Cults*, Oxford University Press, Oxford, New York.

Bruce, S. (2000) "The New Age and Secularisation" in S. Sutcliffe and M. Bowman (eds.), *Beyond New Age: Exploring Alternative Spirituality*, Edinburgh University Press: 220-236.

Bruce, S. (2002) *God is Dead: Secularization in the West*, Blackwell Publishing, Oxford.

Buenfil, A. (1991) *Rainbow Nation Without Borders. Toward an Ecotopian Millennium*, Bear & Company Publishing, Santa Fe, New Mexico.

Campbell, B. (1978) "A Typology of Cults", *Sociological Analysis* 39 (3), 228-240.

Campbell, C. (1972) "The Cult, the Cultic Milieu and Secularization" *Sociological Yearbook of Religion in Britain* (5), 119-136.

Campbell, C. (1978) "The Secret Religion of the Educated Classes", *Sociological Analysis* 39 (2), 146-156.

Capra, F. (1990) *The Turning Point. Science, Society and the Rising Culture*, Fontana Paperbacks, London.

Casanova, J. (1994) *Public Religions in the Modern World*, The University of Chicago Press, Chicago and London.

Castoriadis, C. (1992) "The Retreat from Autonomy: Post-Modernism as Generalised Conformism", *Thesis Eleven* (31), 14-25.

Cavendish, R. (1977) *The Black Arts*, Picador Edition, London.

Champion, F. (1995) "La nébuleuse New Age", *Etudes*, February, 233-242.

Champion F. and C. Françoise (1993) "Recompositions, décompositions. Le renouveau charismatique et la nébuleuse mystique-ésotérique depuis les années soixante-dix", *Débat* (75), 81-89.

Chryssides, G. (1999) *Exploring New Religions,* Cassel, London.

Cohen, Erik, B. Nachman and A. Janet (1987) "Recentering the world: the quest for 'elective' centers in a secularized universe", *Sociological Review* 35 (2), 320-346.

Coleman, N. (1994) *Five Lectures on Perennial Philosophy Today*, Leftbank Portfolios, Melbourne.

Corrywright, D. (2003) *Theoretical and Empirical Investigations into New Age Spiritualities*, Peter Lang, Bern.

Corrywright, D. (2004) "Network Spirituality: The Schumacher-Resurgence-Kumar Nexus", *Journal of Contemporary Religion* 19 (3), 289-310.

Cottom, D. (1991) *Abyss of Reason. Cultural Movements, Revelations, & Betrayals*, Oxford University Press, New York, Oxford.

Daaleman T., A. Cobb and B. Frey (2001) Spirituality and well-being: an exploratory study of the patient perspective *Social Science and Medicine* 53 (1): 1503-1511.

Davie, G. (1994) *Religion in Britain since 1945: Believing without Belonging*, Blackwell, Oxford.

Davies, P. (1995) *About Time. Einstein's Unfinished Revolution*, Penguin Books, England, Australia.

Dawson, L. (1998) "The Cultural Significance of New Religious Movements and

Globalization: A Theoretical Prolegomenon" *Journal for the Scientific Study of Religion* 37 (4) : 580-595.

de Certeau, M. (1998) "The practice of Everyday Life", University of California Press, Berkeley and Los Angeles.

Dinges, W. (2004) "The New (Old) Age Movement: Assessing a Vatican Assessement" *Journal of Contemporary Religion* 19 (3), 273-288.

Dobbelaere, K. (1987) "Some Trends in European Sociology of Religion: The Secularization Debate", *Sociological Analysis* 48 (2), 107-137.

Dobbelaere, K. and L. Voyé (1990) "From Pillar to Postmodernity: The Changing Situation of Religion in Belgium", *Sociological Analysis* (51:S), S1-S13.

Donahue, M. (1993) "Prevalence and Correlates of New Age Beliefs in Six Protestant Denominations", *Journal For The Scientific Study Of Religion* 32 (2), 177-184.

Drury, N. (1985) *Don Juan, Mescalito and Modern Magic*, Penguin Group, Arkana Collection, London.

Dulaure, J.A. (1974) *Les divinités génératrices. Le culte du phallus chez les anciens et les modernes*, Marabout, Verviers, Belgium.

Durand, G. (1996) *Science de l'homme et tradition. "Le nouvel esprit anthropologique"*, Albin Michel, Paris.

Eisler, R. (1990) *The Chalice and the Blade*, Pandora (Harper Collins Publishers), London, San Fransisco.

Eleta, P. (1997) "The Conquest of Magic over Public Space: Discovering the Face of Popular Magic in Contemporary Society", *Journal of Contemporary Religion* 12 (1), 51-67.

Eliade, M. (1957) *Mythes, rêves et mystères*, Editions Gallimard, Paris.

Eliade, M. (1962) *Méphistophélès et l'androgyne*, Editions Gallimard, Paris.

Eslin, J. (1997) "Indépassable religion", *Esprit* (233), 7-19.

Eungi K. (2003) "Religious Influences on Personal and Societal Well-Being" *Social Indicators Research* 62, 63: 149-170.

Ezzy, D. (2001) "The Commodification of Witchcraft", *The Australian Religion Studies Review* 14 (1), 31-44.

Faivre, A. (1992) *L'ésotérisme*, Presses universitaires de France, Paris.

Faivre, A. (1994) *Access to Western Esotericism*, State University of New York Press.

Faivre, A. and J. Needleman (eds.) (1992) *Modern Esoteric Spirituality*, Crossroad, New York.

Faivre, A. and W. Hanegraaff (eds.) (1998) *Western Esotericism and the Science of Religion*, Peeters, Leuven.

Featherstone, M. (1990) "Perspectives on consumer Culture", *Sociology* 24 (1), 5-22.

Featherstone, M. (1991) *Consumer Culture & Postmodernism*, Sage Publications, London.

Feleppa, R. (1986) "Emics, Etics, and Social Objectivity", *Current Anthropology* 27 (3), 243-255.

Ferguson, M. (1981) *Les enfants du Verseau: pour un nouveau paradigme*, Calmann-Lévy, Paris.

Garret, C. (2001) "Transcendental Meditation, Reiki and Yoga: Suffering, Ritual and Self-Transformation" *Journal of Contemporary Religion* 16 (3): 329-342.

Garret, W. (1974) "Troublesome Transcendence: The Supernatural in the Scientific

Study of Religion", *Sociological Analysis* 35 (3), 167-180.

Gauchet, M. (1985) *Le désenchantement du monde. Une histoire politique de la religion*, Editions Gallimard, Paris.

Geoffroy, M. (2001) 'Le Mouvement du Nouvel Age' in J.M. Larouche and G. Ménard (eds.) *L'Etude de la Religion au Québec. Bilan et Prospective*, PUL: 227-235.

Giddens, A. (1991) *Modernity and Self-Identity: self and society in the late modern age*, Polity Press, Cambridge.

Gillen, P. (1987) "The Pleasures of Spiritualism" *ANZJS* 23 (2): 217-232.

Gordon, R. (1995) "Earthstar Magic: A feminist theoretical perspective on the way of the Witches and the path to the Goddess", *Social Alternatives* 14 (4), 9-11.

Green, M. (1992) *Prophets of a New Age. The Politics of Hope from the Eighteenth Through the Twenty-First Centuries*, Macmillan Publishing Company, New York.

Griffin, W. (1995) "The Embodied Goddess: Feminist Witchcraft and Female Divinity", *Sociology of Religion* 56 (1), 35-48.

Guénon, R. (1922) *Le théosophisme: histoire d'une pseudo-religion*, Editions Traditionnelles, Paris.

Guénon, R. (1958) *Symbolism of the Cross*, Luzac & Company, London.

Guitton, J., G. Bogdanov and I. Bogdanov (1991) *Dieu et la science, vers le métaréalisme*, Editions Grasset & Fasquelle, France.

Gurdjieff, G.I. (1984) *Views from the Real World*, Arkana, London, Melbourne.

Habermas, J. (1987) *The Theory of Communcative Action: The Critique of Functionalist Reason – Volume 2*, Polity Press, Cambridge.

Habermas, J. (1991) *The Theory of Communicative Action: Reason and the Rationalization of Society – Volume 1*, Polity Press, Cambridge.

Habermas, J. (1996) *The Habermas Reader* (edited by William Outhwaite), Polity Press, Cambridge.

Habermas, J. (2002) *Religion and Rationality. Essays on Reason, God, and Modernity*, MIT Press, Cambridge, Massachusetts.

Hadden, J. (1987) "Toward Desacralizing Secularization Theory", *Social Forces* (65), 587-611.

Hanegraaff, W. (1996) *New Age Religion and Western Culture. Esoterism in the Mirror of Secular Thought*, E.J. Brill, Leiden, New York.

Hanegraaff, W. (1999) "New Age Spiritualities as Secular Religion", *Social Compass* 46 (2), 145-160.

Hanford, J. (1975) "A Synoptic Approach: Resolving Problems in Empirical And Phenomenological Approaches To the Psychology of Religion", *Journal for the Scientific Study of Religion* 14 (3): 219-227.

Harvey, G. and C. Hardman (1996) *Paganism Today: Wiccans, Druids, the Goddess and Ancient Earth Traditions for the Twenty-First Century*, Thorsons, London.

Hay, D. (1982) *Exploring Inner Space. Is God Still Possible in the Twentieth Century?*, Penguin Books, Middlesex, England.

Hay, D. (1990) *Religious Experience Today. Studying the Facts*, Mowbray, London.

Heelas, P. (1993) "The New Age in Cultural Context: The Premodern, the Modern and the Postmodern", *Religion* (23), 103-116.

Heelas, P. (1996) *The New Age Movement*, Blackwell Publishers, Oxford.

Heelas, P., 1999. "Prosperity and the New Age Movement: The efficacy of spiritual economics" in B. Wilson and J. Cresswell (eds.) *New Religious Movements:*

Challenge and response, Routledge, London: 51-78.

Heelas, P. (2000) "Sources of Significance Beyond Church And Chapel" in S. Sutcliffe and M. Bowman (eds.), *Beyond New Age: Exploring Alternative Spirituality*, Edinburgh University Press: 237-254.

Henderson, L. (1987) "Editor's Statement: Mysticism and Occultism in Modern Art" *Art Journal* 46 (1), 5-8.

Hervieu-Léger, D. (1990) "Religion and Modernity in The French Context: For a New Approach to Secularization", *Sociological Analysis*, (51:S), S15-S25.

Hesse H. (1965) *Steppenwolf*, Penguin Books, London.

Hetherington, K. (1992) "Stonehenge and its Festival. Spaces of Consumption" In R. Shields (ed.), *Lifestyle Shopping: The Subject of Consumption*, Routledge, London.

Hetherington, K. (1994) "The Contemporary Significance of Schmalenbach's Concept of the Bund", *The Sociological Review*, 1-25.

Hill, M. (2004) 'The New Age – A Sociological Assessment' in J. Lewis (ed.) *The Encyclopedic Sourcebook of New Age Religions*, Prometheus Books, New York, 383-390.

Hill, M. and Bowman (1992) "New Zealand's Cultic Milieu: Individualism and the Logic of Consumerism" in B. Wilson (ed.), *Religion: Contemporary Issues. The All Souls Seminars in the Sociology of Religion*, Bellow Publishing, London, 216-236.

Höllinger, F. (2004) "Does the Counter-Cultural Character of New Age Persist? Investigating Social and Political Attitudes of New Age Followers", *Journal of Contemporary Religion* 19 (3), 289-310.

Houk, J. (1996) "Anthropological Theory and the Breakdown of Eclectic Folk Religions", *Journal for the Scientific Study of Religion* 35 (4), 442-447.

Houtman, D. and P. Mascini (2002) "Why Do Churches Become Empty, While New Age Grows? Secularization and Religious Change in the Netherlands", *Journal for the Scientific Study of Religion* 41 (3): 455-473.

Howell, J. (1997) "ASC Induction Technique, Spiritual Experiences, and Commitment to new Religious Movements", *Sociology of Religion* 58 (2), 141-164.

Hughes, P. (2000a) "Spirituality", *Pointers* (10) 1: 1-4

Hugues, P. (2000b) *Australia's Religious Communities: A Multimedia Exploration (Professional Edition)*, The Christian Research Association, Melbourne.

Hume, L. (1995) "Guest Editor's Introduction: Modern Pagans in Australia", *Social Alternatives* 14 (4), 5-8.

Hume, L. (1997) *Witchcraft and Paganism in Australia*, Melbourne University Press, Melbourne.

Hume, L. (1998) "Phenomenology, Reflexivity and Research in the Anthropology of Consciousness", *Australian Religion Studies Review* 11 (1), 39-44.

Hume, L. (1999) "Exporting Nature Religions: Problems in Praxis Down Under" *Nova Religio* 2 (2), 287-298.

Hume, L. (2002) *Ancestral Power: The Dreaming, Consciousness and Aboriginal Australians*, Melbourne University Press, Melbourne.

Huxley, A. (1979) *Les portes de la perception*, Editions du Rocher, Monaco.

Huxley, A. (1994) *The Perennial Philosophy*, Chatto & Windus, London.

Introvigne, M. (2001) "After the New Age: Is there a Next Age?" in M. Rothstein (ed.) *New Age Religion and Globalization,* Aarhus University Press, Denmark: 58-72.

Ireland, R. (1988) *The Challenge of Secularisation*, Collins Dove, Victoria, Australia.

Ireland, R. (1991) *Kingdoms come. Religion and Politics in Brazil*, University of Pittsburgh Press, Pittsburgh.

Ivakhiv, A. (2003) "Nature and Self in New Age Pilgrimage" *Culture and Religion* 4 (1), 93-118.

Jameson, F. (1984) "Postmodernism, or the Cultural Logic of Late Capitalism", *New Left Review* (146), 53-92.

Jeudy, H. (1992) "Société désacralisée et ritualisation", *Autrement* (127), 155- 163.

Johnson, P. (1995) "Shamanism from Ecuador to Chicago: A Case Study in New Age Ritual Appropriation", *Religion* (25), 163-178.

Jonhson, P. (1997) 'Postmodernity, New Age and Christian Mission: Mars Hill revisited' *Lutheran Theological Journal* 31 (3).

Johnson, P. (2004) "Discipling New Age and Do-it-yourself Seekers Through Booth Ministries" in I. Hexham et al. (eds) *Encountering New Religious Movements: A Holistic Evangelical Approach*, Kregel Publications, Grand Rapids, MI: 229-242.

Johnson P. and S. Payne (2004) "Evangelical Countercult Apologist versus Astrology: An Unresolved Conundrum", *Australian Religion Studies Review* 17 (2): 73-97.

Jorgensen, D. (1982) "The Esoteric Community. An Ethnographic Investigation of the Cultic Milieu", *Urban Life* 10 (4), 383-407.

Jung, C. et al. (1978) *Man and his Symbols*, Picador, London.

Karcher, B, J. Balswick and I. Robinson (1981) "Empiricism, Symbolic Realism, and the Mystique of the Extreme", *The Sociological Quarterly* 22 (1), 93.103.

Kellehear, A. (1996) *Experiences Near Death. Beyond Medicine and Religion*, Oxford University Press, New York, Oxford.

Kemp, D. (2003) "NA Law: a legal studies approach to New Age", *Culture and Religion* 4 (1), 141-158.

Kemp, D. (2004) *New Age: A Guide*, Edinburgh University Press.

Kepel, G. (1994) *The Revenge Of God. The Resurgence of Islam, Christianity and Judaism in the Modern World*, The Pennsylvania State University Press.

Kohn, R. (1991) "Radical subjectivity in 'self religions' and the problem of authority" in Alan Black (ed.), *Religion in Australia. Sociological Perspectives*, Allen & Unwin, Sydney, 133-150.

Laibleman, A. (1992) "Ultimate Reality and Meaning According to the Perennial Philosophy: Evidence from the Mathematical and Physical Sciences", *Ultimate Reality and Meaning* 15 (3), 216-236.

Lantier, J. (1970) *La Théosophie ou l'invasion de la spiritualité orientale*, Paris.

Le Cour P. (1995) *L'ère du Verseau. Le Secret du Zodiaque et le Proche Avenir de L'humanité*, Editions Dervy, Paris.

Lee, R. (2003) "The Re-enchantment of the Self: Western Spirituality, Asian Materialism" *Journal of Contemporary Religion* 18 (3): 351-367.

Levi (1964) *The Aquarian Gospel of Jesus The Christ. The Philosophic and Practical Basis of the Religion of the Aquarian Age of the World*, L.N. Fowler & Co. Ltd, London.

Lewis, J. and G. Melton (1992) "The New Age", *Syzygy: Journal of Alternative Religion and Culture* 1 (3), 247-258.

Lewis, J., G. Melton et al. (1992) *Perspectives on the New Age*, State University Of New York Press, New York.

Lipovetsky, G. (1987) *L'empire de l'éphémère. La mode et son destin dans les sociétés modernes*, Gallimard, Paris, collection folio essais.

Lipovetsky, G. (1993) *L'ère du vide. Essais sur l'individualisme contemporain*, Gallimard, Paris, collection folio essais.

Lofland, J. (1995) "Analytical Ethnography: Features, Failings, and Futures", *Journal of Contemporary Ethnography* 24 (1), 30-67.

Luckmann, T. (1967) *The Invisible Religion: The Problems of Religion in Modern Society*, Macmillan Company, New York.

Luckmann, T. (1990) "Shrinking Transcendence, Expanding Religion? The Paul Hanly Furfey Lecture – 1989", *Sociological Analysis* (50) 2, 127-138.

Luhrmann, T. (1993) "The Resurgence of Romanticism. Contemporary Neopaganism, Feminist Spirituality and the Divinity of Nature" In Melton, R. (ed.) *Environmentalism in the View from Anthropologists*, Routledge, London.

Luhrmann, T. (1994) *Persuasions of the Witch's Craft. Ritual Magic in Contemporary England*, Picador, London.

Lynch, F. (1978) "Toward a Theory of Conversion and Commitment to the Occult" in James T. Richardson (ed.) *Conversion Carrers. In and Out of the New Religions*, Sage Contemporary Social Science Issues (47), 91-112.

Lyon, D. (1993) "A Bit of a Circus: Notes on Postmodernity and New Age", *Religion* (23), 117-126.

Lyon, D. (1996) *Postmodernity*, Open University Press, Buckingham.

Maffesoli, M. (1988) *Le temps des tribus. Le déclin de l'individualisme dans les sociétés de masse*, Méridiens Klincksieck, Paris.

Maffesoli, M. (1990) "Post-Modern Sociality", *Telos* (85), 89-92.

Maffesoli, M. (1994) "La raison interne", *Sociétés* (44), 127-144.

Maffesoli, M. (1996) *La contemplation du monde. Figures de style communautaire*, Editions Grasset & Fasquelles, Réédition Le Livre de Poche Biblio.

Maffesoli, M. (1997) *Du Nomadisme : Vagabondages initiatiques*, Le Livre de Poche Biblio.

Mayer, J. (1998) 'Swendenborg: A Herald of the New Age?" *Cesnur, http:// www.cesnur.org/testiu/Swedenborg.htm*, 18/04/00.

Melton, G. (1990) *New Age Encyclopedia*, Gale Research ed., Detroit.

Melton, G. (1992) " European Receptivity to the New Religions", *Syzygy: Journal of Alternative Religion and Culture* 1 (1), 3-13.

Melucci, A. (1996) *Challenging Codes. Collective Actions in the Information Age*, Cambridge University Press, Cambridge.

Mulcock, J. (2001) "(Re)discovering our indigenous selves: the nostalgic appeal of Native Americans and other generic indigenes" *Australian Religion Studies Review* 14 (1): 45-64.

Nasr S. (1987) "Guénon, René" In *The Encyclopedia Of Religion*, V.6. Macmillan Publishing Company, New York, 136-138.

Negrâo, L. (1987) "Kardecism" In *The Encyclopedia Of Religion*, V.8. Macmillan Publishing Company, New York: 259-261.

Nelson, G. (1987) *Cults, New Religions and Religious Creativity*, Routledge And

Kegan Paul, London.

Noll, R. (1996) *The Jung Cult. Origins of a Charismatic Movement,* Fontana Press, London.

Occhiogrosso, P. (1994) *The Joy of Sect. A Spirited Guide to the World's Religious Traditions*, Doubleday, New York.

Olds, L. (1992) "Integrating Ontological Metaphors: Hierarchy and Interrelatedness" *Soundings* 75 (2-3), 403-420.

Olivier de Sardan, J.P. (1992) "Occultism and the Ethnographic 'I'. The exoticizing of magic from Durkheim to 'postmodern' anthropology" *Critique of Anthropology* (12) 1, 5-25.

Otto, R. (1936) *The Idea of The Holy. An Inquiry into the Non-Rational Factor in the Idea of the Divine and its Relation to the Rational*, Oxford University Press, Oxford.

Parkins, W. (2001) "Oprah Winfrey's Change Your Life TV and the Spiritual Everyday", *Continuum: Journal of Media & Cultural Studies* 15 (2): 145-157.

Papus (1994) *The Tarot of the Bohemians*, Studio Editions Ltd, London.

Paschkes-Bell, G. (2004) "Christ Consciousness and the Cosmic Christ" in J. Lewis (ed.) *The Encyclopedic Sourcebook of New Age Religions*, Prometheus Books, New York, 318-322.

Peach, H. (2003) 'Religion, spirituality and health: how should Australia's medical professionals respond?' *Medical Journal of Australia* 178 (January): 86-88.

Peters, T. (1991) *The Cosmic Self*, Harper Collins, San Francisco.

Possamai-Inesedy, A. (2002) 'Beck's Risk Society and Giddens' Ontological Security: A Comparative Analysis between the Assemblies of God and the Anthroposophical Society' *ARS Review* 15 (1), 27-43.

Possamai, A. (1998) *In Search of New Age Spirituality: Toward a Sociology of Perennism*, PhD Thesis, La Trobe University, Melbourne.

Possamai, A. (2002) 'Secrecy and Consumer Culture: An Exploration of Esotericism in Contemporary Western Society Using the Work of Simmel and Baudrillard' *Australian Religion Studies Review* 15 (1): 44-56.

Possamai, A. (2003) 'Alternative Spiritualities and the Logic of Late Capitalism' *Culture and Religion* 4 (1): 31-45.

Possamai, A. (2005) *Religion and Popular Culture: A Hyper-Real Testament?* P.I.E.-Peter Lang, Bruxelles.

Prévost, J.P. (1993) "Le Nouvel Age. Approche historique, sociologique et psychologique", *La Foi et le Temps* XXIII (1), 18-48.

Reid, D. (1992) "The Possessed" in David Reid (ed.), *Sex, Death and God in L.A.*, University of California Press, Berkeley.

Rémy, J. (1996) "Un nouveau paradigme: entre le sensible et l'intelligible, l'innovation et l'institution. De l'intérêt du propos de Michel Maffesoli", *Social Compass* 43 (1), 19-23.

Richardson, J. (1985) 'Studies of Conversion: Secularization or Re-enchantment?" in Phillip E. Hammond (Ed.), *The Sacred in a Secular Age. Toward Revision in the Scientific Study of Religion*, University of California Press, Berkeley and Los Angeles, California.

Richardson, J. (1993) "Definitions of Cult: From Sociological-Technical to Popular-Negative", *Review of Religious Research* 34 (4), 348-356.

Riffard, P. (1990) *L'ésotérisme*, Editions Robert Laffont, Paris.

Ringer, F. (1997) *Max Weber's Methodology. The Unification of the Cultural and Social Sciences*, Harvard University Press.

Ritzer, G. (1999) *Enchanting a disenchanted world. Revolutionizing the means of consumption*, Pine Forge Press, California.

Roberts, R. (1994) "Power and Empowerment: New Age Managers and the Dialects of Modernity/Postmodernity", *Syzygy: Journal of Alternative Religion and Culture* 3 (3-4), 271-288.

Rodgers, B. (1995) "The Radical Faerie Movement: A Queer Spirit Pathway", *Social Alternatives* 14 (4), 34-37.

Roof, W. (1993) "Toward the Year 2000: Reconstructions of Religious Space" *The Annals of the American Academy of Political & Social Science* (527), 155-170.

Roof, W., C. Jackson and D. Roozen (eds.) (1995) *The Post-War Generation and Establishment Religion. Cross-Cultural Perspectives*, Westview Press, Boulder (USA) and London.

Rose, S. (1998) "An Examination of the New Age Movement: Who is Involved and What Constitutes its Spirituality" *Journal of Contemporary Religion* 13 (1), 5-22.

Rosati, M. (2003) "The Making and Representing of Society: Religion, the Sacred and Solidarity among Stranger in a Durkheimian Perspective" *Journal of Classical Sociology* 3 (2): 173-196.

Rosenau, P.M. (1992) *Post-Modernism and the Social Sciences. Insight, Inroads, and Intrusions*, Princeton University Press, Princeton, New Jersey.

Ross, A. (1991) *Strange Weather. Culture, Science, and Technology in the Age of Limits*, Verso, London, New York.

Roszak, T. (1969) *The Making of a Counter Culture. Reflections on the Technocratic Society and its Youthful Opposition*, Anchor Books, New York.

Roszak, T. (1976) *Unfinished Animal. The Aquarian Frontier and the Evolution of Consciousness*, Faber and Faber, London.

Rushing, J. (1985) "E.T. as Rhetorical Transcendence" *Quarterly Journal of Speech* 71 (2), 188-203.

Russell, B. (1957) *History of Western Philosophy and its connection with Political and Social Circumstances from the Earliest Times to the Present Day*, George Allen and Unwin Ltd, London.

Salamon, K. (2001) "Going global from the inside out – Spiritual Globalism in the workplace' in M. Rothstein (ed.) *New Age and Globalization*, Renner Publications & Aarhus University Press, Oxford and Denmark, 150-172.

Salamon, K. (2005, forthcoming) "Possessed by Entreprise. Values and value-creation in Mandrake Management" in O. Löfgren and R. Willim (eds.) *Magic, Culture and the New Economy*, Berh, Oxford.

Saliba, J. (2004) 'A Christian Response to the New Age' in J. Lewis (ed.) *The Encyclopedic Sourcebook of New Age Religion*, Prometheus Books, New York, 307-317.

Salzmann, M. de (1987) "Gurdjieff, G.I." in *The Encyclopedia of Religion*, V.6. Macmillan Publishing Company, New York, 139-140.

Samuel, G. (1996) "Nature Religion Today: Western Paganism, Shamanism and Esotericism in the 1990s. Conference at the Lake District Campus of Lancaster University, 9th to 13th April 1996", *Religion* (26), 373-376.

Schlegel, J.L. (1995) *Religions à la carte*, Hachette, Paris.

Schlegel, Jean-Louis (1997) "Pourquoi on n'en finit pas avec les sectes", *Esprit* (233), 98-112.

Schopp, A. (1997) "Cruising the Alternatives: Homoeroticism and the Contemporary Vampire", *Journal of Popular Culture* 30, 231-243.

Schutz, A. (1970) *On Phenomenology and Social Relations*, The University of Chicago Press, Chicago and London.

Simmel, G. (1991) *Secret et sociétés secrètes*, Editions Circé, Strasbourg.

Smith, H. (1989) *Beyond the Post-Modern Mind*, The Theosophical Publishing House, Wheaton, USA.

St John, G. (1997) "Going Feral: Authentica on the Edge of Australian Culture", *The Australian Journal of Anthropology* 8 (2), 167-189.

St John, G. (2001a) "Heal thy Self – thy Planet: Confest, Eco-Spirituality and the Self/ Earth Nexus" *Australian Religion Studies Review* 14 (1): 97-112.

St John G. (2001b) 'Australian (Alter)Natives: Cultural Drama and Indigeneity' *Social Analysis* 45 (1): 122-140.

Stark, R. and W.S. Bainbridge (1985) *The Future of Religion. 'Secularization', Revival and Cult Formation*, University Of California Press, Berkeley.

Stark, R. and L. Iannaccone (1994) "A Supply-Side Reinterpretation of the "Secularization" of Europe", *Journal for the Scientific Study of Religion* 33 (3), 230-252.

Steyn, C. (1994) *Worldviews in Transition: An Investigation into the New Age Movement in South Africa*, University of South Africa Press, Pretoria.

Sutcliffe, S. (2003a) *Children of the New Age: A History of Spiritual Practices*, Routledge, London.

Sutcliffe, S. (2003b) "Category Formation and the History of 'New Age'" *Culture and Religion* 4 (1), 5-29.

Sutcliffe, S. and M. Bowman (eds.) (2000) *Beyond New Age: Exploring Alternative Spirituality*, Edinburgh University Press.

Tacey, D. (1998) "Jung and the New Age. A Study in Contrasts" *Review of contemporary contributions to Jungian psychology* 5 (4), 1-11.

Tacey, D. (2000) *ReEnchantment. The New Australian Spirituality*, Harper Collins, Sydney.

Tacey, D. (2001) *Jung and the New Age*, Brunner-Routledge, East Sussex.

Talbot, M. (1992) *Mysticism and the New Physics*, Arkana (Penguin Group), London.

Thomas, E. et al. (1993) "Two Patterns of Transcendence: An Empirical Examination of Wilber's and Washburn's Theories", *Journal of Humanistic Psychology* 33 (3), 66-81.

Tiryakian, E. (1974) "Toward the Sociology of Esoteric Culture" In Edward A. Tiryakian (ed.), *On the Margin of the Visible*, New York, 257-281.

Tramacchi, D. (2000) "Field Tripping: Psychedelic *communitas* and Ritual in the Australian Bush", *Journal of Contemporary Religion* 15 (2): 201-213.

Travisano, R. (1970) "Alternation and Conversion as Qualitatively Different Transformations" in Gregory P. Stone and Harvey A. Faberman (eds), *Social Psychology Through Symbolic Interaction*, Ginn-Blaisdell, Wlatham, Massachusetts, 594-606.

Trevelyan, G. (1984) *A Vision of the Aquarian Age. The Emerging Spiritual World*

View, Stillpoint Publishing, Walpole, New Hampshire.

Troeltsch, E. (1950) *The Social Teaching of the Christian Churches*, George Allen and Unwin Ltd, London, Two Volumes.

Truzzi, M. (1974) "Definition and Dimension of the Occult: Towards A Sociological Perspective" in Edward A. Tiryakian (ed.), *On the Margin of the Visible*, New York, 243-257.

Van Hove, H. (1999) "L'émergence d'un 'marché spirituel' religieux" *Social Compass* 46 (2), 161-172.

Vernette, J. (1992) *Le New Age*, Presses universitaires de France, Paris.

Watts, A. (1998) "From Time to Eternity", Internet site: Http:// www.alanwatts.com/ fromtime.htm, 21-01-1998.

Webb, J. (1980) *The Harmonious Circle. The Lives and Works of G.I. Gurdjieff, P.D. Ouspensky, and Their Followers*, Thames and Hudson, London.

Weber, M. (1968) *The Protestant Ethic and the Spirit of Capitalism*, Unwin University Books, London.

Welch, L. (1982) *Orage with Gurdjieff in America*, Routledge & Kegan Paul, Boston, London.

Westley, F. (1978) "The Cult of Man": Durkheim's Predictions and New Religious Movements' *Sociological Analysis* 39 (2), 135-145.

Wilber, K. (1981) *Up from Eden. A Transpersonal View of Human Evolution*, Anchor Press, New York.

Wilber, K. (1996) *Eye to Eye. The Quest for the New Paradigm*, Shambhala Publications, Boston.

Williams, D. (1984) "2001: A Space Odyssey: A Warning Before Its Time", *Critical Studies in Mass Communication* 1, 311-321.

Wilson, C. (1971) *L'occulte*, Albin Michel, Paris.

Witter, R. et al. (1985) "Religion and Subjective Well-Being in Adulthood: a quantitative synthesis" *Review of Religious Research* 26 (4): 332-342.

Wood, M. (2003) "Capital Possession: a comparative approach to 'New Age' an control of the means of possession" *Culture and Religion* 4 (1), 159-182.

York, M. (1995) *The Emerging Network. A Sociology of the New Age and Neo-Pagan Movements*, Rowmann & Littlefield Publishers, Maryland, US.

York, M. (1999) "Le supermarché religieux: ancrages locaux du Nouvel Age au sein du réseau mondial", *Social Compass* 46 (2), 173-179.

York, M. (2004) "New Age Commodification and Appropriation of Spirituality" in J. Lewis (ed.) *The Encyclopedic Sourcebook of New Age Religions*, Prometheus Books, New York, 369-754.

Ziguras, C. (1994) "Cyberdelia", *Arena Magazine*, August-September, 22-26.

Zohar, D. and I. Marshall (1994) *The Quantum Society. Mind, Physics and a New Social Vision*, Flamingo, London.

Index

2001, A Space Odyssey 121

Abellio, R. 82
Action research 2
Age of Aquarius 12, 40, 43, 59, 101, 104, 112, 123
Alexandrian 107
Alexandrism, *see* Sanders, Alex 107
Alternation 24, 38
Angelology 15
Animism 131
Anthropological immersion 2-3, 12, 40
Anthroposophy 73, 80
Aquarian Christ, Maitreya 85-86, 95-96
Aquarian conspiracy 50, 93
Aquarians, *see* Perennists, Aquarian
Aquarius, Age of 85-98, 109
Arcane School 77, 90
Aries, Age of 87
Aristotelian elements 102-103
Aristotle 121
Arnason, J. 116
Astrology 2, 14-16, 19-20, 33, 64-65, 67, 82, 87, 98n, 99, 108-109
  Astrology, mundane 87, 90
  Astrology, religious 87, 90
Athames 102
Atheism 18
Atlantis, journal 87
Australian Meditation Network 96
Automatic writing 14, 18

Bailey, A. *Good Will* 90, 96
Bailey, F. 77
Bainbridge, W.S. 32, 33, 79
Baudrillard 120
Bauman, Z. 32, 82, 115, 125
Beck, U. 37
Beckford, J. 120
Beltaine 103
Bendle, M.
Besant, A. 79, 80
Beyer, P. 9

Blake, W. 122
Blavastky, H. P. 75, 77-80, 83n, 90
Bloch, J. 39
Bowman, M. 11
Brazilian Spiritist Foundation 78
Brigid 103
Bruce, S. 9, 10, 132, 135, 136
Bucke, R.M. 49
Buddha Mind, *see* Monism
Buddhism 15, 18, 40, 48, 70, 77, 123
Buddhism, Zen 14, 123
Buenfil, A. 114, 123
Buffy the Vampire Slayer 120

Caddy, P. 76, 96
Campbell, B. 32, 33, 34, 61
Campbell, C. 31, 38n
Cancer, Age of 87
Capra, F. 125
Capricorn, Age of 91
Casanova, J. 9, 133
Castaneda, C. 122, 123
Castoriadis, C. 115-116
Cavendish, R. 88-89
Cayce, E. 1
Champion, F. 17, 36, 40, 75
Channelling 15, 40
Christ consciousness 96, 98n
Christianity 9, 10, 48, 63, 70, 78, 89-91, 98n
  fundamentalist 18, 99
  rejection of 13, 16, 19, 21
Chryssides, G. 71
Church of All Worlds 100, 120
Church-sect-cult typology 30
Clairvoyance 8, 13, 14
Coincidentia oppositorum, *see* Human Potential Ethic
Coleman, N. 49
Collective evolution 80
Commodification of religion 24, 26-27, 29, 31, 33, 38, 47, 48, 128-134, 139
Confest *see* psychic fairs

Consciousness, cosmic, *see* Monism
Consumption of New Age symbols, *see*
   Religious market consumption
Consumption of spirituality 12
Corporate Social Responsibility
   Movement 137
Corrywright, D. 2, 30, 40, 71
Cosmic Christ 98n
Cosmic unity, *see* Monism
Counter culture movement, 1960s 118,
   122-123
Covens, *see* also Witchcraft 102-104
Creative Evolution 79, 112
Cretia 107
Critical mass 91-97, 101
   through meditation 85, 91-97, 95, 112,
      101, 136
   through social action 93-95, 136, 138
Crowley, A. 107
Crystal manipulation 16, 24, 36, 40
Cultic Milieu 31-39, 139
Cults
   audience 32
   client 32-33
   entertainment 34
   illumination 33-34, 61
   instrumental 33-34, 61
   movements 32-33
   service oriented 38n

Darwinism 78, 79
Davie, G. 10
de Certeau, M. 31
Demonology 15
Divine Mind, *see* Monism
Dobbelaere, K. 11, 22, 119-120
Donahue, M. 2
Dowling, E. S 89
Dowling, L. 89
Druidism 107, 131
Drury, N. 123
Durand, G. 110

Eastern religions 40, 123, 124
Ecology 107, 122
Ecotopia millennium 114
Eisler, R. 107
Eleusis 107
Eliade, M. 7, 50, 110
Encyclopaedist philosophers 88

Energy, *see* Monism
Enlightenment 88
Equinoxes, precession of 87, 88
Esalen 122
Esotericism 12, 39, 71, 73, 76, 79, 81,
   139
Etheric surgery 16, 81
Ethnography 1
Etic and emic approaches 5, 39-41, 46
Eveno, J. 89
Ezzy 135

Faivre, A. 48, 51, 71, 77, 78, 121
Featherstone, Mike 26-27, 122, 127, 133
Feminist spirituality 14, 30, 100, 107-
   109, 122
Ferguson, M. 50, 80, 89, 93
Fetishisation of growth 134
Findhorn Foundation 76, 96, 122
Folk theology 10-11
Fortune, D. 107
Fox sisters 78

Gaia 122
Ganymede 88
Gardner, G. 103, 107
Gardnerism, *See* Gardner, G.
Gauchet, M. 9
Geertz 5
Gemini, Age of 87
Geoffroy, M. 136
Gestalt therapy 124
Giddens, A. 37
Ginsberg, A. 122
Gnosis, *see* Spiritual Knowledge
Gnosticism 39, 48, 76, 105
Gnosticism, neo 39
Goddess worship 101-104, 106, 108
Golden Dawn, Hermetic Order of the 99,
   100, 107, 107
Green, M. 80, 108
Guénon, R. 50, 75, 77, 81
Guénonism 2, 12, 73, 77, 81, 114, 123
Gurdjieff, G.I. 76, 98n

Habermas, J. 127, 134-135
Hallucinogenic drugs 56
Hanegraaff, W. 1, 11, 22, 39, 52, 78
Hardy, Alister, Research Centre 25
Harvest home 103

Hay, D. 8, 10, 25
Healing 51
Heaven's Gate 120
Heelas, P. 1, 11, 22, 23, 34, 39, 40, 71, 75, 104-105, 117, 124, 125, 132, 136
Heinlein, R. 120
Hermetism 48
Hesse H. 50
Hetherington, K. 30, 38n
Higher self 34, 46, 51, 53, 105
Hill, M. 40, 72, 132
Hinduism 40, 51, 63, 105
Historical progress 109
Holarchy, *see* Monism
Holism, *see* Monism
Höllinger, F. 137
Homosexuality 16
Horned God 108
Houtman, D. 2, 10
Hughes, P. 36, 130
Human potential ethic 12, 49-51, 53, 57-62, 66-72, 106, 117, 121-124, 132, 139
Hume, L. 102, 104, 107, 121
Huxley, A. 12, 47-51, 71, 122

Iannacone, L 10
Imbolc 103
Individuation 22, 31, 40, 50-51, 72, 118, 135, 139
Initiation 81-82
Inner Light, Society of the 107
Intelligible reality, *see* Monism
Introvigne, M. 44, 136
Ireland, R. 83n
Isis 79
Islam 9

James, W. 49
Jameson, F. 125, 127, 132
Jediism 115, 120-121
Jesus Christ 86-88, 90, 97
Jivanmukta, *see* Human Potential Ethic
Johnson, P. 98n, 130-131
Jonas, H. 51
Judaism 9
Julevno 89
Jung, C. 49-51, 57, 93, 123, 125
  Jungian movement 118, 124

Kabala 8-9, 80, 82, 107, 123
Kant, E. 7
Kardec, A. 78, 83n
Kellehear, A. 25, 118
Kemp, D. 39, 44, 46, 105, 135
Kepel, G. 9
Kerouac, J. 122
Kraftzeit 110
Krishnamurti 80, 90
Kuhn, T. 93

Lammas 103
Lantier, J. 80
Le Cour, P. 87, 89-92
Leadbeater 90
Leo, Age of 87
Leo, A. 89
Levasseur, M. 120
Levi, E. 80
Lewis, J. 1, 44, 78-80, 105, 123-124
Life crises
  as pathway to new spirituality 24
  linked to mystico-pneumatic experiences 25
Lipovetsky, G. 47, 76, 83n
Litha 103
Logos, *see* Monism
Lovecraft, H. P. 120
Luckmann, T. 9
Lughnasadh 103
Luhrmann, T. 34, 106, 107
Lyon, D. 117
Lyotard, J.F 118

Mabon 103
Macro knowledge 75, 82, 138
Maffesoli, M. 10, 30, 125, 133, 138n
Magic 15, 66, 75, 77, 99, 100, 102, 107
Mandraked economy 132
Marshall, I. 126
Mascini, P 2, 10
Maslow, A. 122, 124
Mathers, S., *The Golden Dawn* 81
Matrix, The, Matrixism 120
McLaine, S. 1
Meditation 7, 13, 18, 33, 36, 51, 69, 73, 95, 101
  Transcendental 14, 37, 92
  Critical mass through 85, 91-97, 95, 112, 101, 136

Mediums 78
Melton, G. 1, 44, 49, 78-81, 80, 105, 106, 123-125, 138
Melucci, A. 115
Mental illness 95
Midsummer 103
Mind, Body and Spirit festivals 130-131
Mind-at-large, *see* Monism
Mithraism 87, 107
Modernism 12, 17, 37, 76, 81, 117, 132, 139
Moebius strip 50
Monism 12, 49-50, 54-57, 66-70, 108, 121, 122, 139
Montgomery, R. 14, 18
Mulcock, J. 135
Mystico-esoteric nebulae 40, 71
Mystico-pneumatic experiences 7, 14, 18, 24, 25, 38, 55, 95

Narcissism 37, 76
Naturopathy 16
Near Death experiences 25
Necromancy 78
Neo-paganism, *see also* Perennism, neo-pagan 2, 11-16, 66, 95, 99-111, 114, 131
Networking 29-38, 138
Networking, affinity
Networks, Bund 30, 38
Networks, Segmented Polycentric Integrated 30, 40
Networks, situationalistic
New Age
    and awareness 43, 44
    as business, commercial 41, 136
    as misnomer 41
    as reaction against materialism 44
    as superficial 42
    as weak-minded 42
    festivals, *see* psychic fairs
    studies, first and second waves 1, 41
    rejection of term 1, 40, 41, 46, 71, 136
    used as umbrella term 1, 11, 40, 104, 139
Noll, R. 123
Non-oiled Mechanical World 124
Noumenon 7, 78, 80
Numerology 15, 64, 82

Occultism 2, 12, 13, 39, 76, 78-81, 99, 106-107, 125
Oimelc 103
Olcott, H. S. 78, 79, 80
Omega-point, *see* Monism
Ontological insecurity and security 37
Orphism 48
OTO 100, 107
Otto, R. 7

Palmistry 15, 127
Panenthism, *see* Monism
Pantheism 131
    acosmic, *see* Monism
Papus 82
Paracelsus 110
Paracletism 90-92
Parapsychology 15
Parousia 15
Payne, S 98n
Pentacles 102
Perennial philosophy, *see* perennism
Perennism 1, 12, 14, 47-8, 48-72, 99-111, 112-125, 139
    Aquarian 13, 101, 104, 112-125
    Aquarian contrasted with new-pagans 104-108
    Christian 90-92
    neo pagan 112-125
    presentist 11-13, 99-111, 112-125
Perls, F. 124
Peters, T. 49, 51, 71, 91
Phenomenological noumenalist approach to research 6-8
Phenomenon 7
Philosophia perennis, *see* perennism
Pisces, Age of 86, 87, 90
Plato 49, 68
Plotinus 49, 110
Possamai, A. 1, 73, 77, 82, 83, 132-133, 138n
Possamai-Inesedy, A. 37
Post modernism 12-13, 17, 32, 53, 73, 76, 82, 110-120, 132
Presentist perennism *see* perennism
Psychedelic drugs 14, 122, 123
Psychic counselling 15, 16
Psychic fairs 13, 15, 16, 29, 31-32, 47, 85, 127-134, 138
Psychic healing 15, 33

Pythagoreanism, neo 48, 76

Qualitative research 2, 17
Quantitative research 2, 17
Quantum mechanics 67
Quantum physics 118, 124-125

Radical Faerie movement 108
Radical subjectivism 23
Rainbow Gatherings 131
Rainbow, warriors 114
Regression 18
Reiki 14, 16, 36, 37
Reincarnation 78, 79, 92
Religious market consumption, *see*
    Commodification of religion
Renaissance 88
Rhine, J. B. 122
Richardson, J. 9, 31
Riffard, P. 48, 76, 77, 81, 82, 88
Rite, Great (witchcraft) 104
Ritzer, G. 133
Rivail, L. 78
Rogers, C. 122, 124
Rose, S. 2, 17, 44
Rosenau, P.M. 52n, 76, 118
Rosicrucians 80
Ross, A. 117, 136
Roszak, T. 79, 118, 120-121, 122
Russell, B. 49

Sabbats 103
Salamon, K. 132
Saliba, J. 52n
Salzmann, M. de 75, 76
Samhain 103
Samuel, G. 104-105
Sanders, A. 103, 107
Satan, Church of 120
Satanism 100, 131
Schlegel, J.-L. 82
Schmalenbach 30
Science fiction 118, 120-122
Scientific method 78
Scientism 48, 118
Secularisation thesis 8-10, 89, 127
Segmented Polycentric Integrated
    Networks 30, 40
Self knowledge 75, 82, 109
Self, as authority 23, 30, 135

Self, higher 34, 46, 51, 53, 105
Shadows, Book of 102
Shamanism 40, 78, 123
    urban 16, 101
    Western 123
Shaw, B., Back to Methuselah 79-80
Simmel, G. 77
Smith, H. 49-50
Snyder, G. 122
Solar Magic 102
Spiritism 78
Spiritual knowledge 12, 49, 51, 62-66,
    66-70, 73-83, 121, 139
Spiritualism 2, 13, 77-81, 110,
    114
St John, G. 38n, 49, 131
Star Trek 120-121
Star Wars 121
Stark, R. 10, 1, 32, 78
Steiner, R. 80
Steppenwolf 50
Stoicism 48
Sufism 81
Sutcliffe, S. 1, 2, 11, 39, 40, 41, 46, 76,
    96, 98n
Swedenborg 78, 98n
Symbols, consumption of, *see* Religious
    market consumption
Synoptic approach to research 4

Tacey, D. 133
Tantrism 14
Tarot 2, 15, 16, 20, 33, 82, 123
Taurus, Age of 87
Technical mysticism 22, 34
Teilhard De Chardin, P. 49
Theosophical Society 12-13, 35, 73, 75,
    77-82, 90, 98n, 105, 110, 114, 123-
    125
The Secret Doctrine 79
Tillich, P. 122
Tiryakian, E. 77
Toynbee, A. 122
Traditional religions, decline of *see*
    Secularisation thesis
Transcendence 82
Transpersonal psychology 124
Trevelyan, G. 82, 91
Triangle mediation 99
Troeltsch, E. 22, 34

Unconscious, collective, *see* Monism
Universal knowledge 74, 82

Vampires 121
Van Hove, H. 132
Vatican Pontifical Councils 52n
Verstehen approach to research 2, 5, 7,
   12
Voltairian philosophers 88
Voyé, L. 22, 118-120

Wachsendzeit 110
Water dowsing 33
Watts, A. 122, 123
Weber, M. 4, 72, 133
Weberian approach to research 4-5, 40,
   115
Welfare State 119-120
Wellbeing, religion and
Western Mysteries 107
Westley, F. 72

Wheel of the Year 102
Wholism, *see* Monism
Wicca, *see* Witchcraft
Wilber, K. 40, 48, 49, 124
Wilson, C. 78
Winfrey, O. 132
Witchcraft 74, 100-104, 107, 131, 135-
   136
   Witchcraft Act 1736 89
   Gothic 121

X-files 120

Yoga 14, 15, 33, 37, 123
York, M. 1-3, 24, 30, 31, 37, 40, 49, 71,
   79, 105, 132
Yule 103

Zodiacal ages 86-87, 108
Zohar, D. 125